Fodor's

BIG ISLAND OF HAWAII

anythink™

A REVOLUTION OF RANGEVIEW LIBRARIES

0083

WELCOME TO BIG ISLAND

NO LONGER PROPERTY OF ANYTHINK RANGEVIEW LIBRARY DISTRICT

takes time to explore the Big Island's stunning landscapes, but the rewards are spectacular. Hawaii's largest island has more than 250 miles of coast from Kona to Hilo and beyond, lined with incredible beaches, elegant resorts, coffee farms, rain forests, and waterfalls. History and culture resonate everywhere, from Kealakekua Bay, Captain Cook's landing site and modern-day snorkeling haven, to the rugged Valley of Kings near Waipio. Above it all, snowcapped Maunakea contrasts with fiery Mauna Loa, the centerpiece of popular Hawaii Volcanoes National Park.

TOP REASONS TO GO

★ **Hawaii Volcanoes National Park:** The world's most active volcano is an amazing sight.

★ **Fun Towns:** Humming Kailua-Kona, cowboy country Waimea, rainbow-streaked Hilo.

★ **Stargazing:** Maunakea's peak is the best place on Earth to stare out into space.

★ **Beaches:** The Big Island offers sand in many shades—black, white, and even green.

★ **Wildlife:** You can watch sea turtles on the beach and humpback whales in the waves.

★ **Kona Coffee:** Farm tours, smooth sips, and a coffee cultural festival are all memorable.

17 ULTIMATE EXPERIENCES

Big Island of Hawaii offers terrific experiences that should be on every traveler's list. Here are Fodor's top picks for a memorable trip.

1 Stargaze on Maunakea

The sunset and stargazing at Maunakea's summit is outstanding. The visitor center (as far as most rental cars are allowed to go) offers free public stargazing four nights a week, but there are also tours. *(Ch. 2)*

2 Tour a Kona Coffee Plantation

Local farmers love to share their passion for farming genuine Kona coffee with the public and offer free tours. Our favorite is Lion's Gate Farm at mile marker 101 in Honaunau. *(Ch. 2)*

3 Be a Cowboy for a Day

Saddle up and get ready to ride the ranges, cliffs, and trails of the Big Island on horseback. It's one of the best ways to take in the island's beautiful scenery. *(Ch. 9)*

4 Hike to the Green Sand Beach

It's worth the effort to drive to the end of South Point Road and hike about three miles to a stunning olivine Papakolea Beach. Take lots of water. *(Ch. 3)*

5 Enjoy a Sunday Stroll in Kailua-Kona

On the third Sunday of every month, Kailua-Kona town closes off to car traffic for a local market, ending with a free Hawaiian concert. *(Ch. 2)*

6 Swim at Night With Manta Rays

These gracious, gentle giants feed on plankton in a spot called "Manta Village." An experienced excursion outfitter can get you there. *(Ch. 8)*

7 Go Bowling on a Volcano

Kilauea Military Camp (KMC), within Hawaii Volcanoes National Park, was established in 1916 for military families, but the public is also welcome to bowl, eat, shop, and pump affordable gas. *(Ch. 2)*

8 Watch Lava Flow at Hawaii Volcanoes National Park

Witness the primal birth of living land from two eruption sites flowing from Kilauea Volcano, currently the world's most active volcano; lava flows are also reachable on foot and by bike. *(Ch. 2)*

9 Sky Dive the Big Island

Jump out of a plane for a true bird's eye view of the incredible northern landscapes of the Big Island—even beginners can do it. You'll feel more like you are floating rather than freefalling. *(Ch. 9)*

10 Visit Kaloko-Honokohau

At this underrated national historic park, boardwalks take visitors past ancient fishponds and ruins in addition to beautiful beaches populated with interesting flora and fauna. *(Ch. 2)*

11 Go Whale Watching

From November through May, take a boat trip to watch migrating humpbacks from Alaska mate, give birth, and nurture their young in the waters off the Hawaiian Islands. *(Ch. 8)*

12 Tour a Royal Palace

Take a docent-led tour of the gorgeous Hulihee Palace, which is on the National Register of Historic Places and one of only three royal palace residences in the United States. *(Ch. 2)*

13 Explore Lava Tubes

While the Thurston Lava Tube in Hawaii Volcanoes National Park is convenient, Kula Kai Caverns and Kilauea Caverns of Fire are also fascinating but require expert guides. *(Ch. 2, 9)*

14 Walk Down to Waipio Valley

This lush, waterfall-laden valley—surrounded by sheer, fluted 2,000-foot cliffs—was once a favorite retreat for Hawaiian royalty. *(Ch. 2)*

15 Check out Sleeping Turtles at a Black Sand Beach

At Punaluu Black Sand beach, rows of endangered Hawaiian green sea turtles (honu) often bask on the hot sand in the sun. *(Ch. 3)*

16 Dine or Drink with a Lava View

The Rim restaurant at the historic Volcano House hotel overlooks the Kilauea caldera. Order a hot buttered rum at the bar or have dinner, and watch the glowing lava. *(Ch. 4)*

17 Visit a 5-Star Beach

The Big Island's most beautiful white sand beaches flank the Kohala Coast, and some, including Anaehoomalu Bay, Hapuna Beach, and Kaunaoa Beach, are among Hawaii's finest. *(Ch. 3)*

Fodor's BIG ISLAND OF HAWAII

Editorial: Douglas Stallings, *Editorial Director*; Margaret Kelly, Jacinta O'Halloran, *Senior Editors*; Kayla Becker, Alexis Kelly, Amanda Sadlowski, *Editors*; Teddy Minford, *Content Editor*; Rachael Roth, *Content Manager*

Design: Tina Malaney, *Design and Production Director*; Jessica Gonzalez, *Production Designer*

Photography: Jennifer Arnow, *Senior Photo Editor*

Maps: Rebecca Baer, *Senior Map Editor*; Henry Colomb and Mark Stroud (Moon Street Cartography), David Lindroth, *Cartographers*

Production: Jennifer DePrima, *Editorial Production Manager*; Carrie Parker, *Senior Production Editor*; Elyse Rozelle, *Production Editor*

Business & Operations: Chuck Hoover, *Chief Marketing Officer*; Joy Lai, *Vice President and General Manager*; Stephen Horowitz, *Director of Business Development and Revenue Operations*; Tara McCrillis, *Director of Publishing Operations*; Eliza D. Aceves, *Content Operations Manager and Strategist*

Public Relations and Marketing: Joe Ewaskiw, *Manager*; Esther Su, *Marketing Manager*

Writers: Karen Anderson, Kristina Anderson

Editor: Douglas Stallings

Production Editor: Carrie Parker

Copyright © 2019 by Fodor's Travel, a division of Internet Brands, Inc.

Fodor's is a registered trademark of Internet Brands, Inc. All rights reserved. Published in the United States by Fodor's Travel, a division of Internet Brands, Inc. No maps, illustrations, or other portions of this book may be reproduced in any form without written permission from the publisher.

6th Edition

ISBN 978-1-64097-080-9

ISSN 1934–5542

All details in this book are based on information supplied to us at press time. Always confirm information when it matters, especially if you're making a detour to visit a specific place. Fodor's expressly disclaims any liability, loss, or risk, personal or otherwise, that is incurred as a consequence of the use of any of the contents of this book.

SPECIAL SALES

This book is available at special discounts for bulk purchases for sales promotions or premiums. For more information, e-mail SpecialMarkets@fodors.com.

PRINTED IN THE UNITED STATES OF AMERICA

10 9 8 7 6 5 4 3 2 1

CONTENTS

Fodor's Features

CONTENTS

ABOUT THIS GUIDE

Fodor's Recommendations

Everything in this guide is worth doing—we don't cover what isn't—but exceptional sights, hotels, and restaurants are recognized with additional accolades. Fodor'sChoice★ indicates our top recommendations. Care to nominate a new place? Visit Fodors.com/contact-us.

Trip Costs

We list prices wherever possible to help you budget well. Hotel and restaurant price categories from $ to $$$$ are noted alongside each recommendation. For hotels, we include the lowest cost of a standard double room in high season. For restaurants, we cite the average price of a main course at dinner or, if dinner isn't served, at lunch. For attractions, we always list adult admission fees; discounts are usually available for children, students, and senior citizens.

Hotels

Our local writers vet every hotel to recommend the best overnights in each price category, from budget to expensive. Unless otherwise specified, you can expect private bath, phone, and TV in your room. For expanded hotel reviews visit Fodors.com.

Top Picks	Hotels &
★ Fodor'sChoice	Restaurants
	☒ Hotel
Listings	↳ Number of
☒ Address	rooms
☒ Branch address	℗ Meal plans
☎ Telephone	✗ Restaurant
🖷 Fax	⟨ Reservations
⊕ Website	🏛 Dress code
✉ E-mail	⊟ No credit cards
🎫 Admission fee	⑤ Price
☉ Open/closed	
times	**Other**
Ⓜ Subway	⇨ See also
✛ Directions or	☞ Take note
Map coordinates	🏌 Golf facilities

Restaurants

Unless we state otherwise, restaurants are open for lunch and dinner daily. We mention dress code only when there's a specific requirement and reservations only when they're essential or not accepted.

Credit Cards

The hotels and restaurants in this guide typically accept credit cards. If not, we'll say so.

EUGENE FODOR

Hungarian-born Eugene Fodor (1905–91) began his travel career as an interpreter on a French cruise ship. The experience inspired him to write *On the Continent* (1936), the first guidebook to receive annual updates and discuss a country's way of life as well as its sights. Fodor later joined the U.S. Army and worked for the OSS in World War II. After the war, he kept up his intelligence work while expanding his guidebook series. During the Cold War, many guides were written by fellow agents who understood the value of insider information. Today's guides continue Fodor's legacy by providing travelers with timely coverage, insider tips, and cultural context.

EXPERIENCE
THE ISLAND

WHAT'S WHERE

1 Kailua-Kona. This seaside town is packed with restaurants, shops, and a busy waterfront bustling with tourists along the main street, Alii Drive.

2 The Kona Coast. This area stretches a bit north of Kailua-Kona and much farther south, including gorgeous Kealakekua Bay. It's the place to take farm tours and taste samples of world-famous Kona coffee.

3 The Kohala Coast. The sparkling coast is home to all those long, white-sand beaches, and the expensive resorts that go with them.

4 Waimea. Ranches sprawl across the cool, upland meadows of the area, known as *paniolo* (cowboy) country.

5 Maunakea. Climb (or drive) this 13,796-foot mountain for what's considered the world's best stargazing, with 13 telescopes perched on top.

6 The Hamakua Coast. Waterfalls, dramatic cliffs, ocean views, ancient hidden valleys, rain forests, and the stunning Waipio Valley are just a few of the treats here.

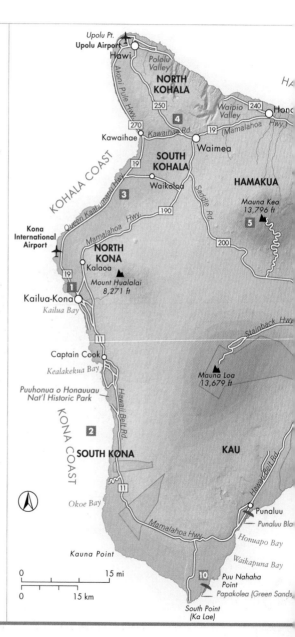

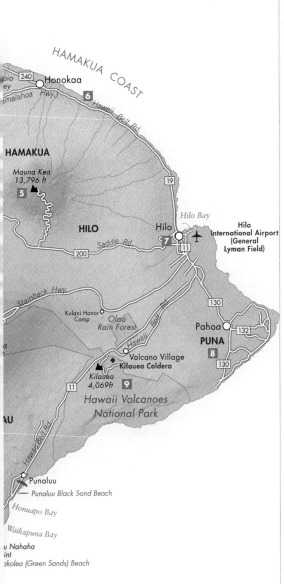

7 **Hilo.** Known as the City of Rainbows for all its rain, Hilo is often skipped by tourists in favor of the sunny Kohala Coast. But for what many consider the "real" Hawaii, as well as incredible rain forests, waterfalls, and the island's best farmers' market, Hilo can't be beat.

8 **Puna.** This remote district has the quirky, hippie town of Pahoa as well as the island's most recent lava flows.

9 **Hawaii Volcanoes National Park and vicinity.** The glow from the lava lake at Halemaumau Crater within Kilauea Caldera is not to be missed. The adjacent hamlet of Volcano Village provides a great base for exploring the park.

10 **Kau and Ka Lae (South Point).** Round the southernmost part of the island for two of the Big Island's most unusual beaches: Papakolea (Green Sands) Beach, and Punaluu Black Sand Beach.

BIG ISLAND AND HAWAII TODAY

You could fit all the other Hawaiian Islands into the Big Island and still have a little room left over—hence the name. Locals refer to the island by side: the Kona (leeward) side to the west and Hilo side to the east. Most of the resorts, condos, hotels, and beaches are located along 30 miles of the sunny Kona side, while the rainy, windward Hilo side offers a much more local and "Old Hawaii" experience.

Hawaiian culture and tradition have experienced a renaissance over the last few decades. Resort hotels often have a Hawaiian cultural expert on staff to ensure cultural sensitivity and to educate visitors.

Nonetheless, development remains an issue for all Islanders—land prices are expensive, putting many areas out of reach for the local population. The cost of living and the cost of doing business make Hawaii one of the more challenging places to live in the United States if you are on a fixed income.

Sustainability
Although sustainability is an effective buzzword and authentic direction for the Islands' dining establishments, 90% of Hawaii's food and energy is imported.

In decades past, the state's predominant agricultural regions were used for monocropping of pineapple or sugarcane, both of which have all but vanished. Sugarcane production on Maui ceased in 2016, while pineapple production has dropped precipitously. Dole, once the largest pineapple company in Hawaii, closed its plants in 1991, and after 90 years, Del Monte stopped pineapple production in 2008. As of 2018, Maui Gold Pineapple Company continues to operate on 1,350 acres on the slopes of Haleakala. The low cost of labor and transportation from Latin American and Southeast Asian pineapple producers are factors contributing to the industry's demise in Hawaii. Although this proves daunting, it also sets the stage for great agricultural change to be explored.

Back-to-Basics Agriculture
Emulating how the Hawaiian ancestors lived and returning to their simple ways of growing and sharing a variety of foods has become a statewide initiative. Hawaii boasts the natural conditions and talent to produce diversity in agriculture, from coffee, avocados, and dragon fruit to flowers, goat cheese, and wine. The seed of this movement thrives through various farmers' markets and partnerships between restaurants and local farmers. Localized efforts such as the Hawaii Farm Bureau Federation are collectively leading the organic and sustainable agricultural renaissance. From home-cooked meals to casual plate lunches to fine-dining cuisine, cooks, farmers, and chefs are blazing a trail of sustainability, helping to enrich the culinary tapestry of Hawaii.

Tourism and the Economy
At over $15.6 billion annually, the tourism industry represents a third of Hawaii's state income. With a record number of 9 million visitors coming to the Islands in 2016, tourism added $1.82 billion in state tax revenue for the year. Arrivals by air in 2016 increased by 3.1 percent thanks to growth in the West Coast and East Coast U.S. markets, as well as Korea. Arrivals via cruise ships, however, declined by 6.6% from 2015 to 2016 due to fewer vessels serving the Islands. Visitor spending contributes to at least 190,000 jobs locally.

Sovereignty

Political issues of sovereignty continue to divide Native Hawaiians, who have formed myriad organizations, each operating with a separate agenda and lacking one collectively defined goal. Ranging from achieving complete independence to solidifying a nation within a nation, existing sovereignty models remain fractured and their future unresolved.

The introduction of the Native Hawaiian Government Reorganization Act of 2009 (The Akaka Bill) attempted to set up a legal framework in which Native Hawaiians can attain federal recognition and coexist as a self-governed entity. Still held up in Congress, the bill has faced innumerable challenges through the years, including among Native Hawaiians who disagree about its merits and mission.

The Arts

The Hawaiian Islands have inspired artistic expression from the time they were first inhabited, whether hula, tapa cloth, carving and petroglyphs or modern pursuits like filmmaking and digital photography. Honolulu is the artistic hub of the state. The Honolulu Museum of Art has an impressive permanent collection and hosts major exhibitions throughout the year. It comprises four locations including the spectacular Shangri La, the former home of heiress Doris Duke, filled with Islamic treasures. The Hawaii Theatre Center in Honolulu—a restored art deco palace—stages theatrical productions, concerts, and films. The Maui Arts & Cultural Center (MACC) has a 1,200-seat theater for concerts, theatrical productions, and film, as well as an amphitheater and art gallery. Numerous art galleries thrive on the Islands.

Latest Eruptions

In May 2018, dramatic changes began happening at Kilauea Volcano. The collapse of the Puʻu Oʻo vent, which has been continuously erupting since 1983, preceded fissure eruptions in a remote neighborhood in Lower Puna, destroying dozens of homes. Meanwhile, back in Hawaii Volcanoes National Park, the lava lake at Halemaʻumaʻu began receding quickly, creating ash plumes above the summit and steam explosions. As with any eruption, no one knows how long the eruption in Lower Puna will last, or what will happen at Halemaʻumaʻu Crater. What's important for the visitor to know is that these events are taking place in remote areas. Most of the Big Island is safe from ongoing eruptions at Kilauea. If you are planning a trip to Lower Puna or Pahoa, do your research first before booking your stay since some places are closed and some roads have been covered by lava flows.

With no end in sight to the Kilauea eruption, much of Hawaii Volcanoes National Park closed on May 11, 2018, and remains closed at this writing. The Kahuku Unit remains open whenever air quality is deemed safe. Park rangers, in the meantime, are stationed at the Hilo Airport and at the Mokupapapa Discovery Center in downtown Hilo.

BIG ISLAND PLANNER

When You Arrive

The Big Island's two main airports are almost directly across the island from each other. Kona International Airport, on the west side, is about a 10-minute drive from Kailua-Kona and 30 to 45 minutes from the Kohala Coast. On the east side, Hilo International Airport, 2 miles from downtown Hilo, is about 40 minutes from Hawaii Volcanoes National Park. A 2½-hour drive connects Hilo and Kailua-Kona.

Visitor Information

Before you go, contact the Island of Hawaii Visitors Bureau to request a free official vacation planner. The Hawaii Island Chamber of Commerce also has links on its website to dozens of museums, attractions, bed-and-breakfasts, and parks. The Kona-Kohala Chamber of Commerce also has resources for the west side of the island.

Contacts **Island of Hawaii Visitors Bureau.** ⊠ *68-1330 Mauna Lani Dr., Ste. 109A* ⊕ *www.gohawaii.com.* **Hawaii Island Chamber of Commerce.** ⊠ *117 Keawe St., Hilo* ☎ *808/935–7178* ⊕ *www.hicc. biz.* **Kona-Kohala Chamber of Commerce.** ⊠ *75-5737 Kuakini Hwy., Suite 208, Kailua-Kona* ☎ *808/329–1758* ⊕ *www. kona-kohala.com.*

Getting Here and Around

It's essential to rent a car when visiting the Big Island. As the name suggests, it's a big island, and it takes a while to get from point A to point B.

For those who want to travel from the west side to the east side, or vice versa, the newly rerouted and repaved Saddle Road creates a nice shortcut across the middle of the island.

⇨ *See Travel Smart Big Island for more information on renting a car and driving.*

Island Driving Times

Before you embark on your day trip, it's a good idea to know how long it will take you to get to your destination. Some areas, like downtown Kailua-Kona and Waimea, can become congested at certain times of day. For those traveling to South Kona, the county has opened a long-awaited bypass road between Keauhou and Keal-akekua, which has alleviated congestion considerably during rush hour. In general, you can expect the following average driving times:

Kailua-Kona to Kealakekua Bay	14 miles/25 min
Kailua-Kona to Kohala Coast	32 miles/40 min
Kailua-Kona to Waimea	40 miles/1 hr
Kailua-Kona to Hamakua Coast	53 miles/1 hr 40 min
Kailua-Kona to Hilo	75 miles/2½ hrs
Kohala Coast to Waimea	16 miles/20 min
Kohala Coast to Hamakua Coast	29 miles/55 min
Hilo to Volcano	30 miles/40 min

Weather-Related Driving Tips

As a result of multiple microclimates and varying elevations, the Big Island experiences its share of diverse weather. On one circle-the-island trip you may experience combinations of the following: intensely heavy tropical downpours; cool, windy conditions; searing heat; and even snow flurries if you happen to be driving up

Maunakea. Be cautious on the mostly single-lane roads through rural areas, as these can be slick, winding, and poorly lit. Pull over to the side of the road to wait out intense bursts of rain that may obscure vision and create other hazardous conditions. These are usually brief and may even end with a rainbow.

FAQs

Will I see flowing lava? Lava often flows on the Big Island, but you may not know until the day of your visit whether the lava flow will be in an accessible location, or even visible from a distance. Your best bet is to call the visitor center at Hawaii Volcanoes National Park before you head out. Without question, the best time to see lava is at night. The nighttime glow of the lava lake within Halemaumau crater, located below the Jaggar Museum, is a jaw-dropping sight and one that should not be missed. Plan your trip to the volcano so that you can be near the crater at dusk. Fortunately, the park is open 24 hours a day, and night visits are allowed. In recent years, active lava flows have been taking place outside the park near Kalapana. When lava is flowing outside park boundaries, hiking is sometimes regulated because trails pass through private land. Pay attention to all warning signs, and take safety advice from park rangers seriously. ■TIP➜ Bring a flashlight, water, and sturdy shoes, and be prepared for some rough going over the lava fields at night.

➪ *For more information about visiting Hawaii Volcanoes National Park, see Chapter 2.*

Will I see manta rays? The Big Island is known for its scuba diving, and the visibility is amazing. If you book a nighttime manta-ray dive, you will likely actually see some majestic manta rays up close and personal in Keauhou Bay, and it's an experience not to be missed.

Will it rain? The Kona side of the Big Island is arid and hot, with mile upon mile of black lava fields lining a shimmering coastline. The Hilo side, on the other hand, gets roughly 130 inches of rain a year, so the chances of getting rained on while driving along the Hamakua Coast to Hilo are pretty good. That said, it tends to rain most in the morning and evening on the Hilo side and clears up during the afternoon, leaving a handful of rainbows behind.

Can I surf? The Big Island is not known for its surf spots, but that doesn't mean that there aren't any, or that there aren't plenty of local surfers. Surf's up in winter, down in summer; the beautiful peaceful beach you went to last summer could be a rough and rowdy surfer beach in the winter.

What other activities are popular? The Big Island is particularly well known for deep-sea fishing (late summer to early fall is peak season), and it is also rapidly building a reputation as the golfer's island. Guided tours are handy for remote attractions like Maunakea stargazing and Waipio Valley. Definitely set aside time and money for as many activities as you can fit into your trip.

GREAT ITINERARIES

Yes, the Big Island is big, and yes, there's a lot to see. If you're short on time, consider flying into one airport and out of the other. That will give you the opportunity to see both sides of the island without ever having to backtrack. Decide what sort of note you'd rather end on to determine your route—if you'd prefer to spend your last few days near the beach, go from east to west; if hiking through rain forests and showering in waterfalls sounds like a better way to wrap up the trip, move from west to east. If you're short on time, head straight for Hawaii Volcanoes National Park and briefly visit Hilo before traveling the Hamakua Coast route and making your new base in Kailua-Kona.

From exploring the shores of green- and black-sand beaches to stargazing atop Maunakea, there's no shortage of ways to spend time immersed in nature on the Big Island. Choose a couple or several of our favorite one-day itineraries to suit your interest and length of stay.

Green Hawaii
Take full advantage of Hawaii's living classroom. Visit one of the island's botanical gardens or take a farm tour in the morning, then head to the Natural Energy Lab, near the Kona International Airport, for a peek at how various enterprises raise shellfish, spirulina, and even seahorses. Wrap it up with an evening spent enjoying the delicious island-grown products at one of Waimea's top restaurants, such as local favorite Merriman's or its nearby neighbor Red Water Cafe.

Black and Green Sand
Check out some of the unusual beaches you'll find only on the Big Island. Start with a hike into Green Sands Beach near South Point and plan to spend some time sitting on the beach, dipping into the bay's turquoise waters, and marveling at the surreal beauty of this spot.

When you've had your fill, hop back in the car and head south about half an hour to Punaluu Black Sand Beach, the favorite nesting place of the endangered Hawaiian hawksbill turtle. Although the surf is often too rough to go swimming with green sea turtles, there are typically at least two or three napping on the beach at any given time.

Sun and Stars
Spend the day lounging on a Kohala Coast beach (Hapuna, Kaunaoa—also known as Maunakea—or Kua Bay), but throw jackets and boots in the car because you'll be catching the sunset from Maunakea's summit. Bundle up and stick around after darkness falls for some of the world's best stargazing.

For the safest, most comfortable experience, book a summit tour or stop in at the Onizuka Center for International Astronomy, a visitor center located at about 9,000 feet, or join the free summit tour at 1 pm on Saturday or Sunday, and return to the center to use the telescopes for evening stargazing.

Hike Volcanoes
Devote a full day (at least) to exploring Hawaii Volcanoes National Park. Head out on the Kilauea Iki trail—a 4-mile loop near Thurston Lava Tube—by late morning. Leave the park to grab lunch at nearby restaurants in Volcano Village just a few minutes away, or plan ahead and pack your own picnic before you start your morning hike. Later you can take a stroll past the steam vents and sulfur banks, and then hit the Jaggar Museum, which offers great views of Halemaumau Crater's glow at night.

Majestic Waterfalls and Kings' Valleys

Take a day to enjoy the splendors of the Hamakua Coast—any gorge you see on the road is an indication of a waterfall waiting to be explored. For a sure bet, head to beautiful Waipio Valley. Book a horseback, hiking, or four-wheel-drive tour, or walk on in yourself (just keep in mind that it's an arduous hike back up—a 25% grade for a little over a mile).

Once in the valley, take your first right to get to the black-sand beach. Take a moment to sit here—the ancient Hawaiians believed this was where souls crossed over to the afterlife. Whether you believe it or not, there's something unmistakably special about this place.

Waterfalls abound in the valley, depending on the amount of recent rainfall. Your best bet is to follow the river from the beach to the back of the valley, where a waterfall and its lovely pool await.

Underwater Day

Explore the colorful reefs populated with tropical fish off the Big Island's coast. We challenge you to stop thinking about the world beneath the waves when you're back on land. Our favorite spots include easily accessible Kahaluu Beach Park (off Alii Drive), Kealakekua Bay, and the Kapoho Tide Pools.

Early morning or late afternoon is the best time to see pods of Hawaiian spinner dolphins that rest in calm bays, but you're likely to encounter turtles any time of day, along with convict tangs, puffer fish, triggerfish, angelfish, spotted moray eels, trumpet fish, and hundreds of other brightly colored species.

Thermal Springs and Waterfalls

Due to its remote location, many visitors skip Puna. They don't know what they're missing. Venture into this isolated area for a morning, and you'll be rewarded with lava-tube hikes (Kilauea Caverns of Fire), volcanically heated pools (Ahalanui Park), and tide pools brimming with colorful coral, fish, and the occasional turtle (Kapoho Tide Pools).

Head to Hilo in the afternoon to visit Rainbow Falls, located right in town, or Akaka Falls, just outside town. Stroll Banyan Drive and Queen Liliuokalani Gardens before dining at one of Hilo's great restaurants.

Pololu and Paniolo Country

North Kohala is a world away from the resorts of the coast. Visit the quaint artists' community of Hawi, then head to the end of the road at Pololu Valley for amazing views.

A steep ½-mile hike leads to a fantastic black-sand beach surrounded by beautiful, sheer green cliffs. Back on the road, head up Highway 250 to Waimea and the rolling hills and pastures of *paniolo* country. Indulge in a memorable meal at one of the town's fantastic restaurants.

Venture Off-Road

Book an ATV tour or take your four-wheel drive for a spin to check out some of the Big Island's isolated beaches. There are green beaches (in addition to *the* Green Sands Beach) waiting in the Kau region and ruggedly beautiful white beaches with perfect turquoise water along the Kohala Coast; deal with the tough, four-wheel-drive-only roads into these beaches and you're likely to be rewarded with a pristine tropical beach all to yourself.

KIDS AND FAMILIES

With dozens of adventures, discoveries, and fun-filled beach days, Hawaii is a blast with kids. Even better, the things to do here don't only appeal to small fry. The entire family, parents included, will enjoy surfing, discovering a waterfall in the rain forest, and snorkeling with sea turtles. And there are plenty of organized activities for kids that will give parents time for a few romantic beach strolls.

Choosing a Place to Stay

Resorts: Most of the big resorts make kids' programs a priority, and it shows. When you are booking your room, ask about "kids eat free" deals and the number of kids' pools at the resort. Also check out the size of the groups in the children's programs, and find out whether the cost of the programs includes lunch, equipment, and activities.

The Hilton Waikoloa Village is every kid's fantasy vacation come true, with multiple pool slides, one lagoon for snorkeling and one filled with dolphins, and even a choice between riding a monorail or taking a boat to your room. Not to be outdone, the Four Seasons Resort Hualalai has a great program that will keep your little ones happy and occupied all day.

Condos: Condo and vacation rentals are a fantastic value for families vacationing in Hawaii. You can cook your own food, which is cheaper than eating out and sometimes easier (especially if you have a finicky eater in your group), and you'll get twice the space of a hotel room for about a quarter of the price. If you decide to go the condo route, be sure to ask about the size of the complex's pool (some try to pawn off a tiny soaking tub as a pool) and whether barbecues are available. One of the best reasons to stay in your own place

is to hold a sunset family barbecue by the pool or overlooking the ocean.

Condos in Kailua-Kona (on or near Alii Drive) are the some of the best values on the Big Island. We like Casa de Emdeko for its oceanfront pool and on-site convenience store. On the Kohala Coast, the Vista Waikoloa complex provides extra-large condos and is walking distance to beautiful Anaehoomalu Bay. Affordable food is available at restaurants in Kona, if you are looking for a family night out or, even better, a date night.

Ocean Activities

On the Beach: Most people like being in the water, but toddlers and school-age kids tend to be especially enamored of it. The swimming pool at your condo or hotel is always an option, but don't be afraid to hit the beach with a little one in tow. There are lots of family-friendly beaches on the Big Island, complete with protected bays and pleasant white sand. As always, use your judgment, and heed all posted signs and lifeguard warnings.

Calm beaches to try include Kamakahonu Beach and Kahaluu Beach Park in Kailua-Kona; Spencer Beach Park, and Waialea Bay in Puako; Ahalanui Beach Park in Puna; and Leleiwi Beach Park in Hilo.

On the Waves: Surf lessons are a great idea for older kids. Beginner lessons are always on safe and easy waves. Most surf schools also offer instruction in stand-up paddleboarding.

For school-age and older kids, book a four-hour surfing lesson with Kahaluu Bay Surf & Sea and either join the kids out on the break or say aloha to a little parents-only time.

The Underwater World: If your kids are ready to try snorkeling, Hawaii is a great place to introduce them to the underwater world. Even without the mask and snorkel, they'll be able to see colorful fish darting this way and that below the surface of the water, and they may also spot turtles at many of the island beaches.

The easily accessible Kahaluu Beach, in Kailua-Kona, is a great introductory snorkel spot because of its many facilities. Protected by a natural breakwater, these shallow reefs attract large numbers of sea creatures, including the Hawaiian green sea turtle. These turtles feed on seaweed near shore and sometimes can be spotted basking on the rocks.

On the southern tip of the island, Punaluu Black Sand Beach provides opportunities to see the sea turtles up close. Though the water can be rough, the hawksbill turtles nest here, and there are nearly always one or two napping on the beach. At nighttime, head to the Sheraton Kona Resort & Spa at Keauhou Bay, or Huggo's on the Rocks in Kailua-Kona, to view manta rays; each place shines a bright spotlight on the water to attract them. Anyone, but especially kids, could sit and watch them glide through the ocean in graceful circles for hours. No snorkel required!

Another great option is to book a snorkel cruise or opt to stay dry inside the Atlantis Submarine that operates out of Kailua-Kona. Kids love crawling down into a real-life submarine and viewing the ocean world through its little portholes.

Land Activities

In addition to beach experiences, Hawaii Island has easy waterfall hikes, botanical gardens, a zoo, and hands-on museums that will keep your kids entertained and out of the sun for a day.

Hawaii Volcanoes National Park is a must for any family vacation. Even grumpy teenagers will acknowledge the coolness of lava tubes, steaming volcanic craters, and a fiery nighttime lava show.

On the Hilo side, the Panaewa Rain Forest Zoo is small, but free, and lots of fun for the little ones, with a small petting zoo on Saturday. Your kids might even get to hold a Hawaiian hawk. Just a few miles north, on the Hamakua Coast, the Hawaii Tropical Botanical Garden makes a beautiful and fun stop for kids, filled with huge lily pads and noisy frogs.

School-age and older kids will get a kick out of the ATV tours on the rim above Waipio Valley, and horseback rides past the waterfalls of Waipio Valley via Naalapa Stables.

After Dark

At night, younger kids get a kick out of attending a luau, and many of the shows incorporate young audience members, adding to the fun. Teens and adults alike are sure to enjoy the music and overall theatrical quality of the Sheraton Kona Resort & Spa's "Haleo," the story of the Keauhou *ahupuaa* (land division).

Stargazing from Maunakea is another treat. The visitor center has telescopes set up for all visitors to use. If you'd rather leave the planning to someone else, book a tour with Hawaii Forest & Trail. Its unbelievably knowledgeable guides are great at sharing that knowledge in a narrative form that kids—and adults, for that matter—enjoy.

TOP 5 BIG ISLAND OUTDOOR ADVENTURES

Getting out for active adventure is one of the top reasons people come to the Big Island.

There are endless options here for spending time outside, enjoying the land, the ocean, or the highest points of mountains and volcanoes. Here are a few of our favorites.

Bike Kulani Trails

Stands of 80-foot eucalyptus. Giant hapuu tree ferns. The sweet song of honeycreepers overhead. Add single-track of rock and root—no dirt here—and we're talking technical. Did we mention this is a rain forest near Hilo? That explains the perennial slick coat of slime on every possible surface. Advanced cyclists only.

Snorkel at Kealakekua Bay

Yes, the snorkeling here is tops for the Big Island. Visibility reaches depths of 80 feet, and you'll spot colorful creatures swimming among jagged pinnacles and pristine coral habitats. But, to be real, the draw here is the Hawaiian spinner dolphins that come to rest in the bay during the daytime.

While it's enticing to swim with wild dolphins, getting too close can disrupt their sleep cycles. Observe from a distance and respect their space while still enjoying a fantastic experience communing with nature.

Search for Lava at Hawaii Volcanoes National Park

It's not too often that you can witness the creation of molten earth in action. That's just what happens at Hawaii Volcanoes National Park. The most dramatic examples occur where lava flows enter the sea. While Madame Pele rarely gives away her itinerary in advance, if you're lucky a hike or boat ride may pay off with spectacular sights. Just before dawn and nighttime make for the best viewing opportunities.

Go Horseback Riding in Waipio Valley

The Valley of the Kings owes its relative isolation and off-the-grid status to the 2,000-foot-high cliffs bookending the valley. Really, the only way to explore this sacred place is on two legs—or four.

We're partial to the horseback rides that wend deep into the rain forest to a series of waterfalls and pools—the setting for a perfect romantic getaway.

Witness Waterfalls on the Hilo Side

The east side of the Big Island—also called the Hilo side (as opposed to the western Kona side)—is essentially a rain forest, with an average rainfall of 130 inches a year. It's no wonder Hilo is called the City of Rainbows—and all that rain means tons of waterfalls. Some of our favorites include Peepee Falls (Boiling Pots) and Rainbow Falls, both easy to access from main roads just above downtown Hilo.

BIG ISLAND'S TOP BEACHES

With over 265 miles of coastline, the Big Island—the largest and youngest island—offers the widest variety of beaches in Hawaii. Take your pick from black sand, soft white sand, crystalline green sand, award-winning beaches, and beaches off the beaten track.

Best Classic Beach

Mauna Kea Beach (Kaunaoa) and nearby Hapuna Beach, Kohala Coast. Long, white stretches of pure soft sand and glistening, azure water are perfect for swimming, snorkeling, and sunbathing. These two beaches are consistently rated among the best in the state. Simply perfect.

Kekaha Kai State Park, Kona Coast. This beautiful beach in a postcard-like setting has outstandingly soft sand and great spots for swimming.

Best for Families

Spencer Park, Kohala Coast. This protected sandy beach has consistently gentle surf so it's usually safe for swimming.

Anaehoomalu Bay, Kohala Coast. In the heart of Waikoloa Beach Resort, this white-sand beach is a spectacular spot for swimming, snorkeling, stand-up paddleboarding, and spotting turtles. The glass-bottom boat ride is cool, too.

Onekahakaha Beach Park, Hilo. Parents can relax on the white-sand beach while kids explore the shallow, enclosed tide pools for exotic sea life.

Best for Interesting Sand

Punaluu Black Sand Beach Park, Kau. It's busy for a reason. Between the turtles and the black sand, it's tough not to camp out all day at this easily accessed beach.

Pololu Valley Beach, Kohala Coast. Jaw-droppingly scenic, this perfect crescent of black sand is backed by sheer green cliffs. The hike down to the beach is definitely worth the trip, but the surf can be treacherous.

Papakolea Beach, Kau. Sure it's a 2-mile hike, but where else are you going to see a beach with green sand? The dry, barren landscape is surreal, and the beach sparkles with olivine crystals formed during volcanic eruptions.

Best Snorkeling

Kahaluu Beach Park, Kailua-Kona. Protective reefs keep the waters calm, and the abundant fish are not shy, as they're used to swimming amid snorkelers.

Punaluu Black Sand Beach Park, Kau. You're almost guaranteed to see sea turtles who nest in the black sand and swim in the waters just offshore.

Best Surfing

Kahaluu Beach Park, Kailua-Kona. When the surf's up, this beach is irresistible for anyone who wants to take a beginner surf lesson.

Kua Bay (Kekaha Kai State Park), Kona Coast. Local surfers and body boarders love the challenge of the rough waves in winter.

Honolii Beach Park, Hilo. Even if you don't surf, Hilo's main drag for surfers is a great place to hang out and watch.

Best Sunsets

We're going to say it one last time: westward-facing **Hapuna Beach** is not to be missed.

WEDDINGS AND HONEYMOONS

There's no question that Hawaii is one of the country's foremost honeymoon destinations. Romance is in the air here, and the white-sand beaches, turquoise water, swaying palm trees, balmy tropical breezes, and perpetual sunshine put people in the mood for love. It's easy to understand why Hawaii is a popular wedding destination as well, especially as the cost of airfare is often discounted, and new resorts and hotels entice visitors. You can plan a traditional ceremony in a place of worship followed by a reception at an elegant resort, or you can go barefoot on the beach and celebrate at a luau. There are almost as many wedding planners in the Islands as real estate agents, which makes it oh-so-easy to wed in paradise, and then, once the knot is tied, stay and honeymoon as well.

The Big Day

Choosing the Perfect Place. When choosing a location, remember that you really have two choices to make: the ceremony location and where to have the reception, if you're having one. For the former, there are beaches, bluffs overlooking beaches, gardens, private residences, resort lawns, and, of course, places of worship. As for the reception, there are these same choices, as well as restaurants and even a luau. If you decide to go outdoors, remember the seasons—yes, Hawaii has seasons. If you're planning a summer wedding outdoors, be sure you have a backup plan (such as a tent) in case it rains. Also, if you're planning an outdoor wedding at sunset—which is very popular—be sure you match the time of your ceremony to the time the sun sets at that time of year. If you choose an indoor spot, be sure to ask for pictures of the location when you're planning. You don't want to plan a pink wedding, say, and wind up in a room

that's predominantly red. Or maybe you do. The point is, it should be your choice.

Finding a Wedding Planner. If you're planning to invite more than an officiant and your loved one to your wedding ceremony, seriously consider an on-island wedding planner who can help select a location; help design the floral scheme and recommend a florist as well as a photographer; help plan the menu and choose a restaurant, caterer, or resort; and suggest Hawaiian traditions to incorporate into your ceremony. And more: Will you need tents, a cake, music? Maybe transportation and lodging? Many planners have relationships with vendors, providing packages—which mean savings.

If you're planning a resort wedding, most have on-site wedding coordinators; however, there are many independents around the Islands and even those who specialize in certain types of ceremonies—by locale, size, religious affiliation, and so on. A simple "Hawaii weddings" Google search will reveal dozens. What's important is that you feel comfortable with your coordinator. Ask for references and call them. Share your budget. Get a proposal—in writing. Ask how long they've been in business, how much they charge, how often you'll meet with them, and how they select vendors. Request a detailed list of the exact services they'll provide. If your idea of your wedding doesn't match their services, try someone else. If you can afford it, you might want to meet the planner in person.

Getting Your License. The good news about marrying in Hawaii is that there is no waiting period, no residency or citizenship requirement, and no blood test or shots required. You can apply and pay the fee online; however, both the bride and groom must appear together in person before a marriage-license agent to receive the marriage license (the permit to get married). You'll need proof of age—the legal age to marry is 18. (If you're 19 or older, a valid driver's license will suffice; if you're 18, a certified birth certificate is required.) Upon approval, a marriage license is immediately issued and costs $60. After the ceremony, your officiant will mail the marriage certificate (proof of marriage) to the state. Approximately four months later, you will receive a copy in the mail. (For $10 extra, you can expedite this process. Ask your marriage-license agent when you apply.) For more detailed information, visit ⊕ *marriage.ehawaii.gov.*

Also—this is important—the person performing your wedding must be licensed by the Hawaii Department of Health, even if he or she is a licensed officiant. Be sure to ask.

Wedding Attire. In Hawaii, basically anything goes, from long, formal dresses with trains to white bikinis. Floral sundresses are fine, too. For men, tuxedos are not the norm; a pair of solid-colored slacks with a nice aloha shirt is. In fact, tradition in Hawaii for the groom is a beautiful white aloha shirt (they do exist) with slacks or long shorts and a colored sash around the waist. If you're planning a wedding on the beach, barefoot is the way to go.

If you decide to marry in a formal dress and tuxedo, you're better off making your selections on the mainland and hand-carrying them aboard the plane. Yes, it can be a pain, but ask your wedding-gown retailer to provide a special carrying bag. After all, you don't want to chance losing your wedding dress in a wayward piece of luggage. And when it comes to fittings, again, that's something to take care of before you arrive in Hawaii

Local Customs. The most obvious traditional Hawaiian wedding custom is the lei exchange in which the bride and groom take turns placing a lei around the neck of the other—with a kiss. Bridal lei are usually floral, whereas the groom's is typically made of *maile,* a green leafy garland that drapes around the neck and is open at the ends. Brides often also wear a *lei po'o*—a circular floral headpiece. Other Hawaiian customs include the blowing of the conch shell, hula, chanting, and Hawaiian music.

The Honeymoon

Do you want champagne and strawberries delivered to your room each morning? A breathtaking swimming pool in which to float? A five-star restaurant in which to dine? Then a resort is the way to go. If, however, you prefer the comforts of a home, try a bed-and-breakfast. A small inn is also good if you're on a tight budget or don't plan to spend much time in your room. On the other hand, maybe you want your own private home in which to romp freely—or just laze around recovering from the wedding planning. Maybe you want your own kitchen so you can whip up a gourmet meal for your loved one. In that case, a private vacation-rental home is the answer. Or maybe a condominium resort. That's another beautiful thing about Hawaii: the lodging accommodations are almost as plentiful as the beaches, and there's one that will perfectly match your tastes and your budget.

THE HISTORY OF HAWAII

Hawaiian history is long and complex; a brief survey can put into context the ongoing renaissance of native arts and culture.

The Polynesians

Long before both Christopher Columbus and the Vikings, Polynesian seafarers set out to explore the vast stretches of the open ocean in double-hulled canoes. From western Polynesia, they traveled back and forth between Samoa, Fiji, Tahiti, the Marquesas, and the Society Isles, settling on the outer reaches of the Pacific, Hawaii, and Easter Island, as early as AD 300. The golden era of Polynesian voyaging peaked around AD 1200, after which the distant Hawaiian Islands were left to develop their own unique cultural practices and subsistence in relative isolation.

The Islands' symbiotic society was deeply intertwined with religion, mythology, science, and artistry. Ruled by an *alii,* or chief, each settlement was nestled in an *ahupuaa,* a pie-shaped land division from the uplands where the *alii* lived, through the valleys and down to the shores where the commoners resided. Everyone contributed, whether it was by building canoes, catching fish, making tools, or farming land.

A United Kingdom

When the British explorer Captain James Cook arrived in Kealakekua Bay in 1778, he was greeted by the Hawaiians as a person of important stature. With guns and ammunition purchased from subsequent foreign trading ships, the Big Island chief, Kamehameha the Great, gained a significant advantage over the other *alii.* He united Hawaii into one kingdom in 1810, bringing an end to the frequent interisland battles that dominated Hawaiian life.

Tragically, the new kingdom was beset with troubles. Native religion was abandoned, and *kapu* (laws and regulations) were eventually abolished. The European explorers brought diseases with them, and within a few decades the Native Hawaiian population was decimated.

New laws regarding land ownership and religious practices eroded the underpinnings of pre-contact Hawaii. Each successor to the Hawaiian throne sacrificed more control over the Island kingdom. As Westerners permeated Hawaiian culture, so did social unrest.

Modern Hawaii

In 1893, the last Hawaiian monarch, Queen Liliuokalani, was overthrown by a group of Americans and European businessmen and government officials, aided by an armed militia. This led to the creation of the Republic of Hawaii, and it became a U.S. territory for the next 60 years. The loss of Hawaiian sovereignty and the conditions of annexation have haunted the Hawaiian people since the monarchy was deposed.

Pearl Harbor was attacked in 1941, which engaged the United States immediately into World War II. Tourism, from its beginnings in the early 1900s, flourished after the war and naturally inspired rapid real estate development in Waikiki. In 1959, Hawaii officially became the 50th state.

HAWAIIAN CULTURAL TRADITIONS HULA, LEI, AND LUAU

HULA: MORE THAN A FOLK DANCE

Hula has been called "the heartbeat of the Hawaiian people" and also "the world's best-known, most misunderstood dance." Both are true. Hula isn't just dance. It is storytelling.

Chanter Edith McKinzie calls it "an extension of a piece of poetry." In its adornments, implements, and customs, hula integrates every important Hawaiian cultural practice: poetry, history, genealogy, craft, plant cultivation, martial arts, religion, protocol. So when 19th-century Christian missionaries sought to eradicate a practice they considered depraved, they threatened more than just a folk dance.

With public performance outlawed and private hula practice discouraged, hula went underground for a generation. The fragile verbal link by which culture was transmitted from teacher to student hung by a thread. Even increasing literacy did not help because hula's practitioners were a secretive and protected circle.

As if that weren't bad enough, vaudeville, Broadway, and Hollywood got hold of the hula, giving it the glitz treatment in

an unbroken line from "Oh, How She Could Wicky Wacky Woo" to "Rock-A-Hula Baby." Hula became shorthand for paradise: fragrant flowers, lazy hours. Ironically, this development assured that hundreds of Hawaiians could make a living performing and teaching hula. Many danced *auana* (modern form) in performance; but taught *kahiko* (traditional), quietly, at home or in hula schools.

Today, decades after the cultural revival known as the Hawaiian Renaissance, language immersion programs have assured a new generation of proficient—and even eloquent—chanters, songwriters, and translators. Visitors can see more, and more authentic, traditional hula than at any other time in the last 200 years.

Like the culture of which it is the beating heart, hula has survived.

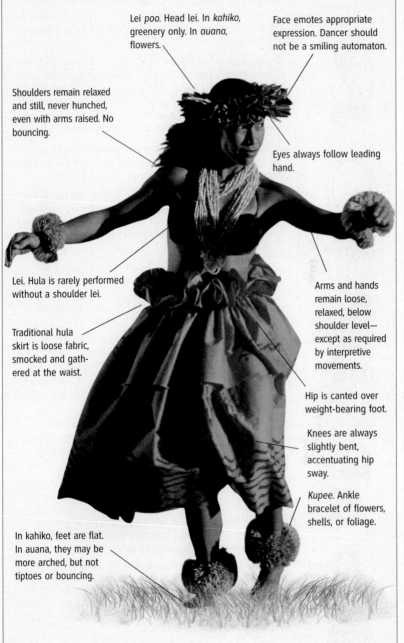

Lei *poo*. Head lei. In *kahiko*, greenery only. In *auana*, flowers.

Face emotes appropriate expression. Dancer should not be a smiling automaton.

Shoulders remain relaxed and still, never hunched, even with arms raised. No bouncing.

Eyes always follow leading hand.

Lei. Hula is rarely performed without a shoulder lei.

Arms and hands remain loose, relaxed, below shoulder level—except as required by interpretive movements.

Traditional hula skirt is loose fabric, smocked and gathered at the waist.

Hip is canted over weight-bearing foot.

Knees are always slightly bent, accentuating hip sway.

Kupee. Ankle bracelet of flowers, shells, or foliage.

In kahiko, feet are flat. In auana, they may be more arched, but not tiptoes or bouncing.

BASIC MOTIONS

Speak or Sing

Moon or Sun

Grass Shack or House

Mountains or Heights

Love or Caress

At backyard parties, hula is performed in bare feet and street clothes, but in performance, adornments play a key role, as do rhythm-keeping implements such as the pahu drum and the *ipu* (gourd).

In hula *kahiko* (traditional style), the usual dress is multiple layers of stiff fabric (often with a pellom lining, which most closely resembles *kapa*, (the paperlike bark cloth of the Hawaiians). These wrap tightly around the bosom but flare below the waist to form a skirt. In pre-contact times, dancers wore only kapa skirts. Men traditionally wear loincloths.

Monarchy-period hula is performed in voluminous muumuu or high-necked muslin blouses and gathered skirts. Men wear white or gingham shirts and black pants.

In hula *auana* (modern), dress for women can range from grass skirts and strapless tops to contemporary tea-length dresses. Men generally wear aloha shirts, but sometimes grass skirts over pants or even everyday gear.

SURPRISING HULA FACTS

■ Grass skirts are not traditional; workers from Kiribati (the Gilbert Islands) brought this custom to Hawaii.

■ In olden-day Hawaii, *mele* (songs) for hula were composed for every occasion—name songs for babies, dirges for funerals, welcome songs for visitors, celebrations of favorite pursuits.

■ Hula *mai* is a traditional hula form in praise of a noble's genitals; the power of the *alii* (royalty) to procreate gave *mana* (spiritual power) to the entire culture.

■ Hula students in old Hawaii adhered to high standards: scrupulous cleanliness, no sex, daily cleansing rituals, certain food prohibitions, and no contact with the dead. They were fined if they broke the rules.

WHERE TO WATCH

If you're interested in "the real thing," there are annual hula festivals on each island. Check the individual island visitors' bureaus websites at ⊕ *www.gohawaii.com*.

If you can't make it to a festival, there are plenty of other hula shows—at most resorts, many lounges, and even at certain shopping centers. Ask your hotel concierge for performance information.

ALL ABOUT LEI

Lei brighten every occasion in Hawaii, from birthdays to bar mitzvahs to baptisms. Creative artisans weave nature's bounty—flowers, ferns, vines, and seeds—into gorgeous creations that convey an array of heartfelt messages: "Welcome," "Congratulations," "Good luck," "Farewell," "Thank you," "I love you." When it's difficult to find the right words, a lei expresses exactly the right sentiment.

WHERE TO BUY THE BEST LEI

Most airports in Hawaii have lei stands where you can buy a fragrant garland upon arrival. Every florist shop in the Islands sells lei; you can also treat yourself to a lei while shopping for provisions at any supermarket or box store. And you'll always find lei sellers at crafts fairs and outdoor festivals.

LEI ETIQUETTE

■ To wear a closed lei, drape it over your shoulders, half in front and half in back. Open lei are worn around the neck, with the ends draped over the front in equal lengths.

■ Pikake, ginger, and other sweet, delicate blossoms are "feminine" lei. Men opt for cigar, crown flower, and ti leaf lei, which are sturdier and don't emit as much fragrance.

■ Lei are always presented with a kiss, a custom that supposedly dates back to World War II when a hula dancer fancied an officer at a U.S.O. show. Taking a dare from members of her troupe, she took off her lei, placed it around his neck, and kissed him on the cheek.

■ It has become a custom for visitors to toss their lei into the ocean before leaving to ensure a return trip, but this poses an entanglement risk to marine life. Instead, cut the lei string and remove the flowers so they can be loosely scattered into the water.

ORCHID

Growing wild on every continent except Antarctica, orchids—which range in color from yellow to green to purple—comprise the largest family of plants in the world. There are more than 20,000 species of orchids, but only three are native to Hawaii—and they are very rare. The pretty lavender vanda you see hanging by the dozens at local lei stands has probably been imported from Thailand.

MAILE

Maile, an endemic twining vine with a heady aroma, is sacred to Laka, goddess of the hula. In ancient times, dancers wore maile and decorated hula altars with it to honor Laka. Today, "open" maile lei usually are given to men. Instead of ribbon, interwoven lengths of maile are used at dedications of new businesses. The maile is untied, never snipped, for doing so would symbolically "cut" the company's success.

ILIMA

Designated by Hawaii's Territorial Legislature in 1923 as the official flower of the island of Oahu, the golden ilima is so delicate it lasts for just a day. Five to seven hundred blossoms are needed to make one garland. Queen Emma, wife of King Kamehameha IV, preferred ilima over all other lei, which may have led to the incorrect belief that they were reserved only for royalty.

PLUMERIA

This ubiquitous flower is named after Charles Plumier, the noted French botanist who discovered it in Central America in the late 1600s. Plumeria ranks among the most popular lei in Hawaii because it's fragrant, hardy, plentiful, inexpensive, and requires very little care. Although yellow is the most common color, you'll also find plumeria lei in shades of pink, red, orange, and "rainbow" blends.

PIKAKE

Favored for its fragile beauty and sweet scent, pikake was introduced from India. In lieu of pearls, many brides in Hawaii adorn themselves with long, multiple strands of white pikake. Princess Kaiulani enjoyed showing guests her beloved pikake and peacocks at Ainahau, her Waikiki home. Interestingly, pikake is the Hawaiian word for both the bird and the blossom.

KUKUI

The kukui (candlenut) is Hawaii's state tree. Early Hawaiians strung kukui nuts (which are quite oily) together and burned them for light; mixed burned nuts with oil to make an indelible dye; and mashed roasted nuts to consume as a laxative. Kukui nut lei may not have been made until after Western contact, when the Hawaiians saw black beads from Europe and wanted to imitate them.

LUAU: A TASTE OF HAWAII

The best place to sample Hawaiian food is at a backyard luau. Aunts and uncles are cooking, the pig is from a cousin's farm, and the fish is from a brother's boat.

But even locals have to angle for invitations to those rare occasions. So your choice is most likely between a commercial luau and a Hawaiian restaurant.

Some commercial luau are less authentic; they offer little of the traditional diet and are more about umbrella drinks, spectacle, and fun.

For greater culinary authenticity, folksy experiences, and rock-bottom prices, visit a Hawaiian restaurant (most are in anonymous storefronts in residential neighborhoods). Expect rough edges and some effort negotiating the menu.

In either case, much of what is known today as Hawaiian food would be as foreign to a 16th-century Hawaiian as risotto or chow mien. The pre-contact diet was simple and healthy—mainly raw and steamed seafood and vegetables. Early Hawaiians used earth ovens and heated stones to cook seafood, taro, sweet potatoes, and breadfruit and seasoned their food with sea salt and ground kukui nuts. Seaweed, fern shoots, sweet potato vines, coconut, banana, sugarcane, and select greens and roots rounded out the diet.

Successive waves of immigrants added their favorites to the ti leaf–lined table. So it is that foods as disparate as salt salmon and chicken long rice are now Hawaiian—even though there is no salmon in Hawaiian waters and long rice (cellophane noodles) is Chinese.

AT THE LUAU: KALUA PORK

The heart of any luau is the *imu*, the earth oven in which a whole pig is roasted. The preparation of an imu is an arduous affair for most families, who tackle it only once a year or so, for a baby's first birthday or at Thanksgiving, when many Islanders prefer to imu their turkeys. Commercial luau operations have it down to a science, however.

THE ART OF THE STONE

The key to a proper imu is the *pohaku*, the stones. Imu cook by means of long, slow, moist heat released by special stones that can withstand a hot fire without exploding. Many Hawaiian families treasure their imu stones, keeping them in a pile in the back-yard and passing them on through generations.

PIT COOKING

The imu makers first dig a pit about the size of a re-frigerator, then lay down *kiawe* (mesquite) wood and stones, and build a white-hot fire that is allowed to burn itself out. The ashes are raked away, and the hot stones covered with banana and ti leaves. Well-wrapped in ti or banana leaves and a net of chicken wire, the pig is lowered onto the leaf-covered stones. *Laulau* (leaf-wrapped bundles of meats, fish, and taro leaves) may also be placed inside. Leaves—ti, banana, even ginger—cover the pig followed by wet burlap sacks (to create steam). The whole is topped with a canvas tarp and left to steam for the better part of a day.

OPENING THE IMU

This is the moment everyone waits for: The imu is unwrapped like a giant present and the imu keep-ers gingerly wrestle out the steaming pig. When it's unwrapped, the meat falls moist and smoky-flavored from the bone, looking just like Southern-style pulled pork, but without the barbecue sauce.

WHICH LUAU?

Most resort hotels have luau on their grounds that include hula, music, and, of course, lots of food and drink. Each island also has at least one "authentic" luau. For lists of the best luau on each island, visit the Hawaii Visitors and Convention Bureau website at ⊕ *www.gohawaii.com*.

MEA AI ONO:
GOOD THINGS TO EAT.

LAULAU
Steamed meats, fish, and taro leaf in ti-leaf bundles: fork-tender, a medley of flavors; the taro resembles spinach.

Laulau

LOMI LOMI SALMON
Salt salmon in a piquant salad or relish with onions and tomatoes.

POI
Poi, a paste made of pounded taro root, may be an acquired taste, but it's a must-try during your visit.

Consider: The Hawaiian Adam is descended from *kalo* (taro). Young taro plants are called "keiki"–children. Poi is the first food after mother's milk for many Islanders. Ai, the word for food, is synonymous with poi in many contexts.

Lomi Lomi Salmon

Not only that, we love it. "There is no meat that doesn't taste good with poi," the old Hawaiians said.

But you have to know how to eat it: with something rich or powerfully flavored. "It is salt that makes the poi go in," is another adage. When you're served poi, try it with a mouthful of smoky kalua pork or salty lomi lomi salmon. Its slightly sour blandness cleanses the palate. And if you don't like it, smile and say something polite. (And slide that bowl over to a local.)

Poi

E HELE MAI AI! COME AND EAT!

Local-style Hawaiian restaurants tend to be inconveniently located in well-worn storefronts with little or no parking, outfitted with battered tables and clattering Melmac dishes, but they personify aloha, invariably run by local families who welcome tourists who take the trouble to find them.

Many are cash-only operations and combination plates, known as "plate lunch," are a standard feature: one or two entrées, two scoops of steamed rice, one scoop of macaroni salad, and—if the place is really old-style—a tiny portion of coarse Hawaiian salt and some raw onions for relish.

Most serve some foods that aren't, strictly speaking, Hawaiian, but are beloved of ka-

maaina, such as salt meat with watercress (preserved meat in a tasty broth), or *akubone* (skipjack tuna fried in a tangy vinegar sauce).

MENU GUIDE

Much of the Hawaiian language encountered during a stay in the Islands will appear on restaurant menus and lists of luau fare. Here's a quick primer.

ahi: *yellowfin tuna.*

aku: *skipjack, bonito tuna.*

amaama: *mullet; it's hard to get but tasty.*

bento: *a box lunch.*

chicken luau: *a stew made from chicken, taro leaves, and coconut milk.*

haupia: *a light, pudding-like sweet made from coconut.*

imu: *the underground oven in which pigs are roasted for luau.*

kalua: *to bake underground.*

kimchee: *Korean dish of fermented cabbage made with garlic, hot peppers, and other spices.*

Kona coffee: *coffee grown in the Kona district of the Big Island.*

laulau: *literally, a bundle. Laulau are morsels of pork, chicken, butterfish, or other ingredients wrapped with young taro leaves and then bundled in ti leaves for steaming.*

lilikoi: *passion fruit, a tart, seedy yellow fruit that makes delicious desserts, juice, and jellies.*

lomi lomi: *to rub or massage; also a type of massage. Lomi lomi salmon is fish that has been rubbed with onions and herbs; commonly served with minced onions and tomatoes.*

luau: *a Hawaiian feast; also the leaf of the taro plant used in preparing such a feast.*

luau leaves: *cooked taro tops with a taste similar to spinach.*

mahimahi: *mild-flavored dolphinfish, not the marine mammal.*

mai tai: *potent rum drink with orange liqueurs and pineapple juice, from the Tahitian word for "good."*

malasada: *a Portuguese deep-fried doughnut without a hole, dipped in sugar.*

manapua: *steamed Chinese buns filled with pork, chicken, or other fillings.*

niu: *coconut.*

onaga: *pink or red snapper.*

ono: *a long, slender mackerel-like fish; also called wahoo.*

ono: *delicious; also hungry.*

opihi: *a tiny limpet found on rocks.*

papio: *a young ulua or jack fish.*

poha: *Cape gooseberry. Tasting a bit like honey, the poha berry is often used in jams and desserts.*

poi: *a paste made from pounded taro root, a staple of the Hawaiian diet.*

poke: *cubed raw tuna or other fish, tossed with seaweed and seasonings.*

pupu: *appetizers or small plates.*

saimin: *long thin noodles and vegetables in broth, often garnished with small pieces of fish cake, scrambled egg, luncheon meat, and green onion.*

sashimi: *raw fish thinly sliced and usually eaten with soy sauce.*

ti leaves: *a member of the agave family. The leaves are used to wrap food while cooking and removed before eating.*

uku: *deep-sea snapper.*

ulua: *a member of the jack family that also includes pompano and amberjack. Also called crevalle, jack fish, and jack crevalle.*

EXPLORING

Updated by Kristina Anderson

Nicknamed "The Big Island," Hawaii Island is a microcosm of Hawaii the state. From long white-sand beaches and crystal-clear bays to rain forests, waterfalls, valleys, exotic flowers, and birds, all things quintessentially Hawaii are well represented here.

An assortment of happy surprises also distinguishes the Big Island from the rest of Hawaii—an active volcano (Kilauea) oozing red lava and creating new earth every day, the clearest place in the world to view stars in the night sky (Maunakea), and some seriously good coffee from the famous Kona district, and also from neighboring Kau.

Home to eight of the world's 13 sub-climate zones, this is the land of fire (thanks to active Kilauea volcano) and ice (compliments of not-so-active Maunakea, topped with snow and expensive telescopes). At just under a million years old, Hawaii is the youngest of the main Hawaiian Islands. Three of its five volcanoes are considered active: Mauna Loa, Hualalai, and Kilauea. The Southeast Rift Zone of Kilauea has been spewing lava regularly since January 3, 1983; another eruption began at Kilauea's summit caldera in March 2008, the first since 1982. Back in 1984, Mauna Loa's eruptions crept almost to Hilo, and it could fire up again any minute—or not for years. Hualalai last erupted in 1801, and geologists say it will definitely do so again within 100 years. Maunakea is currently considered dormant but may very well erupt again. Kohala, which last erupted some 120,000 years ago, is inactive, but on volatile Hawaii Island, you can never be sure.

AGRICULTURE

In the 19th- and mid-20th centuries, sugar was the main agricultural and economic staple of all the Islands, but especially the Big Island. The drive along the Hamakua Coast, from Hilo or Waimea, illustrates diverse agricultural developments on the island. Sugarcane stalks have been replaced by orchards of macadamia-nut trees, eucalyptus, and specialty crops from lettuce to strawberries. Macadamia-nut orchards on the Big Island supply 90% of the state's yield, while coffee continues to be big business, dominating the mountains above Kealakekua Bay. Orchids keep farmers from Honokaa to Pahoa afloat, and small organic farms produce meat, fruits, vegetables, and even goat cheese for high-end resort restaurants.

HISTORY

Hawaii's history is deeply rooted in its namesake island, which was home to the first Polynesian settlements and has the state's best-preserved *heiau* (temples) and *puuhonua* (refuges). Kamehameha, the greatest king in Hawaiian history and the man credited with uniting the Islands, was born here, raised in Waipio Valley, and died peacefully in Kailua-Kona. The other man who most affected Hawaiian history, Captain James Cook, spent the bulk of his time in the Islands here, docked in Kealakekua Bay. (He landed first on Kauai, but had little contact with the residents there.) Thus it was here that Western influence was first felt, and from here that it spread to the rest of Hawaii.

KAILUA-KONA

Kailua-Kona is about 7 miles south of the Kona airport.

A fun and quaint seaside town, Kailua-Kona has the souvenir shops and open-air restaurants you'd expect in a small tourist hub, plus a surprising number of historic sites. Quite a few nice oceanfront restaurants here offer far more affordable fare than those at the resorts on the Kohala Coast and in Waimea.

Except for the rare deluge, the sun shines year-round. Mornings offer cooler weather, smaller crowds, and more birds singing in the banyan trees; you'll see tourists and locals out running on Alii Drive, the town's main drag, by about 5 am every day. Afternoons sometimes bring clouds and light rain, but evenings often clear up for cool drinks, brilliant sunsets, gentle trade winds, and lazy hours spent gazing out over the ocean. Though there are better beaches north of town on the Kohala Coast, Kailua-Kona is home to a few gems, including a fantastic snorkeling beach (Kahaluu) and a tranquil bay perfect for kids (Kamakahonu Beach, in front of the Courtyard King Kamehameha's Kona Beach Hotel).

Scattered among the shops, restaurants, and condo complexes of Alii Drive are Ahuena Heiau, a temple complex restored by King Kamehameha the Great and the spot where he spent his last days (he died here in 1819); the last royal palace in the United States (Hulihee Palace); and a battleground dotted with the graves of ancient Hawaiians who fought for their way of life and lost. It was also here in Kailua-Kona that Kamehameha's successor, King Liholiho, broke and officially abolished the ancient *kapu* (roughly translated as "forbidden," it was the name for the strict code of conduct that islanders were compelled to follow) system by publicly sitting and eating with women. The following year, on April 4, 1820, the first Christian missionaries came ashore here, changing life in the Islands forever.

GETTING HERE AND AROUND

The town closest to Kona International Airport (it's about 7 miles away), Kailua-Kona is a convenient home base from which to explore the island.

Half a day is plenty of time to explore Kailua-Kona, as most of the town's sights are located in or near the downtown area. Still, if you add in a beach trip (Kahaluu Beach has some of the best and easiest snorkeling on the island), it's tempting to while away the day here. Another option for making a day of it is to tack on a short trip up a small hill to the charming, artsy village of Holualoa or to the coffee farms in the mountains just above Kealakekua Bay.

The easiest place to park your car is at Courtyard King Kamehameha's Kona Beach Hotel, but you'll have to pay a daily parking fee. Some free parking is also available: When you enter Kailua via Palani Road (Highway 190), turn left onto Kuakini Highway, drive for a half block, and turn right into the small marked parking lot. Walk *makai* (toward the ocean) on Likana Lane a half block to Alii Drive, and you'll be in the heart of Kailua-Kona.

TOURS

Kona Historical Society. The society sells a 24-page booklet, which has a map and more than 40 historic photos, so you can take a self-guided walking tour to learn more about the village's fascinating past. ⊠ 81-6551 Mamalahoa Hwy., Kealakekua ☎ 808/323–3222 ⊕ www.kona-historical.org.

TOP ATTRACTIONS

Fodor'sChoice ★ **Hulihee Palace.** A lovely two-story oceanfront home surrounded by jewel-green grass and elegant coco palms and fronted by an elaborate wrought-iron gate, Hulihee Palace is one of only three royal palaces in America (the other two are in Honolulu). The royal residence was built by Governor John Adams Kuakini in 1838, a year after he completed Mokuaikaua Church. During the 1880s, it served as King David Kalakaua's summer palace. Built of lava rock and coral lime mortar, it features vintage koa furniture, weaving, portraits, tapa cloth, feather work, and Hawaiian quilts. The palace is on the National Register of Historic Places and is operated by the Daughters of Hawaii, a nonprofit organization dedicated to preserving the culture and royal heritage of the Islands. ⊠ 75-5718 Alii Dr., Kailua-Kona ☎ 808/329–1877 ⊕ www.daughtersofhawaii.org 🖾 $8 self-guided tour, $10 guided.

Kailua Pier. Though most fishing boats use Honokohau Harbor, this pier dating from 1918 is still a hub of ocean activity. Outrigger canoe teams practice and race, shuttles transport cruise ship passengers to and from town, and tour boats depart from these docks daily. Along the seawall, children and old-timers cast their lines. For youngsters, a bamboo pole and hook are easy to come by, and plenty of locals are willing to give pointers. September brings the world's largest long-distance canoe race, while in October, 1,700 elite athletes leave from the pier to swim 2.4 miles as part of the famous Ironman World Championship triathlon. ⊠ Alii Dr., across from King Kamehameha's Kona Beach Hotel, Kailua-Kona.

Fodor'sChoice ★ **Kamakahonu and Ahuena Heiau.** In the early 1800s, King Kamehameha the Great built a royal compound at Kamakahonu, the bay fronting what is now the Courtyard King Kamehameha's Kona Beach Hotel.

DID YOU KNOW?

Most of the over 2,200 plant species found in the Hawaiian Islands are not native to Hawaii. The red-and-green lobster claw is originally from South America.

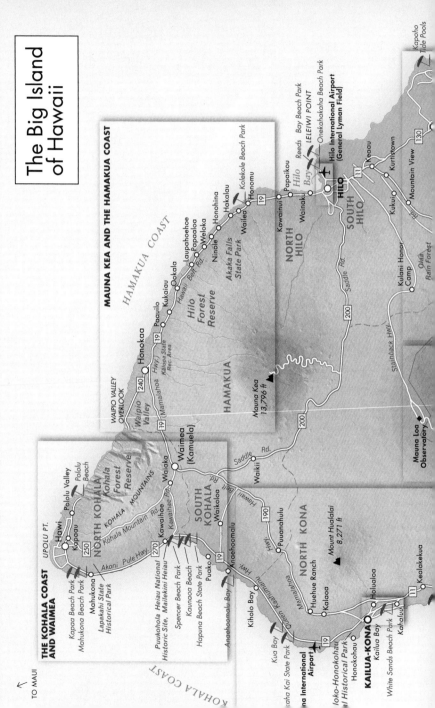

The Big Island of Hawaii

TO MAUI

THE KOHALA COAST AND WAIMEA

UPOLU PT.
Pololu Valley
Pololu Beach
Hawi
Kapaau
Kohala Forest Reserve
KOHALA MOUNTAINS
NORTH KOHALA
Kapaa Beach Park
Mahukona Beach Park
Mahukona
Lapakahi State Historical Park
250
Akoni Pule Hwy.
270
Kawaihae
Kohala Mountain Rd.
Kawaihae Rd.
Waiaka
Waimea (Kamuela)
SOUTH KOHALA
Puukohola Heiau National Historic Site, Mailekini Heiau
Spencer Beach Park
Kaunaoa Beach
Hapuna Beach State Park
Puako
Waikoloa
Anaehoomalu Bay
Anaehoomalu
19
Kiholo Bay
Huehue Ranch
Puuanahulu
NORTH KONA
Mount Hualalai 8,271 ft
Kalaoa
Holualoa
Kua Bay
...aha Kai State Park
...na International Airport
19
...loko-Honokohau ...al Historical Park
Honokohau
KAILUA-KONA
Kailua Bay
White Sands Beach Park
Kahaluu
11
Kealakekua
Kaumana Dr.
Kamehameha Hwy.
Mamalahoa Hwy.
190

MAUNA KEA AND THE HAMAKUA COAST

HAMAKUA COAST
WAIPIO VALLEY OVERLOOK
Waipio Valley
240
19
Honokaa
Hwy.
Mamalahoa Hwy.
Kalopa State Rec. Area
Paauilo
Kukaiau
Ookala
Laupahoehoe
Papaaloa
Hawaii Belt Rd.
Weloka
Ninole
Honohina
Hakalau
Honomu
Kolekole Beach Park
Wailea
Kawainui
Akaka Falls State Park
Hilo Forest Reserve
HAMAKUA
Mauna Kea 13,796 ft
200
Saddle Rd.
Saddle Rd.
Waikii
Hawaii Belt Rd.
190
Saddle Rd.
200
Mauna Loa Observatory
Stainback Hwy.
Kulani Honor Camp
Olaa Rain Forest
NORTH HILO
Papaikou
Kawainui
Wainaku
HILO
Hilo Bay
Reeds Bay Beach Park
LELEIWI POINT
Onekahakaha Beach Park
Hilo International Airport (General Lyman Field)
SOUTH HILO
11
Keaau
Kurtistown
Mountain View
Kuku
130
Kapoho Tide Pools
19

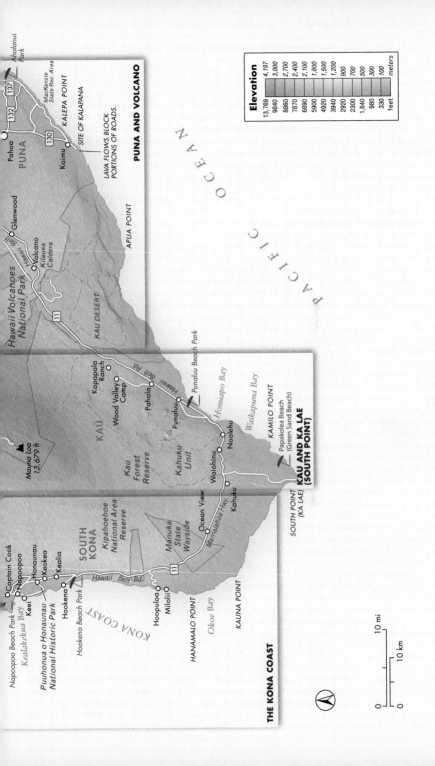

PUNA AND VOLCANO

Ahalanui Park

137 132

MacKenzie
State Rec. Area

KALEPA POINT

130

Pahoa

PUNA

Kaimu

SITE OF KALAPANA

LAVA FLOWS BLOCK
PORTIONS OF ROADS.

APUA POINT

Glenwood

Volcano

Kīlauea
Caldera

Hawaii Volcanoes
National Park

Belt Rd.

Hawaii

11

KAU DESERT

PACIFIC OCEAN

Kapapala
Ranch

Wood Valley
Camp

KAŪ

Pahala

Hawaii Belt Rd.

Punaluu

Punaluu Beach Park

Kau
Forest
Reserve

Kahuku
Unit

Honuapo Bay

Waiohinu

Naalehu

Waikapuna Bay

KAMILO POINT

Papakolea Beach
(Green Sand Beach)

SOUTH POINT
(KA LAE)

KAU AND KA LAE
(SOUTH POINT)

Mauna Loa
13,679 ft

SOUTH KONA

Captain Cook

Napoopoo

Keei

Kealakekua Bay

Honaunau

Keokea

Puuhonua o Honaunau
National Historic Park

Kealia

Hookena

Hookena Beach Park

KONA COAST

Kipahoehoe
National Area
Reserve

Manuka
State
Wayside

Ocean View

Kahuku

Mamalahoa Hwy.

Mamalahoa Hwy.

11

Hawaii Belt Rd.

Hoopuloa

Miloii

Okoe Bay

KAUNA POINT

HANAMALO POINT

THE KONA COAST

Napoopoo Beach Park

Elevation

feet	meters
13,769	4,197
9840	3,000
8860	2,700
7870	2,400
6890	2,100
5900	1,800
4920	1,500
3940	1,200
2920	900
2300	700
1,640	500
980	300
330	100

0   10 mi

0   10 km

Kamakahonu means "eye of the turtle," and it was named for a prominent turtle-shaped rock there, covered in cement when the hotel was built. It was a 4-acre homestead, complete with several houses and religious sites. In 1813, the king rebuilt Ahuena Heiau, a stunning temple dedicated to Lono, the Hawaiian god of peace and prosperity. It was also used as a seat of government. Today the compound is on the National Register of Historic Places and is a National Historic Landmark. One of the most revered and historically significant in all of Hawaii, the site sustained some damage in the 2011 tsunami and has been repaired. (Rather spookily, the tsunami waters caused widespread damage at the hotel but did not impact its rare Hawaiian artifacts or the paintings by famed Hawaiian artist Herb Kane.) ⊠ *75-5660 Palani Rd., Kailua-Kona.*

Fodor's Choice **Mokuaikaua Church.** Site of the first Christian church in the Hawaiian
★ Islands, this solid lava-rock structure, built in 1836, is mortared with burned lime, coral, and kukui oil and topped by an impressive steeple. The ceiling and interior were crafted of timbers harvested from a forest on Hualalai and held together with wooden pegs, not nails. Inside, behind a panel of gleaming koa wood, rests a model of the brig *Thaddeus* as well as a koa wood table crafted by Henry Boshard, pastor for 43 years. The gift shop is open most mornings, and a talk is given by the church historian Sundays at noon. You may also encounter Aloha Greeters within the sanctuary, who love to share the history of Mokuaikaua with visitors. The church still holds services and hosts community events, so please be respectful when entering the building. ⊠ *75-5713 Alii Dr., Kailua-Kona* ☎ *808/329–0655* ⊕ *www.mokuaikaua.org* ⊠ *Free.*

WORTH NOTING

Kuamoo Battlefield and Lekeleke Burial Grounds. In 1819, an estimated 300 Hawaiians were killed on this vast lava field. Their spooky burial mounds are still visible at the south end of Alii Drive (called the "End of the World" by locals). After the death of his father, King Kamehameha, the newly crowned King Liholiho ate at a table with women, breaking the ancient *kapu* (taboo) system. Chief Kekuaokalani, his cousin and co-heir, held radically different views about religious traditions and unsuccessfully challenged Liholiho's forces in battle here. ⊠ *Alii Dr., Kailua-Kona.*

THE KONA COAST

South of Kailua-Kona, Highway 11 hugs splendid coastlines and rural towns, leaving busy streets behind. The winding, upcountry road takes you straight to the heart of coffee country, where fertile plantations and jaw-dropping views offer a taste of what Hawaii was like before the resorts took over. Much of the farmland is in leasehold status, which explains why this part of the Big Island has remained rather untouched by development. Tour one of the coffee farms to find out what the big deal is about Kona coffee, and enjoy a free sample while you're at it.

A 20-minute drive off the highway from Captain Cook leads to beautiful Kealakekua Bay, where Captain James Cook arrived in 1778, dying here not long after. Hawaiian spinner dolphins frolic in the bay, now a Marine Life Conservation District, nestled alongside immensely high green cliffs that jut dramatically out to sea. Snorkeling is superb here, so you may want to bring your gear and spend an hour or so exploring the coral reefs. This is also a nice kayaking spot; the bay is normally extremely calm. ■ TIP➜ One of the best ways to spend a morning is to kayak in the pristine waters of Kealakekua Bay, paddling over to see the spot where Cook died. Guided tours are your best bet, and you'll likely see plenty of dolphins along the way.

North of Kona International Airport, along Highway 19, brightly colored bougainvillea stand out in relief against miles of jet-black lava fields stretching from the mountain to the sea. Sometimes visitors liken it to landing on the moon when they first see it. True, the dry barren landscape may not be what you'd expect to find on a tropical island, but it's a good reminder of the island's evolving volcanic nature.

SOUTH KONA AND KEALAKEKUA BAY

Kealakekua Bay is 14 miles south of Kailua-Kona.

Between its coffee plantations, artsy havens, and Kealakekua Bay—one of the most beautiful spots on the Big Island—South Kona has plenty of activities to occupy a day. Bring a swimsuit and snorkel gear, and hit Kealakekua Bay first thing in the morning. You'll beat the crowds, have a better chance of a dolphin sighting, and see more fish. After a morning of swimming or kayaking, head to one of the homey cafés in nearby Captain Cook to refuel.

The meandering road leading to Kealakekua Bay is home to a historic painted church, as well as coffee-tasting spots and several reasonably priced bed-and-breakfasts with great views. The communities surrounding the bay (Kealakekua and Captain Cook) are brimming with local and transplanted artists. They're great places to shop for gifts or antiques, have some coffee, or take an afternoon stroll.

Several coffee farms around the Kona coffee-belt area welcome visitors to watch all or part of the coffee-production process, from harvest to packaging. Some tours are self-guided and most are free, with the exception of the Kona Coffee Living History Farm.

GETTING HERE AND AROUND

To get to Kealakekua Bay, follow the signs off Highway 11 and park at Napoopoo Beach. It's not much of a beach (it used to be before Hurricane Iniki washed it away in 1992), but it provides easy access into the water.

TOP ATTRACTIONS

Fodor's Choice ★ **Captain Cook Monument.** On February 14, 1779, famed English explorer Captain James Cook was killed here during an apparent misunderstanding with local residents. He had chosen Kealakekua Bay as a landing place in November 1778. Arriving during the celebration of Makahiki, the harvest season, Cook was welcomed at first. Some Hawaiians saw him as an incarnation of the god Lono. Cook's party sailed away in February 1779, but a freak storm forced his damaged ship back to Kealakekua Bay. Believing that no god could be thwarted by a mere rainstorm, the Hawaiians were not so welcoming this time, and various confrontations arose between them and Cook's sailors. The theft of a longboat brought Cook and an armed party ashore to reclaim it. One thing led to another: shots were fired, daggers and spears were thrown, and Captain Cook fell, mortally wounded. A 27-foot-high obelisk marks the spot where he died. You can see it from a vantage point across the bay at Kealakekua Bay State Historical Park, or you can take a guided kayak tour with one of the local licensed operators. ⊠ *Captain Cook* ⊕ *dlnr.hawaii.gov/dsp/parks/hawaii.*

FAMILY **Greenwell Farms.** The Greenwell family played a significant role in the cultivation of the first commercial coffee in the Kona area (as well as the first grocery store). Depending on the season, the 20-minute walking tour of this working farm takes in various stages of coffee production, including a look at the 100-year-old coffee trees. No reservations are required. Sample a cup of their famous Kona coffee at the end; the gift shop stays open until 5. ⊠ *81-6581 Mamalahoa Hwy., ocean side, between mile markers 112 and 111, Kealakekua* ☎ *808/323–2295* ⊕ *www.greenwellfarms.com* ⊠ *Free.*

Holualoa Kona Coffee Company. There is a lot going on at this truly all-organic coffee farm and processing facility, from growing the beans to milling and drying. The processing plant next door to the farm demonstrates how the beans are roasted and packaged. A flock of 50 geese welcomes visitors and "provides fertilizer" for the plantation at no charge. Holualoa also processes beans for 100 coffee farms in the area. ⊠ *77-6261 Old Mamalahoa Hwy., Hwy. 180, Holualoa* ☎ *808/322–9937, 800/334–0348* ⊕ *www.konalea.com* ⊠ *Free* ☉ *Closed weekends.*

Holualoa Town. Hugging the hillside along the Kona Coast, the artsy village of Holualoa is 3 miles up winding Hualalai Road from Kailua-Kona. Galleries here feature all types of artists—painters, woodworkers, jewelers, gourd-makers, and potters—working in their studios in back and selling their wares up front. Look for frequent town-wide events such as art strolls and block parties. Then relax with a cup of coffee in one of the many cafés or stores. Formerly the exclusive domain of coffee plantations, Holualoa still boasts quite a few coffee farms offering free tours and inviting cups of Kona. ⊠ *Holualoa* ⊕ *www. holualoahawaii.com.*

Hula Daddy. On a walking tour of this working coffee farm (by advance reservation only), visitors can witness the workings of a small plantation, pick and pulp their own coffee beans, watch a roasting demonstration, and have a tasting. The gift shop carries whole beans and logo swag including bags, T-shirts and mugs. ⊠ *74-4944 Mamalahoa Hwy., Holualoa* ☎ *808/327–9744, 888/553–2339* ⊕ *www.huladaddy. com* ⊠ *From $10* ☉ *Closed Sun.*

Fodor's Choice **Kealakekua Bay State Historical Park.** This underwater marine reserve is ★ one of the most beautiful spots in the state. Dramatic cliffs surround super-deep, crystal-clear, turquoise water chock-full of stunning coral

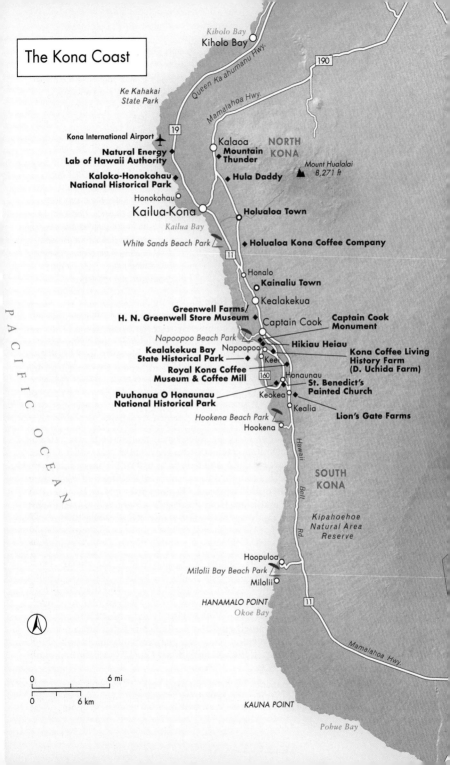

The Kona Coast

Kiholo Bay
Kiholo Bay

190

Queen Ka'ahumanu Hwy.

Mamalahoa Hwy.

Ke Kahakai
State Park

19

Kona International Airport ✈
**Natural Energy
Lab of Hawaii Authority** ◆

**Kaloko-Honokohau
National Historical Park** ◆

Honokohau ○

Kailua-Kona ●

Kailua Bay

White Sands Beach Park ⁄

Kalaoa
**Mountain
Thunder** ◆

Hula Daddy ◆

NORTH
KONA

Mount Hualalai ▲
8,271 ft

Holualoa Town ◆

Holualoa Kona Coffee Company ◆

11

Honalo ○
Kainaliu Town ○

Kealakekua ○

**Greenwell Farms/
H. N. Greenwell Store Museum** ◆
Captain Cook ●

**Captain Cook
Monument**

Napoopoo Beach Park ⁄
**Kealakekua Bay
State Historical Park** ◆
Napoopoo ●
Keei ●

**Royal Kona Coffee
Museum & Coffee Mill**

160

Hikiau Heiau

**Kona Coffee Living
History Farm
(D. Uchida Farm)**

Honaunau ●

**Puuhonua O Honaunau
National Historical Park**

Keokea ●

**St. Benedict's
Painted Church**

Kealia ○

Lion's Gate Farms

Hookena Beach Park ⁄
Hookena ○

Hawaii

Belt

Rd.

SOUTH
KONA

Kipahoehoe
Natural Area
Reserve

Hoopuloa ○
Milolii Bay Beach Park ⁄
Milolii ○

HANAMALO POINT
Okoe Bay

11

PACIFIC OCEAN

Mamalahoa Hwy.

0   6 mi
0   6 km

KAUNA POINT

Pohue Bay

pinnacles and tropical fish. The protected dolphins that frequent the sanctuary should not be disturbed, as they use the bay to escape predators and sleep. There's very little sand at west-facing **Napoopoo Beach,** but this is a nice easy place to enter the water and swim, as it's well protected from currents. There are no lifeguards; at times, you may feel tiny jellyfish stings. Stay at least 300 feet from the shoreline along the cliffs, which have become unstable during recent earthquakes. ⊠ *Beach Rd., off Government Rd. from Puuhonua Rd. (Hwy. 160), Captain Cook* ⊕ *dlnr.hawaii.gov/ dsp/parks/hawaii* ☞ *Bathrooms, limited parking, pavilion, shower.*

HAWAII CHERRIES

Don't scratch your head too much when you see signs advertising "cherries" as you drive around South Kona. It's no use wondering if Hawaii has the proper climate for growing bings; these signs refer to coffee cherries. Coffee beans straight off the tree are encased in fleshy, sweet red husks that make them look like bright little cherries. These are removed in the pulping process and then sun-dried. Farmers who don't process their own can sell 100-pound bags of just-picked cherries to the roasters.

Kona Coffee Living History Farm (D. Uchida Farm). On the National Register of Historic Places, this perfectly preserved farm was completely restored by the Kona Historical Society. It includes a 1913 farmhouse surrounded by coffee trees, a Japanese bathhouse, *kuriba* (coffee-processing mill), and *hoshidana* (traditional drying platform). Caretakers still grow, harvest, roast, and sell the coffee exactly as they did more than 100 years ago. The H.N. Greenwell Store Museum is located on the same property. ⊠ *82-6199 Mamalahoa Hwy., mile marker 110, Captain Cook* ☎ *808/323–2006* ⊕ *www.konahistorical.org* ☜ *$15* ⊘ *Closed weekends.*

Lions Gate Farms. For a century, three generations have grown coffee on this pretty farm with spectacular ocean views in the heart of Honaunau. The coffee is processed in a mill that dates to 1942. Tours given by the friendly proprietors proudly show visitors how coffee and macadamia nuts are cultivated and harvested. The farm also sells packaged coffee, nuts, and jams and jellies from this year's harvest and are passionate about producing only the best estate-grown Kona coffee. ⊠ *Hwy. 11, Mile Marker 105, Honaunau* ☎ *808/989–4883* ⊕ *www.coffeeofkona. com* ☜ *Free.*

Mountain Thunder. This organic coffee producer offers hourly "bean-to-cup" tours, including a tasting and access to the processing plant, which shows dry milling, sizing, coloring, sorting, and roasting. Private VIP tours ($) let you be roast master for a day. Hawaiian teas, handmade chocolate, and macadamia nuts grown on-site are also available. You may also take a self-guided tour. Remember that afternoon rains are common at this elevation so bring an umbrella and sturdy shoes. ⊠ *73-1944 Hao St., Kailua-Kona* ☎ *808/443–7593* ⊕ *www.mountain-thunder.com* ☜ *Free.*

Fodor'sChoice ★ **Puuhonua O Honaunau National Historical Park** (*Place of Refuge*). This 420-acre National Historical Park houses the best preserved *puuhonua*

Kealakekua Bay is one of the most beautiful spots on the Big Island.

(place of refuge) in the state. Providing a safe haven for noncombatants, *kapu* (taboo) breakers, defeated warriors, and others, the *puuhonua* (place of refuge) offered protection and redemption for anyone who could reach its boundaries, by land or sea. The oceanfront, 960-foot stone wall still stands and is one of the park's most prominent features. A number of ceremonial temples, including the restored **Hale o Keawe Heiau** (circa 1700), have served as royal burial chambers. An aura of ancient sacredness and serenity still imbues the place. ⊠ *Rte. 160, Honaunau* ✢ *About 20 miles south of Kailua-Kona* ☎ *808/328–2288* ⊕ *www.nps.gov/puho* ✉ *$5 per vehicle.*

Royal Kona Coffee Museum & Coffee Mill. Take an easy, self-guided tour by following the descriptive plaques located around the coffee mill. Then stop off at the small museum to see coffee-making relics, peruse the gift shop, and watch an informational film. Visitors are also invited to enjoy the beautiful views as well as stroll through a real lava tube on the property. ⊠ *83-5427 Mamalahoa Hwy., next to the tree house, Captain Cook* ☎ *808/328–2511* ⊕ *www.royalkonacoffee.com* ✉ *Free.*

WORTH NOTING

Hikiau Heiau. This stone platform was once an impressive temple dedicated to the god Lono. When Captain Cook arrived in 1778, ceremonies in his honor were held here. It's still considered a religious site, so visit with respect. ⊠ *Bottom of Napoopoo Rd. at bay.*

H.N. Greenwell Store Museum. Established in 1850, the homestead of Henry N. Greenwell served as cattle ranch, sheep station, store, post office, and family home all in one. Now, all that remains is the 1875 stone structure, which is listed on the National Register of Historic

CLOSE UP

Kona Coffee

The Kona coffee belt, some 16 miles long and about a mile wide, has been producing smooth aromatic coffee for more than a century. The slopes of massive Mauna Loa at this elevation provide the ideal conditions for growing coffee: sunny mornings; cloudy, rainy afternoons; and rich, rocky, volcanic soil. More than 600 farms, most just 3 to 7 acres in size, grow the delicious—and luxurious, at generally more than $25 per pound—gourmet beans. Only coffee from the North and South Kona districts can be called Kona (labeling requirements are strict and fiercely defended), and Hawaii is the only state in the U.S. that produces commercially grown coffee.

In 1828, Reverend Samuel Ruggles, an American missionary, brought a cutting over from the Oahu farm of Chief Boki, Oahu's governor. That coffee plant was a strain of Ethiopian coffee called Arabica, which is still produced today, although a Guatemalan strain of Arabica introduced in the late 1800s is produced in far higher quantities.

In the early 1900s, the large Hawaiian coffee plantations subdivided their lots and began leasing parcels to local tenant farmers, a practice that continues. Many tenant farmers were Japanese families. In the 1930s, local schools switched summer vacation to "coffee vacation," August to November, so that children could help with the coffee harvest, a practice that held until 1969.

When coffee trees are flowering, the white blossoms are fondly known as "Kona snow." Once ripened, coffee is harvested as "cherries"—beans encased in a sweet, red shell. Kona coffee trees are handpicked several times each season to guarantee the ripest product. The cherries are shelled, their parchment layer sun-dried and removed, and the beans roasted to perfection. Today most farms—owned and operated by Japanese-American families, West Coast mainland transplants, and descendants of Portuguese and Chinese immigrants—control production from cultivation to cup.

Places. It houses a fascinating museum with exhibits on ranching and coffee farming. It's also headquarters for the **Kona Historical Society,** which archives and preserves the history of the Kona district. An interesting aside: today, direct descendants of Henry Greenwell operate a popular South Kona grocery store, bringing their ancestors' legacy full circle. ⊠ *81-6551 Mamalahoa Hwy., mile marker 112, Kealakekua* ☎ *808/323–3222* ⊕ *www.konahistorical.org* 🖃 *$5* ⊘ *Closed Wed. and Fri.–Sun.*

FAMILY   **Kaloko–Honokohau National Historical Park.** The trails at this sheltered 1,160-acre coastal park near Honokohau Harbor, just north of Kailua-Kona, are popular with walkers and hikers. The free park is a good place to observe Hawaiian archaeological history and intact ruins, including a heiau, house platforms, ancient fishponds, and numerous petroglyphs, along the newly installed boardwalk. The park's wetlands provide refuge to a number of waterbirds, including the endemic Hawaiian stilt and coot. Two beaches here are good for swimming, sunbathing, and

DID YOU KNOW?

Coffee beans are actually the seeds of these cherry-like fruit, appropriately named coffee cherries. Be sure to sample some Kona brew while you're in the area.

Kealakekua Bay is generally considered the best snorkeling spot on the Big Island.

sea turtle spotting: **Aiopio,** a few yards north of the harbor, is a small beach with calm, protected swimming areas (good for kids) near the archaeological site of Puu Oina heiau, while **Honokohau Beach** is a ¾-mile stretch with ruins of ancient fishponds, also north of the harbor. Of the park's three entrances, the middle one leads to a visitor center with helpful rangers and lots of information. Local docents with backgrounds in geology or other subjects are happy to give nature talks. To go directly to the beaches, take the harbor road north of the Gentry retail center, park in the gravel lot, and follow the signs directing you to the park via the sandy path to the water. ⌧ *74-425 Kealakehe Pkwy., off Hwy. 19 near airport, Kailua-Kona* ☎ *808/329–6881* ⊕ *www.nps. gov/kaho* ⌧ *Free.*

Kainaliu Town. This is the first town you encounter to the south heading upcountry from Kailua town. In addition to a ribbon of funky old stores, clothing boutiques, coffee bars, and bistros, a handful of galleries and antiques shops have sprung up in the last few years. Browse around Oshima's, established in 1926, and Kimura's, founded in 1927, to find fabrics and Japanese goods beyond tourist trinkets. Pop into a local café for everything from burgers to New York–style deli. Peek into the 1932-vintage Aloha Theatre, where a troupe of community-theater actors might be practicing a Broadway revue. ⌧ *Hwy. 11, mile markers 112–114, Kainaliu.*

St. Benedict's Painted Church. In the late 1800s, Belgian-born priest and self-taught artist Father John Velge painted the walls, columns, and ceiling of this Roman Catholic church with religious scenes in the style of Christian folk art found throughout the South Pacific. The tiny chapel evokes the European Gothic cathedral tradition and is listed on the Hawaii State Register of Historic Places and the National Register of Historic Places. Mass is offered Saturday and Sunday. ✉ *84-5140 Painted Church Rd., off Hwy. 160, Captain Cook* ☎ *808/328–2227* ⊕ *www.thepaintedchurch.org* ✉ *Free; donations welcome.*

NORTH KONA

The North Kona district is characterized by vast lava fields, dotted with turnoff points to some of the most beautiful beaches in the world. Most of the lava flows here originate from the last eruptions of Hualalai, in 1800 and 1801, although some flows by the resorts hail from Mauna Loa. The stark black lavascapes contrast spectacularly with luminous azure waters framed by coco palms and white-sand beaches. Some of the turnoffs will take you to state parks with parking lots and bathrooms, while others are simply a park-on-the-highway-and-hike-in adventure.

GETTING HERE AND AROUND

Head north from Kona International Airport and follow Highway 19 along the coast. Take caution driving at night between the airport and where resorts begin on the Kohala Coast; it's extremely dark and there are few road signs or traffic lights on this two-lane road, and wild donkeys may appear on the roadway without warning.

WORTH NOTING

Natural Energy Lab of Hawaii Authority. Just south of Kona International Airport, a large mysterious group of buildings with an equally large and mysterious photovoltaic (solar) panel installation resembles some sort of top-secret military station. It's really the site of the Natural Energy Lab of Hawaii Authority, NELHA for short. Here, scientists, researchers, and entrepreneurs make use of a cold, deep-sea pipeline to develop and market everything from desalinated, mineral-rich drinking water and super-nutritious algae products to energy-efficient air-conditioning systems and environmentally friendly aquaculture techniques. Seahorses, abalone, kampachi, and Maine lobsters are also raised here. Take an Inspiring Innovation tour on Mondays, the Ocean Conservation tour on Tuesdays and Thursdays, or the Sustainable Aquaculture tour on Wednesdays and Fridays. ✉ *73-4485 Kahilihili St., Kailua-Kona* ☎ *808/329–8073* ⊕ *www.energyfuturehawaii.org* ✉ *$32 and by donation* ☉ *Closed weekends.*

THE KOHALA COAST

The Kohala Coast is about 32 miles north of Kailua-Kona.

If you had only a weekend to spend on the Big Island, this is probably where you'd want to be. The Kohala Coast is a mix of the island's best beaches and swankiest hotels, yet is not far from ancient valleys and temples, waterfalls, and funky artist enclaves.

The resorts on the Kohala Coast lay claim to some of the island's finest restaurants, golf courses, and destination spas. But the real attraction here is the island's glorious beaches. On a clear day, you can see Maui, and during the winter months, numerous glistening humpback whales cleave the waters just offshore.

Rounding the northern tip of the island, the arid coast shifts rather suddenly to green villages and hillsides, leading to lush Pololu Valley in North Kohala, as the hot sunshine along the coast gives way to cooler temperatures.

As you drive north, you'll find the quaint sugar-plantation-towns-turned-artsy-villages of Hawi and Kapaau. New galleries are interspersed with charming reminders of old Hawaii—wooden boardwalks, quaint local storefronts, ice cream shops, delicious neighborhood restaurants, friendly locals, and a delightfully slow pace. There's great shopping for everything from antiques and designer beachwear to authentic Hawaiian crafts.

GETTING HERE AND AROUND

Two days is sufficient time for experiencing each unique side of Kohala—one day for the resort perks: the beach, the spa, the golf, the restaurants; one day for hiking and admiring the waterfalls and valleys of North Kohala, coupled with a wander around Hawi and Kapaau.

Diving and snorkeling are primo along the Kohala Coast, so bring or rent equipment. If you're staying at one of the resorts, they will usually have any equipment you could possibly want. If you're feeling adventurous, get your hands on a four-wheel-drive vehicle and head to one of the unmarked beaches along the Kohala Coast—you may end up with a beach to yourself.

The best way to explore the valleys of North Kohala is with a hiking tour. Look for one that includes lunch and a dip in one of the area's waterfall pools. There are a number of casual lunch options in Hawi and Kapaau (sandwiches, sushi, seafood, local-style "plate lunch"), and a few good dinner spots.

VISITOR INFORMATION

Contacts North Kohala Welcome Center. ⊠ *55-3393 Akoni Pule Hwy., Hawi* ✛ *Just past the "Welcome to Kohala" sign* ☏ *808/889–5523* ⊕ *www.northkohala.org.*

TOP ATTRACTIONS

Ackerman Gift Gallery. In Kapaau, browse through this longtime gallery's collections of local art, including glass, woodworks, bowls, fine art photography, and paintings. There's also a small café and gift shop a couple of doors away. ⊠ *54-3897 Akoni Pule Hwy., Hwy. 270, Kapaau* ☏ *808/889–5138* ⊕ *www.ackermangalleries.com.*

Hawi and Kapaau. Near the birthplace of King Kamehameha, these North Kohala towns thrived during the plantation days, once bustling with hotels, saloons, and theaters—even a railroad. They took a hit when "Big Sugar" left the island, but both towns are blossoming once again, thanks to strong local communities, tourism, athletic events, and an influx of artists keen on honoring the towns' past. They are full of lovingly restored vintage buildings housing fun and funky shops,

Continued on page 64

BIRTH OF THE ISLANDS

How did the volcanoes of the Hawaiian Islands evolve here, in the middle of the Pacific Ocean? The ancient Hawaiians believed that the volcano goddess Pele's hot temper was the key to the mystery; modern scientists contend that it's all about plate tectonics and one very hot spot.

Plate Tectonics & the Hawaiian Question: The theory of plate tectonics says that the Earth's surface is comprised of plates that float around slowly over the planet's molten interior. The vast majority of earthquakes and volcanic eruptions occur near plate boundaries—the San Francisco earthquakes in 1906 and 1989, for example, were the result of activity along the nearby San Andreas Fault, where the Pacific and North American plates meet. Hawaii, more than 1,988 miles from the nearest plate boundary, is a giant exception. For years scientists struggled to explain the island chain's existence—if not a fault line, what caused the earthquakes and volcanic eruptions that formed these islands?

What's a hotspot? In 1963, J. Tuzo Wilson, a Canadian geophysicist, argued that the Hawaiian volcanoes must have been created by small concentrated areas of extreme heat beneath the plates. Wilson hypothesized that there is a hotspot beneath the present-day position of the Big Island. Its heat produced a persistent source of magma by partly melting the Pacific Plate above it. The magma, lighter than the surrounding solid rock, rose through the mantle and crust to erupt onto the sea floor, forming an active seamount. Each flow caused the seamount to grow until it finally emerged above sea level as an island volcano. Plausible so far, but why then, is there not one giant Hawaiian island?

HAWAIIAN CREATION MYTH

Holo Mai Pele, often played out in hula, is the Hawaiian creation myth. Pele sends her sister Hiiaka on an epic quest to fetch her lover Lohiau. Overcoming many obstacles, Hiiaka reaches full goddess status and falls in love with Lohiau herself. When Pele finds out, she destroys everything dear to her sister, killing Lohiau and burning Hiiaka's ohia groves. Each time lava flows from a volcano, ohia trees sprout shortly after, in a constant cycle of destruction and renewal.

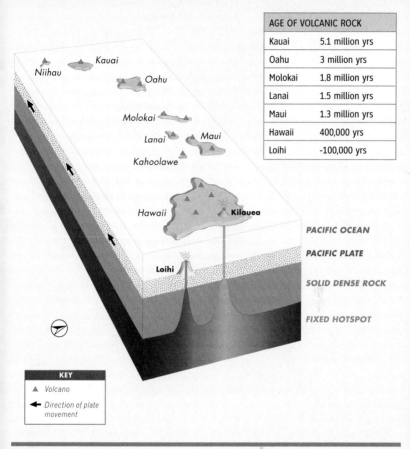

AGE OF VOLCANIC ROCK	
Kauai	5.1 million yrs
Oahu	3 million yrs
Molokai	1.8 million yrs
Lanai	1.5 million yrs
Maui	1.3 million yrs
Hawaii	400,000 yrs
Loihi	-100,000 yrs

PACIFIC OCEAN

PACIFIC PLATE

SOLID DENSE ROCK

FIXED HOTSPOT

KEY

▲ Volcano

◄— Direction of plate movement

Volcanoes on the Move: Wilson further suggested that the movement of the Pacific Plate itself eventually carries the island volcano beyond the hotspot. Cut off from its magma source, the island volcano becomes dormant. As the plate slowly moved, one island volcano would become extinct just as another would develop over the hotspot. After several million years, there is a long volcanic trail of islands and seamounts across the ocean floor. The oldest islands are those farthest from the hotspot. The exposed rocks of Kauai, for example, are about 5.1 million years old, but those on the Big Island are less than .5 million years old, with new volcanic rock still being formed.

An Island on the Way: Off the coast of the Big Island, the volcano known as Loihi is still submerged but erupting. Scientists long believed it to be a retired seamount volcano, but in the 1970s they discovered both old and new lava on its flanks, and in 1996 it erupted with a vengeance. It is believed that several thousand years from now, Loihi will be the newest addition to the Hawaiian Islands.

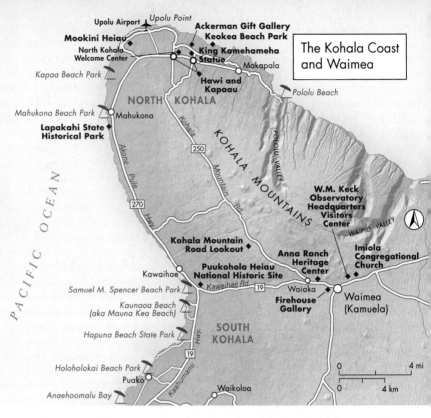

The Kohala Coast and Waimea

galleries, and eateries, and worth a stop or a break for a quick bite. Hawi is internationally known as the turnaround point for the cycling portion of the Ironman event. ⊠ *Along Hwy. 270.*

Keokea Beach Park. A newly renovated pavilion (damaged in the 2006 quake) welcomes visitors to this 7-acre beach park fronting the rugged shore in North Kohala. It's a popular local spot for picnics, fishing, and surfing. ⚠ **Enjoy the scenery, but don't try to swim here—the water is very rough, and be careful on the hairpin curve going down.** ⊠ *Hwy. 270, on the way to Pololu Valley near mile marker 27, Kapaau.*

Kohala Mountain Road Lookout. The road between North Kohala and Waimea is one of the most scenic drives in Hawaii, passing Parker Ranch, open pastures, rolling hills, and tree-lined mountains. There are a few places to pull over and take in the view; the lookout at mile marker 8 provides a splendid vista of the Kohala Coast and Kawaihae Harbor far below. On clear days, you can see well beyond the resorts to Maui, while other times an eerie mist drifts over the view. ⊠ *Kohala Mountain Rd. (Hwy. 250), Waimea (Hawaii County).*

Lapakahi State Historical Park. A self-guided, 1-mile walking tour leads through the ruins of the once-prosperous fishing village Koaie, which dates as far back as the 15th century. Displays illustrate early Hawaiian fishing and farming techniques, salt gathering, games, and legends.

Because the shoreline near the state park is an officially designated Marine Life Conservation District (and part of the site itself is considered sacred), swimming, swim gear, and sunscreen are not allowed in the water. Portable restrooms are available but not drinking water. ⚠ **Use caution: the water is often rough here.** ⊠ *Hwy. 270, mile marker 14 between Kawaihae and Mahukona, Waimea (Hawaii County)* ☎ *808/327–4958* ⊕ *www.hawaiistateparks.org* 🎫 *Free.*

Mookini Heiau. This isolated National Historic Landmark within Kohala Historical Sites State Monument is so impressive in size and atmosphere that it's guaranteed to give you what locals call "chicken skin" (goose bumps). Dating as early as AD 480, the parallelogram structure is a stunning example of a *luakini* heiau, used for ritualized human sacrifice to the Hawaiian war god Ku. The place feels haunted, more so if you are the only visitor and the skies are dark and foreboding. Visit with utmost care and respect. Nearby is Kapakai Royal Housing Complex, the birthplace of Kamehameha the Great. Although now under the care of the National Park Service, the site is still watched over by family descendents. ⚠ **Don't drive out here if it's been raining; even with a four-wheel drive, you could easily get stuck.** ⊠ *Coral Reef Pl./Upolu Point Rd., , off Upolu Airport Rd. and Hwy. 270 (Akoni Pule Hwy.), Hawi* ✥ *Turn at sign for Upolu Airport, near Hawi, and hike or drive 1½ miles southwest* ☎ *808/961–9540* ⊕ *www.nps.gov* ⊘ *Closed Wed.*

Fodor's Choice ★ **Puukohola Heiau National Historic Site.** Quite simply, this is one of the most historic and commanding sites in all of Hawaii. It was here in 1810, on top of Puukohala (Hill of the Whale), that Kamehameha the Great built the war heiau that would serve to unify the Hawaiian Islands, ending 500 years of almost continually warring chiefdoms. The oceanfront, fortresslike site is foreboding and impressive. A paved ½-mile, looped trail runs from the visitor center to the main temple sites. An even older temple, dedicated to the shark gods, lies submerged just offshore, where sharks can be spotted swimming, usually first thing in the morning. A new museum displays ancient Hawaiian weapons, including clubs, spears, a replica of a bronze cannon that warriors dragged into battle on a Hawaiian sled, and three original paintings by artist Herb Kane. Rangers are available to answer questions, or you can take a free audio tour on your own smartphone. Plan about an hour to see everything. ⊠ *62-3601 Kawaihae Rd., Kawaihae* ☎ *808/882–7218* ⊕ *www.nps. gov/puhe/index.htm* 🎫 *Free.*

WORTH NOTING

King Kamehameha Statue. A statue of Kamehameha the Great, the legendary king who united the Hawaiian Islands, stands watch over his descendants in North Kohala. The 8½-foot-tall figure bears the king's sacred feather *kihei*, *mahiole*, and *kaei* (cape, helmet, and sash). It's actually the original of the statue fronting the Judiciary Building on King Street in Honolulu. Cast in Florence in 1880, it was lost at sea. A replica was commissioned and shipped to Honolulu, but the original statue was found later in a Falklands Island junkyard. It now stands in front of the old Kohala Courthouse in Kapaau, next to the highway on the way toward Pololu Valley. Every year on King Kamehameha Day (June 11), Kohala residents honor their most famous son with a celebration that involves a parade and draping the statue in dozens of handmade floral lei. ✉ *54-3900 Kapaau Rd., Kapaau.*

WAIMEA

Waimea is 40 miles northeast of Kailua-Kona and 10 miles east of the Kohala Coast.

Thirty minutes over the mountain from Kohala, Waimea offers a completely different experience than the rest of the island. Rolling green hills, large open pastures, light rain, cool evening breezes and morning mists, along with abundant cattle, horses, and regular rodeos are just a few of the surprises you'll stumble upon here in *paniolo* (Hawaiian for "cowboy") country.

Waimea is also where some of the island's top Hawaii regional-cuisine chefs practice their art using local ingredients, which makes it an ideal place to find yourself at dinnertime. In keeping with the recent restaurant trend toward featuring local farm-to-table ingredients, a handful of Waimea farms and ranches supply most of the restaurants on the island, and many sell to the public as well. With its galleries, coffee shops, brewpubs, restaurants, beautiful countryside, and *paniolo* (cowboy) culture, Waimea is well worth a stop if you're heading to Hilo or Maunakea. ■TIP➔ And the short highway, or mountain road, that connects Waimea to North Kohala (Highway 250) affords some of our favorite Big Island views.

GETTING HERE AND AROUND

You can see most of what Waimea has to offer in one day, but if you're heading up to Maunakea for stargazing—which you should—it could easily be stretched to two. If you stay in Waimea overnight (there are many bed-and-breakfast options), spend the afternoon browsing through town or touring some of the area's ranches and historic sites. Then indulge in a gourmet dinner before heading up the Daniel K. Inouye Highway, also known as the Saddle Road, for world-renowned stargazing on Maunakea.

A word to the wise—there are no services or gas stations on Saddle Road, the only way to reach the summit of Maunakea. Fill up on gas and bring water, snacks, and warm clothes with you (there are plenty of gas stations, cafés, and shops in Waimea).

TOP ATTRACTIONS

FodorsChoice ★ **Anna Ranch Heritage Center.** This stunning heritage property, on the National and State Registers of Historic Places, belonged to the "first lady" of Hawaii ranching, Anna Lindsey Perry-Fiske. Here is a rare opportunity to see a fully restored cattle ranch compound and learn about the life of this fascinating woman, who butchered cattle by day and threw lavish parties by night. Wander the picturesque grounds and gardens on a self-guided walk, watch a master saddle maker and

DID YOU KNOW?

Accessed by a steep hiking trail, the remote Pololu Valley Beach, on the North Kohala peninsula, is one of the Big Island's most striking gray-sand beaches.

Maunakea's snowcapped summit towers ahead on a drive south from Waimea.

an ironsmith in action, and take a guided tour (by appointment only) of the historic house, where Anna's furniture, gowns, and elaborate *pau* (parade riding) costumes are on display. The knowledgeable staff shares anecdotes about Anna's amazing life. (Some staff and visitors have even reported strange goings-on in the main house, suggesting that Anna herself may still be "around.") ✉ *65-1480 Kawaihae Rd., Waimea (Hawaii County)* ☎ *808/885–4426* ⊕ *www.annaranch.org* ✉ *Grounds and Discovery Trail free; historic home tours $10* ☉ *Closed Sat.–Mon.*

WORTH NOTING

Firehouse Gallery. Local Big Island artwork is featured at this historical gallery, an 80-year-old fire station at the intersection of Lindsey Road and old Mamalahoa Highway. Supporting the Waimea Arts Council, the gallery is home to annual juried shows as well as solo and group exhibitions by its many award-winning multimedia artists and artisans. ✉ *67-1201 Mamalahoa Hwy., across from Waimea Chevron, Waimea (Hawaii County)* ☎ *808/887–1052* ⊕ *www.waimeaartscouncil.org* ✉ *Free* ☉ *Closed Mon.–Tues.*

Imiola Congregational Church. Highlights of this church, which was established in 1832 and rebuilt in 1857, are a gleaming, restored koa interior and unusual wooden calabashes hanging from the ceiling. Be careful not to walk in while a service is in progress, as the front entry is behind the pulpit. ✉ *65-1084 Mamalahoa Hwy., on "Church Row", Waimea (Hawaii County)* ☎ *808/885–4987* ⊕ *www.imiolachurch.com* ✉ *Free.*

W. M. Keck Observatory Headquarters Visitor Center. The twin, 10-meter optical/infrared telescopes (among the largest and most scientifically productive in the world) are also some of the most technologically advanced. Top global astronomy teams have used the scopes to make astounding discoveries, thanks in part to their location atop Maunakea, far above the turbulence of the atmosphere. The visitor center docents offer personalized tours and show you models of the telescopes and the Observatory, as well as one of the original instruments. You can peruse the exhibits and interpretive infographics at your own pace. About six times per year, highly renowned speakers, including Nobel Prize laureates, give free astronomy talks to the public. It's a great stop if you want to learn more about the telescopes without making the long journey up the mountain. ✉ *65-1120 Mamalahoa Hwy., across from hospital, Waimea (Hawaii County)* ☎ *808/885–7887* ⊕ *www.keckobservatory.org* ✆ *Free* ☉ *Closed Sat.–Mon.*

> **WAIMEA OR KAMUELA?**
>
> Both, actually. Everyone knows it as Waimea, but the sign on the post office says Kamuela, which is Hawaiian for "Samuel," referring to Samuel Parker, the son of the founder of Parker Ranch. That designation is used to avoid confusion with communities named Waimea on the islands of Kauai and Oahu. But the official name of the town is Waimea.

MAUNAKEA

Maunakea's summit is 18 miles southeast of Waimea and 34 miles northwest of Hilo.

Fodor's Choice
★

Maunakea ("white mountain") offers the antithesis of the typical tropical island experience. Freezing temperatures and arctic conditions are common at the summit, and snow can fall year-round. You can even snowboard or ski up here. Seriously. But just because you can doesn't mean you'll want to. You should be in very good shape and a close-to-expert boarder or skier to get down the slopes near the summit and then up again in the thin air with no lifts. During the winter months, lack of snow is usually not a problem.

But winter sports are the least of the reasons that most people visit this starkly beautiful mountain. From its base below the ocean's surface to its summit, Maunakea is the tallest island mountain on the planet. It's also home to little Lake Waiau, one of the highest natural lakes in the world, though lately, the word "pond" is closer to the truth.

Maunakea's summit—at 13,796 feet—is the best place in the world for viewing the night sky. For this reason, the summit is home to the largest and most productive astronomical observatories in the world—and $1 billion (with a "B") worth of equipment. Research teams from 11 different countries operate 13 telescopes on Maunakea, several of which are record holders: the world's largest optical–infrared telescopes (the dual Keck telescopes), the world's largest dedicated infrared telescope (UKIRT), and the largest submillimeter telescope (the JCMT). A still-larger 30-meter telescope (TMT) had been cleared for construction and was slated to open its record-breaking eye to the heavens until it got delayed by some Native Hawaiian protests. It's since been cleared again for construction.

Maunakea is tall, but there are higher mountains in the world, so what makes this spot so superb for astronomy? It has more to do with atmosphere than with elevation. A tropical-inversion-cloud layer below the summit keeps moisture from the ocean and other atmospheric pollutants down at the lower elevations. As a result, the air around the Maunakea summit is extremely dry, which helps in the measurement of infrared and submillimeter radiation from stars, planets, and the like. There are also rarely clouds up here; the annual number of clear nights here blows every other place out of the water. And, because the mountain is far away from any interfering artificial lights (not a total coincidence—in addition to the fact that the nearest town is nearly 30 miles away, there's an official ordinance limiting certain kinds of streetlights on the island), skies are dark for the astronomers' research. To quote the staff at the observatory, astronomers here are able to "observe the faintest galaxies that lie at the very edge of the observable universe."

Teams from various universities around the world gather on an 18-month waiting list to get the chance to use the telescopes on Maunakea. They have made major astronomical discoveries, including several about the nature of black holes, the discovery of new satellites around Jupiter and Saturn, new Trojans (asteroids that orbit, similar to moons) around Neptune, new moons and rings around Uranus, and new moons around Pluto. Their studies of galaxies are changing the way scientists think about time and the evolution of the universe.

What does all this mean for you? A visit to Maunakea is a chance to see more stars than you've likely ever seen before, and an opportunity to learn more about mind-boggling scientific discoveries in the very spot where these discoveries are being made. For you space geeks, a trip to Maunakea may just be the highlight of your trip.

If you're in Hilo, be sure to visit the Imiola Astronomy Center, which is near the University of Hawaii at Hilo. It offers presentations and planetarium films about the mountain and the science being conducted there, as well as exhibits describing the deep knowledge of the heavens possessed by the ancient Hawaiians.

GETTING HERE AND AROUND

The summit of Maunakea isn't terribly far, but the drive takes about 90 minutes from Hilo and an hour from Waimea thanks to the steep road. Between the ride there, sunset on the summit, and stargazing, allot at least five hours for a Maunakea visit.

To reach the summit, you must take Saddle Road (Highway 200, now known as the Daniel K. Inouye Highway), which has been rerouted and repaved and is now a beautiful shortcut across the middle of the island. At mile marker 28, John A. Burns Way, the access road to the visitor center (9,200 feet), is fine, but the road from there to the summit is a lot more precarious because it's unpaved washboard and very steep. Only four-wheel-drive vehicles with low range should attempt

MAUNA LOA

Mauna Loa is the world's largest active volcano, and it makes up more than 50% of the Big Island of Hawaii. The volcano is so massive and heavy that it creates a depression in the sea floor (actually part of the Pacific tectonic plate) of 8 kilometers (five miles). In fact, if measured from its base on the ocean floor, Mauna Loa would dwarf Everest. It's been erupting for nearly 700,000 years and shows no signs of stopping, although it's currently in a long "quiet" period. Yet it remains fairly enigmatic to visitors (and locals) and is not often visited. On the rare days when the summit is visible from the southeast highway, the view does not appear very commanding; indeed, you might drive right on by and either not notice that you are seeing the world's largest volcano, or simply think it's just a rather large hill.

Looks can be deceiving. Mauna Loa is one of 16 "Decade Volcanoes," so designated by the International Association of Volcanology and Chemistry of Earth's Interior. These volcanoes are particularly dangerous to populated areas. Needless to say, the volcano looms large both in the history and daily life of the Hawaiian islands.

VISITING MAUNA LOA

Although equal in height and superlative in mass to Maunakea, nearby twin peak Mauna Loa is often forgotten in the typical visitor's itinerary. There are several reasons for this. For one thing, it's a very long drive on a single lane road to reach the summit. A paved, 17.5-mile road, accessed from Mile Marker 28 on the Daniel K. Inouye Highway, takes you to the 11,150-foot summit Mauna Loa Observatory, where the road ends. It's then a steep, rugged 6.4-mile hike to the summit, a trek recommended only for the fit, the well-prepared, and the adventurous. There is a cabin located at the summit caldera, called Mokuaweoaweo Caldera (13,250 feet), and you may sleep there if you obtain a permit (available from the Kilauea Visitor Center). But there are no services whatsoever in this sub-freezing wilderness environment. It was from this vantage that several campers were awakened with the shock of their lives in 1984, when the summit erupted and sent lava flows within six miles of Hilo.

this journey. Two-wheel-drive cars are unsafe, especially in winter conditions. Unsuitable cars may experience engine failure as a result of the low oxygen levels. Legislation is pending regarding a total ban of anything but four-wheel-drive vehicles on the summit. And if you're driving back down in the dark, slow and cautious is the name of the game. ⚠ Most rental car companies will not permit you to drive to the summit of Maunakea. Driving there without permission will void your contract and leave you responsible for damages. This happens more often than you'd think.

Also remember that Maunakea's extreme altitude can cause altitude sickness, leading to disorientation, headaches, and light-headedness. Keeping hydrated is crucial. Scuba divers must wait at least 24 hours before traveling to the summit. Children under 16, pregnant women, and those with heart, respiratory, or weight problems should not go higher than the visitor center. While you can park at the visitor center and hike to the summit if you are in good shape, the trip takes approximately seven hours one way, and no camping is allowed. That means you must leave in the pre-dawn hours to be back before dark; a permit is also required for this hike.

The last potential obstacle: it's cold—as in freezing—usually with significant wind chill, ice, and snow. Winds have been clocked at well over 100 miles per hour. Most summit tour operators provide down parkas and ski gloves.

TOURS

Companies that provide organized tours of Maunakea and its summit are headquartered in both Hilo and Kailua-Kona.

Arnott's Lodge & Hiking Adventures. This outfitter takes you to the summit for sunset and then stops along the way down the mountain, where guides give visual lectures (dependent on clear skies) using lasers. They focus on major celestial objects and Polynesian navigational stars. The excursion departs from Hilo and includes parkas and hot beverages. Pickup is available from Hilo hotels. If you drive yourself and park at Puu Huluhulu, across Maunakea Access Road, the cost is lower. The price is even lower if you stay at their traveler's lodge, which offers a variety of rooms, and even tent camping. ⊠ *98 Apapane Rd., Hilo* ☎ *808/339–0921* ⊕ *www.arnottslodge.com* ⊠ *From $150.*

Fodor's Choice ★ **Hawaii Forest & Trail.** The ultra-comfortable, highly educational Summit & Stars tour packs a lot of fun into a few hours. Guides are knowledgeable about astronomy and Hawaii's geologic and cultural history, and the small group size (max of 14) encourages camaraderie. Included in the tour are dinner at an old ranching station, catered by a favorite local restaurant; sunset on the summit; and a fantastic private star show mid-mountain. The company's powerful 11-inch Celestron Schmidt-Cassegrain telescope reveals lots of interesting celestial objects, including seasonal stars, galaxies, and nebula. The moon alone, if present, will knock your socks off. Everything from water bottles, parkas, and gloves to hot chocolate and brownies is included. Their new Maunakea sunrise tour begins in the wee hours before the sun comes up and includes a hike among the endangered silverswords as well as breakfast at the visitor center. And of course, the main event—a spectacular sunrise on the summit. The company also offers a daytime version of the summit tour. ⊠ *73-5598 Olowalu St., Kailua-Kona* ☎ *808/331–8505, 800/464–1993* ⊕ *www.hawaii-forest.com* ⊠ *From $220.*

Mauna Kea Summit Adventures. As the first company to specialize in tours to the mountain, Mauna Kea Summit Adventures is a small outfit that focuses on stars. Cushy vans with panoramic windows journey first to the visitor center, where participants enjoy a hearty lasagna dinner on the lanai and acclimatize for 45 minutes before donning hooded arctic-style parkas and ski gloves for the sunset trip to the 14,000-foot summit. With the help of knowledgeable guides, stargazing through a powerful Celestron telescope happens mid-mountain, where the elevation is more comfortable and skies are just as clear. The tour includes dinner, hot cocoa and biscotti, west-side pickup and runs 364 days a year, weather

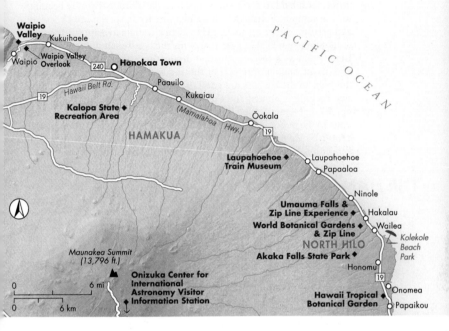

PACIFIC OCEAN

Waipio Valley Kukuihaele
Waipio **Waipio Valley Overlook** **Honokaa Town**
240
Paauilo
Hawaii Belt Rd. Kukaiau
19 (Mamalahoa Hwy.)
Kalopa State Recreation Area ◆ Ōokala
19
HAMAKUA

Laupahoehoe Train Museum ◆ Laupahoehoe
Papaaloa
Ninole
Umauma Falls & Zip Line Experience ◆ Hakalau
World Botanical Gardens & Zip Line ◆ Wailea
Kolekole
NORTH HILO Beach Park
Maunakea Summit (13,796 ft.) **Akaka Falls State Park** ◆
Honomu
▲ **Onizuka Center for** 19
0 6 mi **International** Onomea
Astronomy Visitor **Hawaii Tropical** ◆
0 6 km ◆ **Information Station** **Botanical Garden** ◇ Papaikou

permitting. ■ TIP→ Book at least one month prior, as these tours sell out fast. ⊠ *Kailua-Kona* ☎ *808/322–2366, 888/322–2366* ⊕ *www.maunakea.com* ⊡ *From $216.*

TOP ATTRACTIONS

Head to the summit before dusk so you can witness the stunning sunset and emerging star show. Only the astronomers are allowed to use the telescopes and other equipment, but the scenery is available to all. After the sun sinks, head down to the visitor center to warm up and stargaze, or do your stargazing first and then head up here. If you were blown away by the number of stars crowding the sky over the visitor center, this vantage point will leave you speechless.

If you haven't rented a four-wheel-drive vehicle from Harper's—the only rental company that allows their vehicles on the summit—don't want to deal with driving to the summit, or don't want to wait in line to use the handful of telescopes at the visitor center, the best thing to do is book a commercial tour. Operators provide transportation to and from the summit along with expert guides; some also provide parkas, gloves, telescopes, dinner, hot beverages, and snacks.

Fodor's Choice   **Onizuka Center for International Astronomy Visitor Information Station.** At
★   9,200 feet, this excellent amateur observation site has a handful of
telescopes and a knowledgeable staff. You can enjoy stargazing sessions from 6 to 10 pm on Tuesday, Wednesday, Friday, and Saturday,
or just stop here to acclimate yourself to the altitude if you're heading
for the summit. Fortunately, it's a pleasure to do so. Sip hot chocolate
and peruse exhibits on ancient Hawaiian celestial navigation, about the
mountain's significance as a quarry for the best basalt in the Hawaiian
Islands and as a revered spiritual destination, on modern astronomy,
and about ongoing projects at the summit. Nights are clear 90% of
the year, so the chances are good of seeing some amazing sights in the
sky. Parking is limited and the staff may turn you away if the lot fills
up. ■TIP→ Keep in mind that most summit telescope facilities are not
open to the public, so your best bet for actual stargazing is at the visitor
center. ⊠ *Mauna Kea* ☎ *808/961–2180, 808/935–6268 Current road
conditions* ⊕ *www.ifa.hawaii.edu/info/vis* ✉ *Free, donations welcome.*

THE HAMAKUA COAST

The Hamakua Coast is about 25 miles east of Waimea.

The spectacular waterfalls, mysterious jungles, emerald fields, and stunning ocean vistas along Highway 19 northwest of Hilo are collectively
referred to as the Hilo–Hamakua Heritage Coast. Brown signs featuring
a sugarcane tassel reflect the area's history: thousands of former acres
of sugarcane are now idle, with little industry to support the area since
"King Sugar" left the island in the early 1990s.

This is a great place to wander off the main road and see "real"
Hawaii—untouched valleys, overgrown banyan trees, tiny coastal villages, and little plantation towns Papaikou, Laupahoehoe, and Paauilo
among them. Some small communities are still hanging on quite nicely,
well after the demise of the big sugar plantations that first engendered
them. They have homey cafés, gift shops, galleries, and a way of life
from a time gone by.

The dramatic Akaka Falls is only one of hundreds of waterfalls here,
many of which tumble into refreshing swimming holes, so bring your
swimsuit when you explore this area. The pristine Waipio Valley was
once a favorite getaway spot for Hawaiian royalty. The isolated valley floor has maintained the ways of old Hawaii, with taro patches,
wild horses, and a handful of houses. The view from the lookout is
breathtaking.

GETTING HERE AND AROUND

Though Highway 19 is the fastest route through the area, any turnoff
along this coast could lead to an incredible view, so take your time and
go exploring up and down the side roads. If you're driving from Kailua-
Kona, rather than around the northern tip of the island, cut across on
the Mamalahoa Highway (Highway 190) to Waimea, and then catch
Highway 19 to the coast. It takes a little longer but is worth it.

Signs mark various sites of historical interest, as well as scenic views
along the 40-mile stretch of coastline. Keep an eye out for them and

DID YOU KNOW?

The dramatic Akaka Falls is only one of hundreds of waterfalls on the Hamakua Coast. Many falls tumble into pristine swimming holes, so bring your swimsuit when you explore this area.

DID YOU KNOW?

At the mouth of the Waipio Valley, the Waipio River meets the ocean. The pristine valley used to be a favorite getaway spot for Hawaiian royalty.

try to stop at the sights mentioned—you won't be disappointed.
■TIP→ **The "Heritage Drive," a 4-mile loop just off the main highway, is well worth the detour.**

Once back on Highway 19, you'll pass the road to Honokaa, which leads to the end of the road bordering Waipio Valley.

If you've stopped to explore the quiet little villages with wooden board-walks and dogs dozing in backyards, or if you've spent several hours in Waipio Valley, night will undoubtedly be falling. Don't worry: the trip to Hilo via Highway 19 takes only about an hour, or you can go in the other direction to stop for dinner in Waimea before heading to the Kohala Coast (another 25 to 45 minutes). Although you shouldn't have any trouble exploring the Hamakua Coast in a day, a handful of romantic bed-and-breakfasts are available if you want to spend more time.

GUIDED TOURS

A guided tour is one of the best ways to see Waipio Valley. You can walk down and up the steep narrow road yourself, but you won't see as much. And as locals say, it's 15 minutes to walk down, but about 45 minutes to walk back up. The cost for a tour depends on both the company and the transport mode.

Waipio Naalapa Stables. Friendly horses and friendly guides take guests on tours of the valley floor. The 2½-hour tours run Monday through Saturday (the valley rests on Sunday) with check-in times of 9 am and 12:30 pm. Riders meet at Waipio Valley Artworks, near the lookout, where they are transported to the valley floor in a four-wheel-drive van. ⊠ *48-5416 Kukuihale Rd., Waipio Valley Artworks Bldg., Honokaa* ☎ *808/775–0419* ⊕ *www.naalapastables.com* ◪ *From $90.*

Waipio on Horseback. This outfit offers guided, 2½-hour horseback-riding tours on the Waipio Valley floor. Riders experience lush tropical foliage, flowering trees, a scenic beach, tranquil streams, and 3,000-foot-tall cliff walls. Paniolo guides share the history, culture, and mythology of this magical valley and also give you a sneak peek of a traditional family farm. ⊠ *Hwy. 240, mile marker 7.5, northwest of Honokaa* ☎ *808/775–7291, 877/775–7291* ⊕ *www.waipioonhorseback.com* ◪ *From $105.*

Waipio Valley Shuttle. Not up for hiking in and out of the valley on foot? These informative, 1½- to 2-hour, four-wheel-drive tours do the driving for you, exploring the valley with lots of stops and run Monday through Saturday. The windows on the van are removed, allowing guests to snap unobstructed photos. You have the option to stay at the beach for two to four hours and come back up with the next tour. ⊠ *48-5416 Kukuihaele Rd., Honokaa* ☎ *808/775–7121* ⊕ *www. waipiovalleyshuttle.com* ◪ *From $59.*

Waipio Valley Wagon Tours. Mule-drawn wagon tours take visitors through the valley Monday through Saturday at 10:30, 12:30, and 2:30; the excursion lasts 1½ hours. Narration by friendly guides offers history and cultural background. Reservations are highly recommended. The pickup spot is at the Last Chance Store, 8 miles outside Honokaa. ⊠ *48-5300 Kukuihaele Rd., Honokaa* ☎ *808/775–9518* ⊕ *www.waipiovalleywagontours.com* ◪ *$62.50.*

TOP ATTRACTIONS

Fodor'sChoice   **Akaka Falls State Park.** A paved, 10-minute loop trail (approximately
★   ½ mile) takes you to the best spots to see the spectacular cascades of
Akaka. The majestic upper Akaka Falls drops more than 442 feet,
tumbling far below into a pool drained by Kolekole Stream amid a
profusion of fragrant white, yellow, and red torch ginger and other
tropical foliage. Another 400-foot falls is on the lower end of the trail.
Restroom facilities are available but no drinking water. ⚠ A series of
steps along parts of the trail may prove challenging for some visitors.
⊠ *Off Hwy. 19, 4 miles inland, near Honomu* ☎ *808/974–6200* ◧ *$5
per vehicle (nonresidents); $1 for nonresident walk-ins.*

Hawaii Tropical Botanical Garden. Eight miles north of Hilo, stunning
coastline views appear around each curve of the 4-mile scenic jungle
drive that accesses this privately owned nature preserve next to Onomea
Bay. Paved pathways in the 17-acre botanical garden lead past ponds,
waterfalls, and more than 2,000 species of plants and flowers, including
palms, bromeliads, ginger, heliconia, orchids, and ornamentals. The garden is well worth a stop, and your entry fee helps the nonprofit preserve
plants, seeds, and rain forests for future generations. ⊠ *27-717 Old
Mamalahoa Hwy., Papaikou* ☎ *808/964–5233* ⊕ *www.hawaiigarden.
com* ◧ *$15.*

FAMILY   **Kalopa State Recreation Area.** North of the old plantation town of Paauilo,
at a cool elevation of 2,000 feet, lies this sweet 100-acre state park.
There's a lush forested area with picnic tables and restrooms, and an
easy ¾-mile loop trail with additional paths in the adjacent forest
reserve. Small signs identify some of the plants, including the gothic-
looking native ohia. Three campground areas with full-service kitchen
as well as four cabins can be reserved online. ⊠ *44-3375 Kalopa Mauka
Rd., Honokaa* ✛ *12 miles north of Laupahoehoe and 3 miles inland off
Hwy. 19* ☎ *808/775–8852* ◧ *Free.*

Fodor'sChoice   **Waipio Valley.** Bounded by 2,000-foot cliffs, the "Valley of the Kings"
★   was once a favorite retreat of Hawaiian royalty. Waterfalls drop 1,200
feet from the Kohala Mountains to the valley floor, and the sheer cliff
faces make access difficult. The lush valley is breathtaking in every way
and from every vantage. Though almost completely off the grid today,
Waipio was once a center of Hawaiian life; somewhere between 4,000
and 20,000 people made it their home between the 13th and 17th centuries. In addition, it is a highly historical and culturally signifcant site
as it housed *heiau* (temples) and *puuhonua* (places of refuge) in addition to royal residences. King Kamehameha the Great launched a great
naval battle from here, which marked the start of his unification (some
would say conquest) and reign of the Hawaiian Islands. To preserve
this pristine part of the island, commercial-transportation permits are
limited—only a few outfitters offer organized valley floor trips.

A paved road leads down from the **Waipio Valley Overlook,** but no
car-rental companies on the island allow their cars to be driven down.
The distance is actually less than a mile from the lookout point—just
keep in mind the climb back gains 1,000 feet in elevation and is highly
strenuous, so bring water and a walking stick. Area landowners do not

look kindly on public trespassing to access Hiilawe Falls at the back of the valley, so stick to the front by the beach. Hike all the way to the end of the beach for a glorious vantage. Swimming, surfing, and picnics are all popular activities here, conditions permitting. You can also take the King's Trail from the end of the beach to access another waterfall not far down the trail. (Waterfalls can come and go depending on the level of recent rains.) If you do visit here, respect this area, as it is considered highly sacred to Hawaiians and is still home to several hundred full-time residents who cultivate taro on family farms. ⊠ *Hwy. 240, 8 miles northwest of Honokaa* ⊙ *Closed Sun.*

WORTH NOTING

Honokaa Town. This quaint, cliff-top village fronting the ocean was built in the 1920s and 1930s by Japanese and Chinese workers who quit the nearby plantations to start businesses that supported the sugar economy. The intact historical character of the buildings, bucolic setting, and friendliness of the merchants provide a nice reason to stop and stroll. Cool antiques shops, a few interesting galleries, funky gift shops, and good cafés abound. There's even a vintage theater that often showcases first-rate entertainment. Most restaurants close by 8 pm. ⊠ *Hwy. 240, Honokaa* ⊕ *www.honokaa.org.*

QUICK BITES
Tex Drive-In. This place is famous for its *malasada,* a puffy, doughy, deep-fried Portuguese doughnut without a hole, best eaten hot. They also come in cream-filled versions, including vanilla, chocolate, and coconut. **Known for: the island's best malasadas; food that is cooked to order; long waits.** ⊠ **45-690 Pakalana St., at Hwy. 19, Honokaa** ☎ **808/775–0598** ⊕ **www. texdriveinhawaii.com.**

Laupahoehoe Train Museum. Behind a stone loading platform of the once-famous Hawaii Consolidated Railway, constructed about 1900, the former manager's house is a poignant reminder of the era when sugar was the local cash crop. Today this museum displays artifacts from the sugar plantation era, the 1946 tsunami, local railway history, and the rich culture of the Hamakua Coast. The museum's Wye railyard has a vintage switch engine, large standard-gauge caboose, and narrow-gauge explosives box car. The trains even run a few yards along the restored tracks on special occasions. ⊠ *36-2377 Mamalahoa Hwy., Laupahoehoe* ☎ *808/962–6300* ⊕ *www.thetrainmuseum.com* ⊠ *$6* ⊙ *Closed Mon.–Wed. (except by appointment).*

FAMILY **Umauma Falls & Zip Line Experience.** The only place to see the triple-tier Umauma Falls, this kid-friendly 200-acre park has 14 waterfalls and a classy visitor center. Options include a zip and rappel, where zip liners can zip, swim, and rappel over caves, waterfalls, and pools; the standard zip adventure; and the zip and dip, a refreshing swim in a private waterfall pool after a nine-line zip. Visitors can also choose various à la carte adventures, such as a walk through the tropical grounds, a flume trail hike, kayaking, and a giant swing. ⊠ *Hwy. 19, Mile Marker*

16, Honomu ☎ 808/930–9477 ⊕ *www.ziplinehawaii.com* ✉ *$10 river walk and gardens, $189 zip line; $285 zip and rappel.*

FAMILY **World Botanical Gardens & Zip Line.** Just off the highway, this garden park is on more than 300 acres of former sugarcane land. With wide views of the countryside and the ocean, this is the place to see the beautiful Kamaee waterfalls. You can also follow a walking trail with old-growth tropical gardens including orchids, palm trees, ginger, hibiscus, and heliconia; visit the 10-acre arboretum, which includes a maze made of orange shrubs; explore the river walk; ride the zip line; and take the only off-road Segway adventure on the island. Admission into the gardens (not including zip line and Segway) is good for seven days, and admission to the two adventures gives you a free pass to the gardens for seven days. If you skip the zip line, you can see it all in a few hours. ✉ *31-240 Old Mamalahoa Hwy., just past mile marker 16 from Hilo, on mountain side, Hakalau* ☎ *808/963–5427* ⊕ *www.botanicalworld. com* ✉ *$15 garden, $167 zip line, Segway from $57.*

HILO

Hilo is 55 miles southeast of Waimea, 95 miles northeast of Kailua-Kona, and just north of the Hilo Airport.

In comparison to Kailua-Kona, Hilo is often deemed "the old Hawaii." With significantly fewer visitors than residents, more historic buildings, and a much stronger identity as a long-established community, this quaint, traditional town does seem more authentic and local. It stretches from the banks of the Wailuku River to Hilo Bay, where a few hotels line stately Banyan Drive. The vintage buildings that make up Hilo's downtown have been spruced up as part of a revitalization effort.

Nearby, the 30-acre Liliuokalani Gardens, a formal Japanese garden with arched bridges, stepping stones and waterways, were created in the early 1900s to honor the area's Japanese sugar-plantation laborers. They also became a safety zone after a devastating tsunami swept away businesses and homes on May 22, 1960, killing 61 people.

With a population of almost 50,000 in the entire district, Hilo is the fourth-largest city in the state and home to the University of Hawaii at Hilo. Although it is the center of government and commerce for the island, Hilo is clearly a residential town. Mansions with yards of lush tropical foliage share streets with older, single-walled plantation-era houses with rusty corrugated roofs. It's a friendly community, populated primarily by descendants of the contract laborers—Japanese, Chinese, Filipino, Puerto Rican, and Portuguese—brought in to work the sugarcane fields during the 1800s.

One of the main reasons visitors have tended to steer clear of the east side of the island is its weather. With an average rainfall of 130 inches per year, it's easy to see why Hilo's yards are so green and its buildings so weatherworn. Outside of town, the Hilo District boasts scenic beach valleys, rain forests and waterfalls, a terrain unlike the hot and dry white-sand beaches of the Kohala Coast. But when the sun does shine—usually part of nearly every day—the town sparkles, and, during winter, the snow glistens on Maunakea, 25 miles in the distance. Best of all is when the mists fall and the sun shines at the same time, leaving behind the colorful arches that earn Hilo its nickname: the City of Rainbows.

The Merrie Monarch Hula Festival takes place in Hilo every year during the second week of April, and dancers and admirers flock to the city from all over the world. If you're planning a stay in Hilo during this time, be sure to book your room and car rentals well in advance.

GETTING HERE AND AROUND

Hilo is a great base for exploring the eastern and southern parts of the island; just be sure to bring an umbrella for—sporadic and sometimes torrential—showers. If you're just passing through town or making a day trip, make the first right turn into the town off Highway 19 (it comes up fast) and grab a parking spot in the lot on your left or on any of the surrounding streets. Downtown Hilo is best experienced on foot.

There are plenty of gas stations and restaurants in the area. Hilo is a good spot to load up on food and supplies—just south of downtown there are several large budget retailers. If you're here on Wednesday or Sunday, be sure to stop by the expansive Hilo Farmers' Market to peruse stalls and stalls of produce, flowers, baked goods, coffee, honey, and more.

TOP ATTRACTIONS

Boiling Pots. Four separate streams fall into a series of circular pools here, forming the Peepee Falls. The resulting turbulent action—best seen after a good rain—has earned this scenic stretch of the Wailuku River the nickname Boiling Pots. There's no swimming allowed at Peepee Falls or anywhere in the Wailuku River, due to extremely dangerous currents and undertows. The falls are 3 miles northwest of Hilo off Waianuenue Avenue; keep to the right when the road splits and look for the sign. Gate opens at 7 am and closes at 6 pm. ⚠ **You may be tempted, as you watch others ignore the signs and climb over guard rails, to jump in, but resist. Swimming is expressly prohibited and unsafe, and people have died here.** ⊠ *Wailuku River State Park, Peepee Falls Dr., Hilo* ⊕ *dlnr.hawaii.gov/dsp/parks/hawaii/wailuku-river-state-park/*.

Fodor'sChoice **Imiloa Astronomy Center.** Part Hawaiian cultural center, part astronomy
★ museum, this center provides an educational and cultural complement to the research being conducted atop 14,000-foot Maunakea. Although visitors are welcome at Maunakea, its primary function is as a research facility—not observatory, museum, or education center. Those roles have been taken on by Imiloa in a big way. With its interactive exhibits, full-dome planetarium shows, and regularly scheduled talks and events, the center is a must-see for anyone interested in the stars, the planets, or Hawaiian culture and history. Five minutes from downtown Hilo, near the University of Hawaii at Hilo, the center also provides an important link between the scientific research being conducted at Maunakea and its history as a sacred mountain for the Hawaiian people. Admission includes one planetarium show and an all-day pass to the exhibit hall, which features more than 100 interactive displays. The lunch buffet at the adjoining Sky Garden Restaurant is popular and affordable. ⊠ *600*

Imiloa Pl., at UH Hilo Science & Technology Park, off Nowelo and Komohana, Hilo ☎ *808/969–9700* ⊕ *www.imiloahawaii.org* ✉ *$17.50* ☾ *Closed Mon.*

Liliuokalani Gardens. Designed to honor Hawaii's first Japanese immigrants and named after Hawaii's last reigning monarch, Liliuokalani Gardens' 30 acres of fish-filled ponds, stone lanterns, half-moon bridges, elegant pagodas, and a ceremonial teahouse make it a favorite Sunday destination. You'll see weddings, picnics, and families as you stroll. The surrounding area, once a busy residential neighborhood, was destroyed by a 1960 tsunami that caused widespread devastation and killed 61 people. ✉ *Banyan Dr., at Lihiwai St., Hilo* ✉ *Free.*

FAMILY

Fodor's Choice
★

Panaewa Rainforest Zoo & Gardens. Billed as "the only natural tropical rain forest zoo in the United States," this sweet zoo features native Hawaiian species such as the state bird, the nene goose, and the *io* (hawk), as well as lots of other rare birds, monkeys, sloths, and lemurs. Two Bengal tigers have also been added to the collection. The white-faced whistling tree ducks are a highlight. There's a petting zoo Saturdays from 1:30 to 2:30. It's a joy to stroll the grounds, which are landscaped with hundreds of species of lush and unusual tropical plants. To get here, turn left on Mamaki off Highway 11; it's just past the "Kulani 19, Stainback Hwy." sign. ✉ *800 Stainback Hwy., Hilo* ☎ *808/959–7224* ⊕ *www.hilozoo.com* ✉ *Free, donations encouraged.*

Rainbow Falls. After a hard rain, these impressive falls thunder into the Wailuku River gorge, often creating magical rainbows in the mist. Rainbow Falls, sometimes known as the "Hilo Town Falls," are located just above downtown Hilo. Take Waianuenue Avenue west for a mile; when the road forks, stay right and look for the Hawaiian warrior sign. They remain open during daylight hours.

At another point inside the park along the Wailuku River, four separate streams fall into a series of circular pools, forming the Peepee Falls. The resulting turbulent action—best seen after a good rain—has earned this scenic stretch of the river the nickname Boiling Pots. There's no swimming allowed at Peepee Falls or anywhere in the Wailuku River, due to extremely dangerous currents and undertows. The falls are 3 miles northwest of Hilo off Waianuenue Avenue; keep to the right when the road splits and look for the sign. The gate opens at 7 am and closes at 6 pm. ⚠ You may be tempted, as you watch others ignore signs and climb over guard rails, to jump in, but resist. More than a few people have died here. ✉ *Wailuku River State Park, Rainbow Dr., Hilo* ⊕ *dlnr. hawaii.gov/dsp/parks/hawaii.*

WORTH NOTING

Hilo Coffee Mill. With all the buzz about Kona coffee, it's easy to forget that estate-grown coffee is produced throughout the rest of the island. The Hilo Coffee Mill, located on 24 acres in lush Mountain View, is a pleasant reminder of that. In addition to farming its own coffee on-site, the mill has partnered with several small coffee farmers in East Hawaii in an effort to put the region on the world's coffee map. You can sample their efforts, tour the mill, and watch the roasters in action.

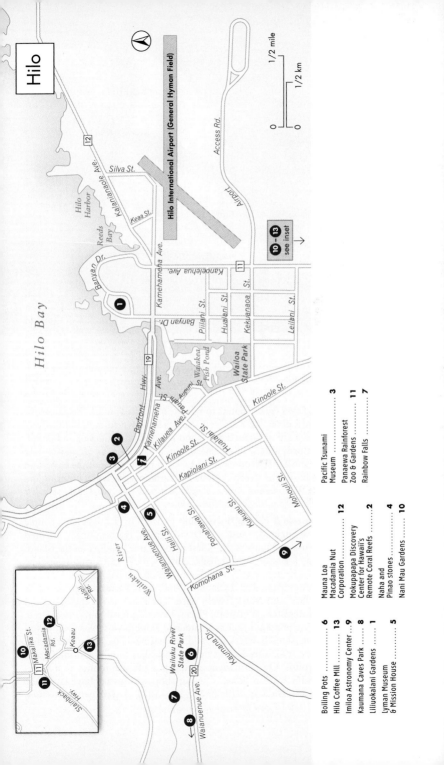

Hilo

Hilo Bay

Hilo Harbor

Reeds Bay

Hilo International Airport (General Hyman Field)

Silva St.

Keaa St.

Kanoelehua Ave.

Access Rd.

Airport

10 – 13 see inset

Piilani St.

Hualani St.

Kekuanaoa St.

Leilani St.

Kamehameha Ave.

Banyan Dr.

Kalanianaole Ave.

12

Banyan Dr.

1

2

3

7

Wailoa State Park

Waiakea Fish Pond

Kinoole St.

Kinoole St.

Hualani St.

Kapiolani St.

Ponahawai St.

Kilauea Ave.

Piilani St.

Manono St.

Komohana St.

Kaumana Dr.

4

5

9

Bayfront Hwy.

US Hwy.

Kamehameha Ave.

19

Wailuku River

Waianuenue Ave.

Haili St.

20

6

7

8

Wailuku River State Park

Saddleback Hwy.

Kipi Rd.

Macadamia Rd.

Keaau

Makalika St.

10

11

12

13

11

0   1/2 mile
0   1/2 km

Boiling Pots **6**
Hilo Coffee Mill **13**
Imiloa Astronomy Center .. **9**
Kaumana Caves Park **8**
Liliuokalani Gardens **1**
Lyman Museum
& Mission House **5**

Mauna Loa
Macadamia Nut
Corporation **12**
Mokupapapa Discovery
Center for Hawai'i's
Remote Coral Reefs **2**
Naha and
Pinao stones **4**
Nani Mau Gardens **10**

Pacific Tsunami
Museum **3**
Panaewa Rainforest
Zoo & Gardens **11**
Rainbow Falls **7**

The world's largest optical and infrared telescopes are located at the Keck Observatory on Maunakea's summit.

✉ *17-995 Volcano Rd. (Hwy. 11), between mile markers 12 and 13, Mountain View* ☎ *808/968–1333* ⊕ *www.hilocoffeemill.com* 💲 *Free* 🕙 *Closed Sun.–Mon.*

Kaumana Caves Park. Thanks to Hilo's abundant rainfall, this lava tube is lush with plant life. Concrete stairs lead down to the 2½-mile-long tube. There are no lighted areas and the ground is uneven and damp, so wear sturdy shoes, bring a flashlight, and explore as far as you dare to go. There are restrooms and a covered picnic table at the cave, and parking across the street. ⚠ **Heed all warning signs when entering the caves.** ✉ *Waianuenue Ave., on right just past mile marker 4 (veer left going toward Saddle Rd.), Hilo* 💲 *Free.*

Lyman Museum & Mission House. Built in 1839 by a missionary couple from New England, Sarah and David Lyman, the beautifully restored Lyman Mission House is the oldest wood-frame building on the island. On display are household utensils, artifacts, tools, and furniture used by the family, giving visitors a peek into the day-to-day lives of Hawaii's first missionaries. The Lymans hosted such literary dignitaries as Isabella Bird and Mark Twain here. The home is on the State and National Registers of Historic Places. Docent-guided tours are offered. An adjacent museum houses wonderful exhibits on volcanoes, island formation, island habitats and wildlife, marine shells, and minerals and gemstones. It also showcases native Hawaiian culture and immigrant ethnic groups. On permanent exhibit is a life-size replica of a traditional 1930s Korean home. The gift shop sells great Hawaiian-made items. ✉ *276 Haili St., Hilo* ☎ *808/935–5021* ⊕ *www.lymanmuseum. org* 💲 *$10* 🕙 *Closed Sun.*

2

CLOSE UP

A Walking Tour of Hilo

Put on some comfortable shoes, because all of the best downtown destinations are within easy walking distance of each other. Start your excursion in front of the public library, on Waianuenue Avenue, four blocks from Kamehameha Avenue. Here, you'll find the massive Naha and Pinao stones, which legend says King Kamehameha I was able to move as a teenager, thus foretelling that someday he would be a powerful king. Cross the road to walk southeast along Kapiolani Street, and turn right on Haili Street to visit the historic Lyman Museum & Mission House. Back on Haili Street, follow this busy road toward the ocean; on your right you'll pass Haili Church.

Soon you'll reach Keawe Street with its vintage, early-1900s shop fronts.

Stop at the Big Island Visitors Bureau on the right-hand corner for maps and brochures before taking a left. You'll bump into Kalakaua Street; for a quick respite turn left and rest on the benches in Kalakaua Park.

Continue *makai* (toward the ocean) on Kalakaua Street to visit the Pacific Tsunami Museum on the corner of Kalakaua and Kamehameha avenues. After heading three blocks east along the picturesque bayfront, you'll come across the S. Hata Building, which has interesting shops and restaurants. On the corner of Kamehameha and Waianuenue Avenue you'll find the free Mokupapapa Discovery Center for Hawaii's Remote Coral Reefs. You can't miss the Hilo Farmers, bustling with vendors and customers.

Mauna Loa Macadamia Nut Corporation. Acres of macadamia-nut trees lead to a giant roasting facility and processing plant with viewing windows and self-guided tours. You can even watch demonstrations showing how they coat nuts and shortbread cookies with milk chocolate to create their famous products. There are free samples and plenty of gift boxes with mac nuts in every conceivable form of presentation for sale in the visitor center. There is no factory processing on weekends or holidays. Children can burn off extra energy on a nature trail. ✉ *16-701 Macadamia Rd., off Hwy. 11, Hilo ✛ 5 miles south of Hilo* ☎ *808/966–8618, 888/628–6256* ⊕ *www.maunaloa.com.*

FAMILY **Mokupapapa Discovery Center for Hawai i's Remote Coral Reefs.** This is a great place to learn about the stunning Papahanaumokuakea Marine National Monument, which encompasses nearly 140,000 square miles in the Northwestern Hawaiian Islands and is the only mixed UNESCO World Heritage site in the United States. Giant murals, 3-D maps, and hands-on interactive kiosks depict the monument's extensive wildlife, including millions of birds and more than 7,000 marine species, many of which are found only in the Hawaiian archipelago. Knowledgeable staff and volunteers are on hand to answer questions. A new 3,500-gallon aquarium and short films give insight into the unique features of the monument, as well as threats to its survival. Located in the refurbished F. Koehnen Building, the center is worth a stop just to get an up-close look at its huge stuffed albatross with wings outstretched, or the new monk seal exhibit. (And the price is right.) ✉ *F. Koehnen*

CLOSE UP The Trees of Hilo's Banyan Drive

The history of the giant trees lining Hilo's Banyan Drive is one of the Big Island's most interesting and least known stories. Altogether, some 50 or so banyans were planted by VIP visitors to Hilo between 1933 and 1972.

The majority are Chinese banyans, and each one is marked with a sign naming the VIP who planted it and the date on which it was planted. The first trees were planted on October 20, 1933, by a Hollywood group led by director Cecil B. DeMille, who was in Hilo making the film *Four Frightened People*. Soon after, on October 29, 1933, another banyan was planted by the one and only George Herman "Babe" Ruth, who was in town playing exhibition games.

President Franklin D. Roosevelt planted a tree on his visit to Hilo on

July 25, 1934. And in 1935, famed aviator Amelia Earhart put a banyan in the ground just days before she became the first person to fly solo across the Pacific Ocean.

Trees continued to be planted along Banyan Drive until World War II. The tradition was then revived in 1952, when a young and aspiring U.S. senator, Richard Nixon of California, planted a banyan tree. Nixon's tree was later toppled by a storm and was replanted by his wife, Pat, during a Hilo visit in 1972. On a bright sunny day, strolling down Banyan Drive is like walking through a green, shady tunnel. The banyans form a regal protective canopy over Hilo's own "Walk of Fame." Be careful if you walk at dusk, as thousands of mynah birds begin to roost and may drop some surprises from overhead.

Bldg., 76 Kamehameha Ave., Hilo ☎ *808/933–8180* ⊕ *www.papah-anaumokuakea.gov/education/center.html* ✉ *Free* ☼ *Closed Sun.–Mon.*

Naha and Pinao stones. These two huge, oblong stones are legendary. The Pinao stone is purportedly an entrance pillar of an ancient temple built near the Wailuku River. King Kamehameha is said to have moved the 5,000-pound Naha stone when he was still in his teens. Legend decreed that he who did so would become king of all the islands. The stones are in front of the Hilo Public Library. ✉ *300 Waianuenue Ave., Hilo.*

Nani Mau Gardens. The name means "forever beautiful" in Hawaiian, and that's a good description of this 2-acre botanical garden filled with several varieties of fruit trees, rare palms, and hundreds of varieties of ginger, orchids, anthuriums, and other exotic plants. It was originally planted by a Japanese immigrant. Take a stroll and stay for lunch. (Some locals like to visit the garden just for the affordable lunch.) ■TIP→ **The restaurant offers a daily buffet lunch plus garden admission package, with discounts for seniors and kids.** ✉ *421 Makalika St., off Hwy. 11, Hilo* ☎ *808/959–3500* ⊕ *www.nanimaugardens.com* ✉ *$10.*

FAMILY **Pacific Tsunami Museum.** In downtown Hilo, it may seem odd that businesses tend to be far from the scenic bay front, but there's a reason for this. Tsunamis have killed more people in Hawaii than any other natural event, especially in Hilo. A small but informative museum in a vintage First Hawaiian Bank building designed by a famous Hawaii architect provides newly updated tsunami education and scientific information. Visitors can peruse the poignant history of these devastating disasters, with accounts taken from tsunami survivors from Hawaii and worldwide. Exhibits include a wave machine and interactive tsunami warning center simulation as well as films and pictographs detailing recent tsunamis in Japan, Alaska, and Indonesia. A new safety-wall exhibit demonstrates how to be prepared and what steps to take during an evacuation. ⌧ *130 Kamehameha Ave., Hilo* ☎ *808/935–0926* ⊕ *www. tsunami.org* ⌧ *$8* ⊘ *Closed Sun.–Mon.*

PUNA

Puna is about 6 miles south of Hilo.

The Puna District is wild in every sense of the word. The jagged black coastline is changing all the time; the trees are growing out of control, forming canopies over the few paved roads; the land is dirt cheap and there seem to be few building codes; and the people—well, there's something about living in an area that could be destroyed by lava at any moment (as Kalapana was in 1990, or Kapoho in 1960, or parts of Pahoa Town in 2014) that makes the norms of modern society seem silly. Vets, surfers, hippies, yoga teachers, and other free spirits abound. And also a few ruffians. So it is that Puna has its well-deserved reputation as an "outlaw" region of the Big Island.

That said, it's well worth a detour, especially if you're near this part of the island anyway. Volcanically heated springs and tide pools burst with interesting sea life, and some mighty fine people-watching opportunities exist in Pahoa, a funky little town that the "Punatics" call home.

This is also farm country for both legal and illicit crops. Local farmers grow everything from orchids and anthuriums to papayas, bananas, and macadamia nuts. Several of the island's larger, rural, residential subdivisions are nestled between Keaau and Pahoa, including Hawaiian Paradise Park, Orchidland Estates, Hawaiian Acres, and Hawaiian Beaches.

When dusk falls here, the air fills with the high-pitched symphony of thousands of coqui frogs. Though they look cute on the signs and seem harmless, the invasive frogs are pests both to local crops and to locals tired of their shrieking, all-night calls.

GETTING HERE AND AROUND

The sprawling Puna District includes part of the Volcano area and stretches northeast down to the coast. If you're staying in Hilo for the night, driving around wild lower Puna is a great way to spend a morning.

The roads connecting Pahoa to Kapoho and the Kalapana coast form a loop that's about 25 miles long; driving times are from two to three hours, depending on the number of stops you make and the length of time at each stop. There are restaurants, stores, and gas stations in Pahoa, but services elsewhere in the region are spotty. Long stretches of the road may be completely isolated at any given point; this can be a little scary at night but beautiful and tranquil during the day.

Compared to big-city living, it's pretty tame, but there is a bit of a "locals-only" vibe in parts of Puna, and some areas suffer crime and drug problems. Don't wander around alone at night or get lost on backcountry roads.

WORTH NOTING

Kapoho Tide Pools. This network of tide pools at the end of Kapoho-Kai Road has been a popular destination for locals and visitors for over 50 years. Created from a lava flow in 1960, the tide pools bordered the Vacationland Hawaii subdivision and Kapoho Bay. The subdivision has now been completely cut off from the rest of the island, many of the homes and apartments destroyed, and the entirety of Kapoho Bay now filled in with the recent lava flow. Locals and tourists will miss the tide pools and the beauty of the bay. ⊠ *Off Hwy. 137, at the end of Kapoho-Kai Rd., Hilo.*

Lava Tree State Monument. Tree molds that rise like blackened smokestacks formed here in 1790, when a lava flow swept through the ohia forest. Some reach as high as 12 feet. A meandering trail provides close-up looks at some of Hawaii's tropical plants and trees. There are restrooms and a couple of picnic pavilions and tables. ⚠ **Mosquitoes live here in abundance, so come prepared.** ⊠ *Hwy. 132, Pahoa* ☎ *808/974–6200* 🖼 *Free.*

MacKenzie State Recreation Area. This coastal park, on rocky shoreline cliffs in a breezy, cool ironwood grove, has a pavilion, picnic tables, and restrooms but no drinking water. The park is significant for the restored section of the old King's Highway trail system, which circled the coast in the era before Hawaii was discovered by the Western world. In those days, regional chiefs used the trails to connect coastal villages, collect taxes, and maintain control over people. Views take in the rugged coast, rocky beach, and coastal dry forest. There's good shore fishing here, so you might see some locals with a line or two in the water. ⊠ *Hwy. 137, Pahoa* ⊕ *dlnr.hawaii.gov/dsp/parks/hawaii.*

Pahoa Town. This eclectic little town is reminiscent of the Wild West, with its wooden boardwalks and vintage buildings—not to mention a reputation as a pot growers' haven. Founded originally to serve the sugar plantation community, today it's a free-spirited throwback to the '60s and '70s. You'll see plenty of hippies, vets, survivalists, woofers (workers on organic farms), yoga students, and other colorful characters pursuing alternative lifestyles. Secondhand stores, tie-dye/hemp clothing boutiques, smoke shops, and art/antiques galleries add to the "trippy" experience. In 2014, lava flows from Kilauea intruded into the town, overrunning the dump and cemetery and destroying a couple of buildings. Residents began saying goodbye to their town and packed up as smoke from the flows billowed in the near distance and the flows glowed after dark. Then it all abruptly stopped within 500 yards of Pahoa Village Road, once again ensuring the town's status as a survivor—for now. Pahoa's funky main street—with buildings dating to 1910—boasts a handful of excellent, local-style eateries. (In 2017, a fire swept through parts of the boardwalk and buildings, which are now

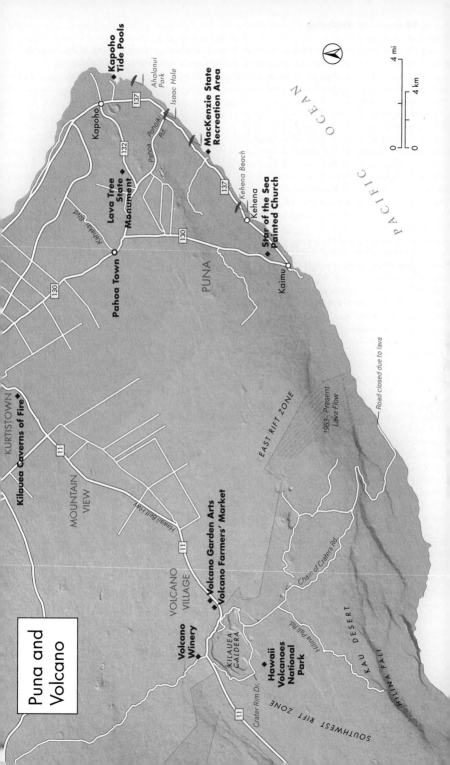

Puna and Volcano

Kapoho
Tide Pools

Ahalanui Park

Isaac Hale

137

132

Kapoho

Pahoa-Pohoiki Rd.

MacKenzie State
Recreation Area

Lava Tree State
Monument

Kahakai Blvd.

30

Kehena Beach

137

Star of the Sea
Painted Church

Kehena

Pahoa Town

PUNA

130

Kaimu

KURTISTOWN

Kilauea Caverns of Fire

111

MOUNTAIN
VIEW

EAST RIFT ZONE

1983-Present
Lava Flow

Road closed due to lava

PACIFIC

OCEAN

Hawaii Bell Hwy.

111

VOLCANO
VILLAGE

Volcano Garden Arts
Volcano Farmers' Market

Chain of Craters Rd.

Volcano Winery

KILAUEA
CALDERA

Hilina Pali Rd.

Hawaii
Volcanoes
National
Park

KAU DESERT

HILINA PALI

Crater Rim Dr.

SOUTHWEST RIFT ZONE

111

4 mi

4 km

0

0

being rebuilt.) To get here, turn southeast onto Highway 130 at Keaau, and drive 11 miles and follow signs to the Village. ⊠ *Pahoa.*

Star of the Sea Painted Church. This historic church, now a community center, was moved to its present location in 1990 just ahead of the advancing lava flow that destroyed the Kalapana area. Dating from the 1930s, the church was built by a Belgian Catholic missionary priest, Father Evarist Gielen, who also painted the detailed scenes on the church's interior. Though similar in style, the Star of the Sea and St. Benedict's were painted by two different Belgian priests. Star of the Sea also boasts several lovely stained-glass windows and is on the National Register of Historic Places. ⊠ *12-4815 Pahoa Kalapana Road, Kaimu, Hawaii 96778, Kalapana ✛ 1 mile north of Kalapana* ⊠ *Free, donations welcome.*

HAWAII VOLCANOES NATIONAL PARK AND VICINITY

Hawaii Volcanoes National Park is about 22 miles southwest from the start of the Puna district, and about 27 miles southwest of Hilo.

Fodor's Choice
★

Few visitors realize that in addition to "the volcano" (Kilauea)—that mountain oozing new layers of lava onto its flanks—there's also Volcano, the village. Conveniently located next to Hawaii Volcanoes National Park, Volcano Village is a charming little hamlet in the woods that offers dozens of excellent inns and bed-and-breakfasts, a great diner, and a handful of things to see and do that don't include the village's namesake.

For years, writers, artists, and meditative types have been coming to the volcano to seek inspiration, and many of them have settled in and around the village. Artist studios (open to the public by appointment) are scattered in the forest, laden with ferns and mists.

Do plan to visit the Halemaumau summit crater at night. It's fun to start with a sunset cocktail at the Volcano House, where you can sit by a large picture window and watch the glow of the crater fill the room. Then after dark (stay for dinner if you wish), head over to the Jaggar Museum, where you can stand at the crater's edge and see the live eruption in all its glory, as park rangers and docents give impromptu talks.

GETTING HERE AND AROUND
There is a handful of dining options, a couple of stores, and gas stations available in Volcano Village, so most of your needs should be covered. If you can't find what you're looking for, Hilo is about a 35-minute drive away, and the Keaau grocery store and fast-food joints are 25 minutes away.

Many visitors choose to stay the night in Volcano to see the dramatic glow at the summit caldera, which has been filling and dropping repeatedly in recent years. (If you do stay, bring a fleece or sweater, as temperatures drop at night and mornings are usually cool and misty.) Currently, there are two active eruption sites: one at the summit caldera (Halemaumau, sometimes known by locals as the lava lake) and the

You may see flowing lava from Kilauea, the Big Island's youngest and most active volcano.

other from the Puu oo vent in the southeast rift zone. Chain of Craters Road intersects with Crater Rim Drive and is open for the full 19 miles to the ocean.

Speed limits in this area are very reduced for a reason. Not only is the region seismically active, the park wishes to maintain protection for the endangered Hawaiian nene goose and for the safety of all visitors.

Parts of the national park were closed in mid-2018 due to ongoing erruptions of Kilauea. Check with the park before planning any trips here.

TOP ATTRACTIONS

Fodor's Choice
★

Hawaii Volcanoes National Park. Kilauea Volcano has been spewing lava rather dramatically since its current eruption began in 1983, and it shows no signs of abating. Hawaii Volcanoes National Park encompasses two of the volcanoes (Kilauea and Mauna Loa) that helped form the Big Island nearly half a million years ago. If you do nothing else on the Big Island, make an effort to see the live active volcano. Many people spend a few nights in the Volcano area just to witness the lava flow glowing against the night sky.

Begin your visit at the visitor center, where you'll find a store selling maps, books, and DVDs; information on trails, ranger-led talks and walks, and special events; and current weather, road, and lava-viewing conditions. Free volcano-related film showings, lectures, and other presentations are regularly scheduled. Rangers lead daily walks at 10:30 am and 1:30 pm into different areas; check with the visitor center for

Continued on page 98

HAWAII VOLCANOES NATIONAL PARK

Exploring the surface of the world's most active volcano—from the moonscape craters at the summit to the red-hot lava flows on the coast to the kipuka, pockets of vegetation miraculously left untouched—is the ultimate ecotour and one of Hawaii's must-dos.

The park sprawls over 520 square miles and encompasses Kilauea and Mauna Loa, two of the five volcanoes that formed the Big Island nearly half a million years ago. Kilauea, youngest and most rambunctious of the Hawaiian volcanoes, erupted at its summit from the 19th century through 1982. Since then, the top of the volcano had been more or less quiet, frequently shrouded in mist; an eruption in the Halemaumau Crater in 2008 ended this period of relative inactivity.

Kilauea's eastern side sprang to life on January 3, 1983, shooting molten lava four stories high. This eruption has been ongoing, and lava flows are generally steady and slow, appearing and disappearing from view. Over 500 acres have been added to Hawaii's eastern coast since the activity began, and scientists say this eruptive phase is not likely to end anytime soon.

If you're lucky, you'll be able to catch creation at its most elemental—when molten lava meets the ocean, cools, and solidifies into brand-new stretches of coastline. Even if lava-viewing conditions aren't ideal, you can hike 150 miles of trails and camp amid wide expanses of *aa* (rough) and *pahoehoe* (smooth) lava. There's nothing quite like it.

✉ 1 Crater Rim DG,
   National Park, HI 96718

☎ 808/985-6000

🌐 www.nps.gov/havo

💲 $25 per vehicle; $12 for pedestrians and bicyclists. Ask about passes. Admission is good for seven consecutive days.

🕐 The park is open daily, 24 hours. Kilauea Visitor Center: 9 am–5 pm. Thomas A. Jaggar Museum: 10–8. Volcano Art Center Gallery: 9–5.

(top) Kilauea Iki Trail
(left) Fuming rim of Puu Oo, source of the current eruption

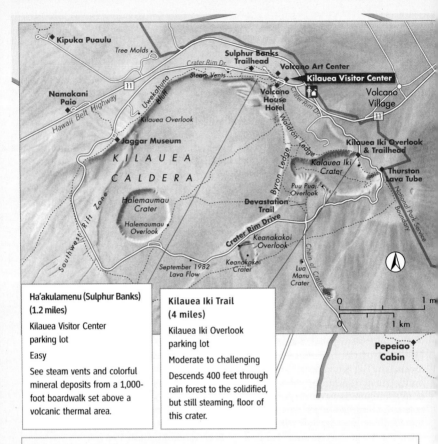

**Ha'akulamenu (Sulphur Banks)
(1.2 miles)**

Kilauea Visitor Center
parking lot

Easy

See steam vents and colorful
mineral deposits from a 1,000-
foot boardwalk set above a
volcanic thermal area.

**Kilauea Iki Trail
(4 miles)**

Kilauea Iki Overlook
parking lot

Moderate to challenging

Descends 400 feet through
rain forest to the solidified,
but still steaming, floor of
this crater.

SEEING THE SUMMIT

The best way to explore the summit of Kilauea is to cruise along Crater Rim Drive to Kilauea Overlook. From Kilauea Overlook you can see all of Kilauea Caldera and Halemaumau Crater, an awesome depression in Kilauea Caldera measuring 3,000 feet across and nearly 300 feet deep. It's a huge and breathtaking view with pluming steam vents. At this writing, lava flows in the Southwest Rift Zone have closed parts of the 11-mile loop road indefinitely, including Halemaumau Overlook.

Near Kilauea Overlook is the Thomas A. Jaggar Museum, which offers simi-

lar views, plus geologic displays, video presentations of volcanic eruptions, and exhibits of seismographs once used by volcanologists at the adjacent Hawaiian Volcano Observatory (not open to the public).

Other Highlights along Crater Rim Drive include sulfur and steam vents, a walk-through lava tube, and deep fissures, fractures, and gullies along Kilauea's flanks. Kilauea Iki Crater, on the way down to Chain of Crater's Road, is smaller, but just as fascinating when seen from Puu Pai Overlook.

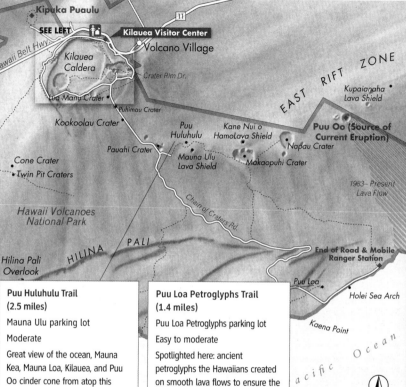

Kipuka Puaulu

SEE LEFT

Kilauea Visitor Center

Volcano Village

Hawaii Belt Hwy

Kilauea Caldera

Crater Rim Dr.

Loa Manu Crater

Puhimau Crater

Kookoolau Crater

Pauahi Crater

Puu Huluhulu

Kane Nui o HamoLava Shield

Mauna Ulu Lava Shield

Makaopuhi Crater

Napau Crater

Puu Oo (Source of Current Eruption)

Kupaianaha Lava Shield

EAST RIFT ZONE

1983– Present Lava Flow

Cone Crater

Twin Pit Craters

Hawaii Volcanoes National Park

HILINA PALI

Hilina Pali Overlook

Chain of Craters Rd.

End of Road & Mobile Ranger Station

Puu Loa

Holei Sea Arch

Kaena Point

Pacific Ocean

Puu Huluhulu Trail (2.5 miles)

Mauna Ulu parking lot

Moderate

Great view of the ocean, Mauna Kea, Mauna Loa, Kilauea, and Puu Oo cinder cone from atop this cinder cone formed 400 years ago.

Puu Loa Petroglyphs Trail (1.4 miles)

Puu Loa Petroglyphs parking lot

Easy to moderate

Spotlighted here: ancient petroglyphs the Hawaiians created on smooth lava flows to ensure the health and safety of their children.

SEEING LAVA

Before you head out to find flowing lava, pinpoint the safe viewing spots at the Visitor Center. One of the best places usually is at the end of 18-mile Chain of Craters Road. Magnificent plumes of steam rise where the rivers of liquid fire meet the sea.

There are three guarantees about lava flows in HVNP. First: They constantly change. Second: Because of that, you can't predict when and where you'll be able to see them. Third: New land formed when lava meets the sea is highly unstable and can collapse at any time. Never go into areas that have been closed.

■ **TIP→** The view of brilliant red-orange lava flowing from Kilauea's east rift zone is most dramatic at night.

People watching lava flow at HVNP

PLANNING YOUR TRIP TO HVNP

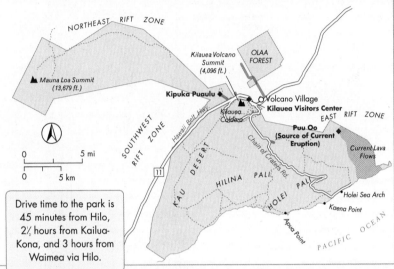

NORTHEAST RIFT ZONE

Kilauea Volcano Summit (4,096 ft.)

OLAA FOREST

▲ Mauna Loa Summit (13,679 ft.)

Kipuka Puaulu ◆

Volcano Village

Kilauea Visitors Center

Kilauea Caldera

SOUTHWEST RIFT ZONE

EAST RIFT ZONE

Hawaii Belt Hwy.

Puu Oo (Source of Current Eruption)

Current Lava Flows

0   5 mi

0   5 km

11

KAU DESERT

HILINA PALI

HOLEI PALI

Chain of Craters Rd.

Holei Sea Arch

Kaena Point

Apua Point

PACIFIC OCEAN

Drive time to the park is 45 minutes from Hilo, 2½ hours from Kailua-Kona, and 3 hours from Waimea via Hilo.

Lava entering the ocean

WHERE TO START

Begin your visit at the Visitor Center, where you'll find maps, books, and DVDs; information on trails, ranger-led walks, and special events; and current weather, road, and lava-viewing conditions. Free volcano-related film showings, lectures, and other presentations are regularly scheduled.

WEATHER

Weather conditions fluctuate daily, sometimes hourly. It can be rainy and chilly even during the summer; the temperature usually is 14° cooler at the 4,000-foot-high summit of Kilauea than at sea level.

Expect hot, dry, and windy coastal conditions at the end of Chain of Craters Road. Bring rain gear, and wear layered clothing, sturdy shoes, sunglasses, a hat, and sunscreen.

Halemaumau Crater, Kilauea

FOOD
It's a good idea to bring your own favorite snacks and beverages; stock up on provisions in Volcano Village, 1½ miles away or at the store in Kilauea Military Camp.

PARK PROGRAMS
Rangers lead daily walks at 10:30 and 1:30 into different areas; check with the Visitor Center for details as times and destinations depend on weather conditions and eruptions.

Over 60 companies hold permits to lead hikes at HVNP. Good choices are Hawaii Forest & Trail (www.hawaii-forest.com), Hawaiian Walkways (www.hawaiianwalkways.com), and Native Guide Hawaii (www.nativeguide hawaii.com).

CAUTION
"Vog" (volcanic smog) can cause headaches; breathing difficulties; lethargy; irritations of the skin, eyes, nose, and throat; and other health problems. Pregnant women, young children, and people with asthma and heart conditions are most susceptible, and should avoid areas such as Halemaumau Crater where fumes are thick.

Wear long pants and boots or closed-toe shoes with good tread for hikes on lava. Stay on marked trails and step carefully. Lava is composed of 50% silica (glass) and can cause serious injury if you fall.

Carry at least 2 quarts of water on hikes. Temperatures near lava flows can rise above 100°F, and dehydration, heat exhaustion, and sunstroke are common consequences of extended exposure to intense sunlight and high temperatures.

Remember that these are active volcanoes, and eruptions can cause parts of the park to close at any time. Check the park's website or call ahead for last-minute updates before your visit.

Volcanologists inspecting a vent in the East Rift Zone

details as times and destinations depend on weather conditions and eruptions. Over 60 companies hold permits to lead hikes at HVNP.

One of the busiest attractions in the park is the Jaggar Museum of volcanology, which displays historical scientific instruments, as well as equipment and protective clothing that has actually been used by scientists here (and which has sometimes gotten too close to the lava), and even working seismographs. At the museum's lookout, you might even spot the rare endangered nene (Hawaii's state bird).

Visitors with limited time may want to just take Crater Rim Drive, which has both scenic viewpoints and short trails into the lava fields. About five miles of Crater Rim Drive (after Jaggar Museum and intersecting with Chain of Craters Road) has been closed since 2008 due to hazardous volcanic gases and particulates being ejected from Halemaumau Crater. If you have a bit more time, you can see the far side of the park on the 19-mile Chain of Craters Road.

Even if lava-viewing conditions aren't ideal, you can hike and camp amid wide expanses of *aa* (rough) and *pahoehoe* (smooth) lava, a fascinating experience.

Weather conditions fluctuate daily, sometimes hourly. It can be rainy, foggy, and chilly even during the summer; the temperature usually is 14° cooler at the 4,000-foot-high summit of Kilauea than at sea level. Expect hot, dry, and windy coastal conditions at the end of Chain of Craters Road. Bring rain gear, and wear layered clothing, sturdy shoes, sunglasses, a hat, and sunscreen. Also bring snacks and water if you plan to hike or stay a while.

"Vog" (volcanic smog) can cause headaches; breathing difficulties; lethargy; irritations of the skin, eyes, nose, and throat; and other health problems. Pregnant women, young children, and people with asthma and heart conditions are most susceptible, and should avoid areas such as Halemaumau Crater, where fumes can be thick. Wear long pants and boots or closed-toe shoes with good tread for hikes on lava. Stay on marked trails and step carefully. Lava is composed of 50% silica (glass) and can cause serious injury if you fall. Remember that these are active volcanoes, and eruptions can cause parts of the park to close at any time. ⚠ **Check the park's website or call ahead for last-minute updates before your visit.** ✉ *Hwy. 11, Volcano* ☎ *808/985–6000* ⊕ *www.nps. gov/havo* 💲 *$25 per car for 7 days, $12 for pedestrians and bicyclists.*

WORTH NOTING

Kilauea Caverns of Fire. This way-out adventure explores the underbelly of the world's most active volcano via the Kazamura Lava Tube system. The longest lava tube system in the world—more than 40 miles long, with sections up to 80 feet wide, and 80 feet tall—it is 500 to 700 years old and filled with bizarre lava formations and mind-blowing colors. Tours are customized to groups' interest and skill level; tours focus on conservation and education and take visitors through the fascinating and beautiful lava caves unlike any others in the world. Tours by reservation only and are well worth the extra detour (about 40 minutes off the main highway) and planning. At the time you make your reservation, you will be given detailed directions to the location. Equipment is included. ⊠ *Hawaiian Acres, off Hwy. 11, between Kurtistown and Mountain View* ☏ *808/217–2363* ⊕ *www.kilaueacavernsoffire.com* 🖃 *$29 for one-hour walking tour, $89 for three-hour adventure tour.*

Volcano Farmers' Market. Local produce, flowers, crafts, and food products, including fresh-baked breads, pastries, coffee, pancakes, fresh coconuts with straws, and homemade Thai specialties are available every Sunday morning at one of the better farmers' markets on the island. It's best to get there early, before 7 am, as vendors tend to sell out of the best stuff quickly. There's also a great bookstore (paperbacks 50¢, hardbacks $1, and magazines 10¢) and a thrift store with clothes and knickknacks. The market is held in the covered Cooper Center, so it's safe from the rain. ⊠ *Cooper Center, 19-4030 Wright Rd., Volcano* ☏ *808/936–9705* ⊕ *www.thecoopercenter.org* ☉ *Closed Mon.–Sat.*

Volcano Garden Arts. This delightful gallery and garden lend credence to Volcano's reputation as an artists' haven. Located on beautifully landscaped grounds dotted with intriguing sculptures, this charming complex includes an eclectic gallery representing more than 100 artists, an excellent organic café housed in redwood buildings built in 1908, and a cute, one-bedroom artist's cottage, available for rent. If you're lucky, you'll get to meet the eccentric owner/"caretaker" of this enclave, the multitalented Ira Ono, known for his whimsical art, recycled trash creations, and friendly personality. ⊠ *19-3834 Old Volcano Rd., Volcano* ☏ *808/985–8979* ⊕ *www.volcanogardenarts.com* 🖃 *Free* ☉ *Garden closed Sun.–Mon.*

Volcano Winery. Volcanic soil may not seem ideal for the cultivation of grapes, but that hasn't stopped this winery from producing some interesting vintages. The Macadamia Nut Honey wine is a nutty, very sweet after-dinner drink. The Infusion pairs estate-grown black tea with South Kona's fermented macademia nut honey for a smooth concoction perfect for brunch through early evening. Though this isn't Napa Valley, the vintners take their wine seriously, and the staff is friendly and knowledgeable. Wine tasting is available; you can also get wine and cheese to eat in the picnic area, and a gift store has a selection of local crafts. ⊠ *35 Pii Mauna Dr., , past entrance to Hawaii Volcanoes National Park, by golf course, Volcano* ☏ *808/967–7772* ⊕ *www.volcanowinery.com.*

KAU AND KA LAE

Ka Lae (South Point) is 50 miles south of Kailua-Kona.

Perhaps the most desolate region of the island, Kau is nevertheless home to some spectacular sights. Mark Twain wrote some of his finest prose here, where macadamia-nut farms, remote green-sand beaches, and tiny communities offer rugged, largely undiscovered beauty. The drive from Kailua-Kona to windswept Ka Lae (South Point) winds away from the ocean through a surreal moonscape of lava plains and patches

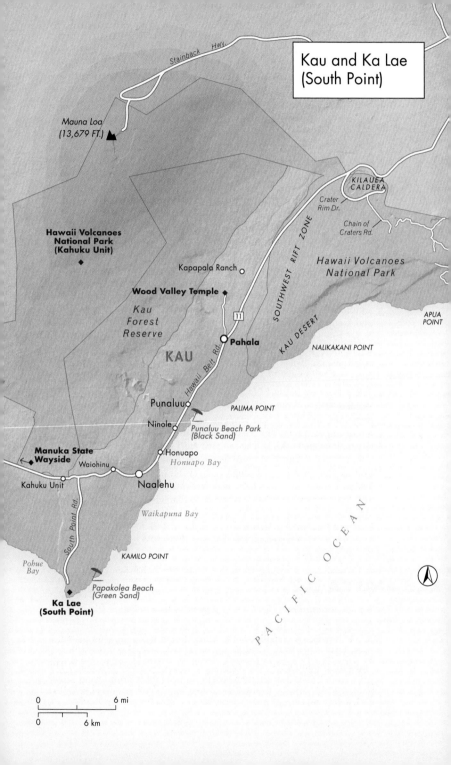

Kau and Ka Lae
(South Point)

Stainback Hwy

Mauna Loa
(13,679 FT.)

KILAUEA
CALDERA

Crater
Rim Dr.

Chain of
Craters Rd.

Hawaii Volcanoes
National Park
(Kahuku Unit)

SOUTHWEST RIFT ZONE

Kapapala Ranch

Hawaii Volcanoes
National Park

Wood Valley Temple

APUA
POINT

Kau
Forest
Reserve

11

KAU DESERT

KAU

NALIKAKANI POINT

Hawaii Belt Rd.

Pahala

Punaluu

PALIMA POINT

Ninole

Punaluu Beach Park
(Black Sand)

Manuka State
Wayside

Honuapo

Honuapo Bay

← Waiohinu

Kahuku Unit

Naalehu

Waikapuna Bay

South Point Rd.

PACIFIC OCEAN

Pohue
Bay

KAMILO POINT

Papakolea Beach
(Green Sand)

Ka Lae
(South Point)

0   6 mi

0   6 km

of scrub forest. Coming from Volcano, as you near South Point, the barren lavascape gives way to lush vistas from the ocean to the hills.

At the end of the 12-mile, two-lane road to Ka Lae, you can park and hike about an hour to Papakolea Beach (Green Sands Beach). Back on the highway, the coast passes verdant cattle pastures and sheer cliffs and the village of Naalehu on the way to the black-sand beach of Punaluu, a common nesting place of the Hawaiian green sea turtle.

GETTING HERE AND AROUND

Kau and Ka Lae are destinations usually combined with a quick trip to the volcano from Kona. This is probably cramming too much into one day, however. Visiting the volcano fills up at least a day (two is better), and the sights of this southern end of the island are worth more than a cursory glance.

Instead, make Green Sands Beach or Punaluu a full beach day, and see some of the other sights on the way there or back. Bring sturdy shoes, water, and a sun hat if Green Sands Beach is your choice (reaching the beach requires a hike). You can pay some enterprising locals $5 a head to give you a ride in their pickups to the beach. And be careful in the surf here. Don't go in unless you're used to ocean waves. There are no lifeguards at this remote beach. It's decidedly calmer and you can sometimes snorkel at Punaluu, but use caution at these and all Hawaii beaches.

The drive from Kailua-Kona to Ka Lae is a long one (roughly 2½ hours); from Volcano it's approximately 45 minutes. You can fill up on gas and groceries in Ocean View, or you can eat, fuel up, and get picnic fixings in Naalehu. Weather tends to be warm, dry, and windy.

TOP ATTRACTIONS

Hawaii Volcanoes National Park: Kahuku Unit. Located off Highway 11 at mile marker 70.5, the Kahuku section of the park takes visitors over many trails through ancient lava flows and native forests. Endangered plants and animals are on display in this beautiful but isolated region of Hawaii Volcanoes National Park, encompassing more than 116,000 acres of protected parklands. Guided hikes with knowledgeable rangers are a regularly scheduled highlight. ⊠ *Hwy 11, Mile Marker 70.5, Kau* ⊕ *www.nps.gov/havo/planyourvisit/kahuku-hikes. htm* ⊗ *Closed Mon.–Thurs.*

Ka Lae (South Point). It's thought that the first Polynesians came ashore at this southernmost point of land in the United States, also a National Historic Landmark. Old canoe-mooring holes, visible today, were carved through the rocks, possibly by settlers from Tahiti as early as AD 750. To get here, drive 12 miles on the turnoff road, past rows of giant electricity-producing windmills powered by the nearly constant winds sweeping across this coastal plain. Bear left when the road forks, and park in the lot at the end. Walk past the boat hoists toward the little lighthouse. South Point is just past the lighthouse at the southernmost cliff. You may see brave locals jumping off the cliffs and then climbing up rusty old ladders, but swimming here is not recommended. Don't leave anything of value in your car. It's isolated and without services. ⊠ *South Point Rd., off Mamalahoa Hwy. near mile marker 70, Naalehu* ⌻ *Free.*

FAMILY **Manuka State Wayside.** This lowland forest preserve spreads across several relatively recent lava flows. A semi-rugged trail follows a 2-mile loop past a pit crater, winding around interesting trees such as *hau* and *kukui*. It's a nice spot to get out of the car and stretch your legs—you can wander through the well-maintained arboretum, snap a few photos of the eerie forest, and let the kids scramble around trees so large they can't get their arms around them. The pathways can get muddy and rough, so bring appropriate shoes if you plan to hike. Large populations of the Hawaiian hoary bat inhabit the area, which, in totality, encompasses 25,000 of forest reserve. Restrooms, picnic areas, and camping sites (by permit) are available. ⊠ *Hwy. 11, north of mile marker 81* ☎ *808/974–6200* ⊕ *dlnr.hawaii.gov/dsp/parks/hawaii* ⌻ *Free.*

QUICK BITES

Punaluu Bakeshop. Billed as the southernmost bakery in the United States, it's a good spot to grab a snack, and the heavenly smell alone is worth the stop. Try the new house favorite, lilikoi-glazed *malasadas* (Portuguese doughnuts)—sweet with a touch of tart. (Be forewarned: one is never enough.) Local-style plate lunches and sandwiches on the bakeshop's famous sweetbread buns go well with Kau coffee. **Known for:** plate lunches and sandwiches; goods all baked on-site; busy with the tourist trade. ⊠ *5642 Mamalahoa Highway, Naalehu* ☎ *808/929-7343, 866/366-3501* ⊕ *www.bakeshophawaii.com.*

Pahala. About 16 miles east of Naalehu, beyond Punaluu Beach Park, Highway 11 passes directly by this little town. You'll miss it if you blink. Pahala, once a booming sugar plantation company town, is sleepy today but still inhabited by retired cane workers and their descendants. Behind it, along a wide, paved cane road, is Wood Valley, once a prosperous community, now just a peaceful road heavily scented by eucalyptus trees, coffee blossoms, and night-blooming jasmine and often laden in mist. ⊠ *Pahala.*

Wood Valley Temple (*Nechung Temple*). Behind the remote town of Pahala, this serene and beautiful Tibetan Buddhist temple, established in 1973, has hosted more than 50 well-known lamas, including the Dalai Lama on two occasions. Known as Nechung Dorje Drayang Ling, or "Immutable Island of Melodious Sound," this peaceful place welcomes all creeds. You can visit and meditate, leave an offering, walk the lush gardens shared by strutting peacocks, browse the gift shop, or stay in the temple's guesthouse, available for peaceful, nondenominational retreats taught by masters. ⊠ *Pahala* ☎ *808/928–8539* ⊕ *www.nechung.org* ⌻ *$5.*

BEACHES

Updated
by Kristina
Anderson

Don't believe anyone who tells you that the Big Island lacks beaches. It's just one of the myths about Hawaii's largest island that has no basis in fact. It's not so much that the Big Island has fewer beaches than the other islands, just that there's more island, so getting to the beaches can be slightly less convenient.

That said, there are plenty of those perfect white-sand stretches you think of when you hear "Hawaii," and the added bonus of black- and green-sand beaches, thanks to the relative young age of the island and its active volcanoes. New beaches appear and disappear regularly, created and destroyed by volcanic activity. In 1989, a black-sand beach, Kamoamoa, formed when molten lava shattered as it hit cold ocean waters; it was enjoyed for a few years before it was closed by new lava flows in 1992. It's part of the ongoing process of the volcano's creation-and-change dynamic.

Hawaii's largest coral reef systems lie off the Kohala Coast. Waves have battered them over millennia to create abundant white-sand beaches on the northwest side of the island. Black-, mixed-, and green-sand beaches lie in the southern regions and along the coast nearest the volcano. On the eastern side of the island, beaches tend to be of the rocky-coast–surging-surf variety, but there are still a few worth visiting, and this is where the Hawaii shoreline is at its most picturesque.

KAILUA-KONA

There are a few good sandy beaches in and near town. However, the coastline is generally rugged black lava rock, so don't expect long stretches of white sand. The beaches in Kailua-Kona get lots of use by local residents, and visitors enjoy them, too. Excellent opportunities for snorkeling, scuba diving, swimming, kayaking, and other water sports are easy to find.

Kahaluu Beach Park. This shallow and easily accessible salt-and-pepper beach is one of the Big Island's most popular swimming and snorkeling

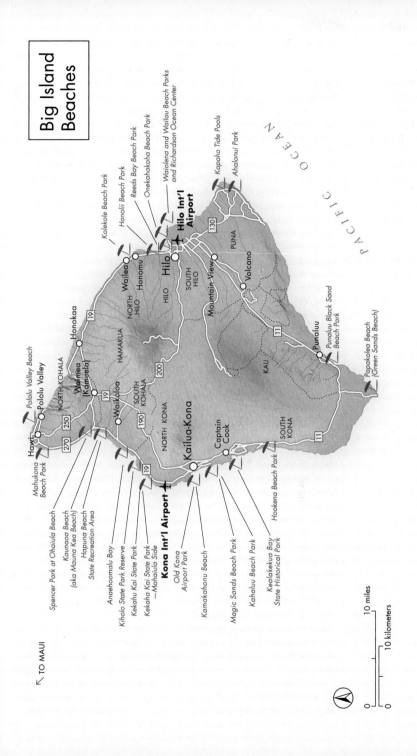

Big Island Beaches

TO MAUI

Mahukona Beach Park
Spencer Park at Ohaiula Beach
Kaunaoa Beach (aka Mauna Kea Beach)
Hapuna Beach State Recreation Area
Anaehoomalu Bay
Kiholo State Park Reserve
Kekahu Kai State Park
Kekaha Kai State Park —Mahaiula Side
Old Kona Airport Park
Kamakahonu Beach
Magic Sands Beach Park
Kahaluu Beach Park
Keolakekua Bay State Historical Park
Hookena Beach Park

Pololu Valley Beach
Kolekole Beach Park
Honolii Beach Park
Reeds Bay Beach Park
Onekahakaha Beach Park
Waiolena and Wailau Beach Parks and Richardson Ocean Center
Kapoho Tide Pools
Ahalanui Park
Papakolea Beach (Green Sands Beach)
Punaluu Black Sand Beach Park

Hawi
Pololu Valley
Honokaa
Waimea (Kamuela)
Waikoloa
Kailua-Kona
Captain Cook

Wailea
Honomu
Hilo
Hilo Int'l Airport
Mountain-View
Volcano
Punaluu

Kona Int'l Airport

NORTH-KOHALA
SOUTH KOHALA
NORTH KONA
SOUTH KONA
HAMAKUA
NORTH HILO
SOUTH HILO
HILO
PUNA
KAU

PACIFIC OCEAN

250
270
19
190
200
11
130
11

10 miles
10 kilometers

sites, thanks to the fringing reef that helps keep the waters calm, visibility high, and reef life—especially turtles and colorful fish—plentiful. Because it is so protected, it's great for first-time snorkelers, but outside the reef, very strong rip currents can run, so caution is advised. Never hand-feed the unusually tame reef fish here; it upsets the balance of the reef. You will see a lot of *honu*—the endangered green sea turtles. Resist the urge to get too close to them; they are protected from harassment by federal and state law. ■ TIP➜ Experienced surfers find good waves beyond the reef, and scuba divers like the shore dives—shallow ones inside the breakwater, deeper ones outside. Snorkel equipment and boards are available for rent nearby, and surf schools operate here. Kahaluu was a favorite of the Hawaiian royal family, especially King Kalakaua. **Amenities:** food and drink; lifeguards; parking (no fee); showers; toilets. **Best for:** snorkeling; swimming; surfing. ✉ *78-6720 Alii Dr., Kailua-Kona* ✢ *5½ miles south of Kailua-Kona, across from Beach Villas* ☎ *808/961–8311.*

FAMILY **Kamakahonu Beach.** This is where King Kamehameha spent his final days—the restored Ahuena Heiau sits on a platform across from the sand. Fronting the Courtyard King Kamehameha's Kona Beach Hotel and adjacent to Kailua Pier, this scenic crescent of white sand is one of the few beaches in downtown Kailua-Kona. The water here is almost always calm and the beach clean, making this a perfect spot for kids. For adults, it's a great place for a swim, some stand-up paddleboarding (SUP), watching outrigger teams practice, or enjoying a lazy beach day. It can get crowded on weekends. Snorkeling can be good north of the beach, and snorkeling, SUP, and kayaking equipment can be rented nearby. ■ TIP➜ A little family of sea turtles likes to hang out next to the seawall, so keep an eye out. There's lots of grass and shade, and free parking in county lots is a short stroll away. **Amenities:** food and drink; showers; toilets; water sports. **Best for:** snorkeling; swimming. ✉ *75-5660 Palani Rd., at Alii Dr., Kailua-Kona.*

Magic Sands Beach Park (*White Sands Beach*). Towering coconut trees provide some shade and lend a touch of tropical beauty to this pretty little beach park (also called Laaloa), which may well be the Big Island's most intriguing stretch of sand. A migratory beach of sorts, it can disappear in winter, when waves wash away the small white-sand parcel (hence the name "Magic Sands"). In summer, the beach re-forms; you'll know you've found it when you see the body- and board surfers. Just south of Anthony's by the Sea Restaurant, this is a popular summer hangout for young locals. It's often quite crowded, no matter what time of year. **Amenities:** lifeguards; parking (no fee); showers; toilets. **Best for:** sunsets; surfing. ✉ *77-6470 Alii Dr., Kailua-Kona* ✢ *4½ miles south of Kailua-Kona* ☎ *808/961–8311.*

FAMILY **Old Kona Airport Park.** Hugging the long shoreline adjacent to the runway that served Kona's airport until 1970 (the old terminal is used for community events), this beach is flat, generally clean, and dotted with rocks and coral pieces. Calm waters make for good snorkeling, and a few accessible small coves of white sand offer safe water entry and tide pools for children. Shady areas are good for picnics or admiring the Kona skyline, complete with a whale (in season) and a cruise ship

Calm Kailua Bay is an excellent spot for kayaking, snorkeling, and swimming.

or two. A well-tended community jogging trail and dog park opposite the runway are worth checking out. Just north, an offshore surf break known as Old A's is popular with local surfers. It's usually not crowded, but this area can get busy on weekends. **Amenities:** parking (no fee); showers; toilets. **Best for:** sunsets; walking. ⊠ *North end of Kuakini Hwy., where the road ends, Kailua-Kona* ☎ *808/961–8561.*

THE KONA COAST

This ruggedly beautiful coastline harbors a couple of scenic beaches that take you off the beaten track. Napoopoo and Hookena offer great swimming, snorkeling, diving, and kayaking.

NORTH KONA

Kekaha Kai State Park—Kua Bay Side. This lovely beach is on the northernmost stretch of the park's coastline on an absolutely beautiful bay. The water is crystal clear, deep aquamarine, and peaceful in summer, but the park's paved entrance, amenities, and parking lot make it very accessible and, as a result, often crowded. Fine white sand sits in stark contrast to old black lava flows with little shade—bring umbrellas as it can get hot. Rocky shores on either side protect the beach from winds in the afternoon. Gates open daily from 8 to 7. ⚠ **In winter, surf can get very rough and often the sand washes away. Amenities:** parking (no fee); showers; toilets. **Best for:** surfing; swimming. ⊠ *Hwy. 19, north of mile marker 88, Kailua-Kona* ⊕ *Across from Veterans Cemetery.*

Fodor's Choice **Kekaha Kai State Park—Mahaiula Side.** It's slowgoing down a 1.8-mile,
★ bumpy but paved road off Highway 19 to this beach park, but it's worth
it. This state park encompasses three beaches (from south to north,
Mahaiula, Makalawena, and Kua Bay, which has its own entrance).
Mahaiula and Makalawena are beautiful, wide expanses of white-sand
beach with dunes; there's a lot of space so you won't feel crowded.
Makalawena has great swimming and boogie boarding. (Note: Makalawena, sandwiched between the two state parks, is private property
and falls under the jurisdiction of Kamehameha Schools Bishop Estates.
They have their own access "road," which is even rougher to traverse,
and we don't recommend it!) From there, a 4½-mile trail leads to Kua
Bay. If you're game, work your way to the top of Puu Kuili, a 342-foot-
high cinder cone whose summit offers a fantastic view of the coastline.
(No vehicle access to the Puu.) However, be prepared for the heat and
bring lots of water, as none is available. Open daily 8–7. (Gates close
promptly at 7 pm, so you need to leave the lot by 6:30.) ⚠ **Watch out
for rough surf and strong currents. Amenities:** toilets. **Best for:** swimming. ⊠ *Hwy. 19, turnoff is about 2 miles north of Keahole–Kona
International Airport, Kailua-Kona* ☎ *808/327–4958, 808/974–6200.*

SOUTH KONA

FAMILY **Hookena Beach Park.** The 2½-mile road to this quiet, secluded little gem
feels like you're venturing off the beaten path. The area is rich in history, with remnants of an old steamship pier testifying to its former
role as a thriving port town, complete with (now gone) post office,
church, and stores. Today, though much quieter, it's still an active
Hawaiian fishing village, beloved by residents and tended to by a local
nonprofit community organization. It has a clean, soft mix of dark
brown and gray sand and is backed by steep emerald embankments and
a dramatic sloping *pali* (cliff) making for picturesque tropical vistas.
The bay is usually calm, tranquil and clear with small surf—good for
swimming, snorkeling, and kayaking. The park partnership oversees
beach concessions, camping permits, and security. You can rent snorkeling equipment, kayaks, beach chairs, umbrellas and SUPs. **Amenities:**
food and drink; parking (no fee); showers; toilets; water sports. **Best
for:** snorkeling; swimming. ⊠ *Hwy. 11, between mile markers 101 and
102, Captain Cook* ✣ *23 miles south of Kailua-Kona* ☎ *808/961–8311*
⊕ *www.hookena.org.*

Fodor's Choice **Kealakekua Bay State Historical Park.** When Hurricane Iniki slammed
★ into Hawaii in 1992, this park lost all of its sand, which is slowly
returning decades later. The shoreline is rocky but don't let that deter
you. The area is surrounded by high green cliffs, creating calm conditions for superb swimming, snorkeling, and diving. Among the variety
of marine life are dolphins, which come to rest and escape predators
during the day. They are protected from harassment by federal law, so
please don't chase or disturb them. This popular spot is also historically significant. Captain James Cook first landed in Hawaii here in
1778. When he returned a year later, he was killed in a skirmish with
Hawaiians, now marked by a monument on the north end of the bay.

Rocky but walkable trails lead to Hikiau Heiau, a sacred place for the Hawaiian people. Please proceed respectfully and do not walk on it or enter it. Parking is very limited. ⚠ **Be aware of the off-limits area (in case of rockfalls) marked by orange buoys. Amenities:** parking (no fee); showers; toilets. **Best for:** snorkeling; swimming. ✉ *Napoopoo Rd., off Hwy. 11, just south of mile marker 111, Kealakekua* ☎ *808/961–9544.*

KOHALA COAST

3

Most of the Big Island's white sandy beaches are found on the Kohala Coast, which is also called the "Gold Coast" and is, understandably, home to the majority of the island's world-class resorts. Hawaii's beaches are public property and the resorts are required to provide public access, so don't be frightened off by a guard shack and a fancy sign. Most resorts do have public parking, although it's limited. Resort beaches aside, there are some real hidden gems, accessible only by boat, four-wheel drive, or a 15- to 20-minute hike. It's well worth the effort to get to at least one of these. ■ TIP➔ **The west side of the island tends to be calmer, but the surf still gets rough in winter.**

FAMILY

Fodor'sChoice

★

Anaehoomalu Bay (*A-Bay*). Also known as "A-Bay," this expansive stretch of white sand, classically fringed with coco palms, fronts the Waikoloa Beach Marriott and is a perfect spot for swimming, windsurfing, snorkeling, and diving. Unlike some Kohala Coast beaches near hotel properties, this one is very accessible to the public and offers plenty of free parking. The bay is well protected, so even when surf is rough or trades are blasting, it's fairly calm here. (Mornings are calmest.) Snorkel gear, kayaks, and boogie boards are available for rent at the north end. Behind the beach are two ancient Hawaiian fishponds, **Kuualii** and **Kahapapa,** that once served ancient Hawaiian royalty. A walking trail follows the coastline to the Hilton Waikoloa Village next door, passing by tide pools, ponds, and a turtle sanctuary where sea turtles can often be spotted sunbathing on the sand. Footwear is recommended for the trail. **Amenities:** food and drink; parking (no fee); showers; toilets; water sports. **Best for:** snorkeling; swimming; sunsets; walking. ✉ *69-275 Waikoloa Beach Dr., Waikoloa* ✛ *Just south of Waikoloa Beach Marriott; turn left at Kings' Shops.*

FAMILY

Fodor'sChoice

★

Hapuna Beach State Recreation Area. One of Hawaii's finest beaches, Hapuna is a ½-mile-long stretch of white perfection. The turquoise water is calm in summer with just enough rolling waves to make body-surfing and body-boarding fun. Watch for the undertow; in winter it can be rough. There is excellent snorkeling around the jagged rocks that border the beach on either side, but high surf brings strong currents. Known for awesome sunsets, this is one of the best places on the island to see the "green flash" as the sun dips below a clear horizon. The north end of the beach fronts the Hapuna Beach Prince Hotel, which rents water-sports equipment and has a food concession with shaded picnic tables. There is ample parking, although the lot can fill up by midday and the beach can get crowded on holidays. Lifeguards, on duty during peak hours, cover only the state park section, not areas north of the rocky cliff that juts out near the middle of the beach. Renovations have temporarily closed off portions of the parking lot. **Amenities:** food and drink; lifeguards; parking (fee); showers; toilets; water sports. **Best for:** sunset; surfing; swimming; walking. ⌂ *Hwy. 19, near Mile Marker 69, Waimea (Hawaii County)* ⊹ *Just south of the Hapuna Beach Prince Hotel* ☎ *808/961–9544* ⌂ *$5 per vehicle.*

FAMILY

Fodor's Choice

★

Kaunaoa Beach (*Mauna Kea Beach*). Handsdown one of the most beautiful beaches on the island, if not the whole state, Kaunaoa features a long crescent of pure white sand framed by coco palms. The beach, which fronts the Mauna Kea Beach Hotel, slopes very gradually, and there's great snorkeling along the rocks. Classic Hawaii postcard views abound, especially in winter, when snow tops Mauna Kea to the east. When conditions permit, waves are good for body- and board surfing also. Currents can be strong in winter, so be careful. Get a cocktail at the beach cabana and enjoy the sunset. ■ TIP➔ Public parking is limited to a few spaces, so arrive before 10 am or after 4 pm. If the lot is full, head to nearby Hapuna Beach, where there's a huge parking lot ($5 per vehicle). Try this spot again another day—it's worth it! **Amenities:** parking (no fee); showers; toilets; water sports. **Best for:** sunset; swimming; walking. ⌂ *62-100 Mauna Kea Beach Dr., entry through gate to Mauna Kea Beach Hotel, Waimea (Hawaii County).*

Kiholo State Park Reserve. One of the state park system's newest treasures, Kiholo Bay is still in the planning stage, so facilities are not yet complete. The brilliant turquoise waters of this stunning bay, set against stark black lava fields, are a cooling invitation on a warm Kohala day. The shore is rocky and the water's a bit cold and hazy due to freshwater springs, but there are tons of green sea turtles in residence year-round. The swimming and snorkeling are excellent when the tide is calm. Thanks to the eruptions of Mauna Loa, what was once the site of King Kamehameha's gigantic fishpond is now several freshwater ponds encircling the bay, with a picturesque lava-rock island in the middle. Along the shoreline southwest toward Kona, just past the big yellow house, is another public beach with naturally occurring freshwater pools inside a lava tube. This area, called Queen's Bath, is as cool as it sounds. Bring plenty of drinking water. Gates are locked promptly at 7 pm; weekend camping is allowed with fee and permit. **Amenities:** parking (no fee); toilets. **Best for:** snorkeling; swimming; walking. ⌂ *Hwy. 19, between mile markers 82 and 83, Waimea (Hawaii County)* ⊹ *Just south of the lookout* ☎ *808/974–6200* ⊕ *dlnr.hawaii.gov/dsp/parks/hawaii/kiholo-state-park-reserve.*

Mahukona Beach Park. Snorkelers and divers make exciting discoveries in the clear waters of this park. Long ago, when sugar was the economic staple of Kohala, this harbor was busy with boats waiting for overseas shipments. Now it's a great swimming hole and an underwater museum of sorts. Remnants of shipping machinery, train wheels and parts, and what looks like an old boat are easily visible in the clear water. There's no actual beach here, but a ladder off the old dock makes getting in the water easy. ⚠ It's best to venture out only on tranquil days, when the water is calm; conditions can get windy and the ocean choppy. A popular place for locals, Mahukona is busy on weekends. A camping area on the south side of the park has picnic tables and an old covered

Kua Bay is protected from wind by the rocky shores that surround it.

pavilion. A trail also leads to nearby Lapakahi State Park, about a ½-mile hike. **Amenities:** showers; toilets. **Best for:** snorkeling; swimming. ⊠ *Hwy. 270, between mile markers 14 and 15, Hawi* ✛ *About 7 miles south of Hawi* ☎ *808/961–8311.*

Pololu Valley Beach. On the North Kohala peninsula, this is one of the Big Island's most scenic black-sand beaches. After about 8 miles of lush, winding road past Hawi Town, Highway 270 ends at the overlook of Pololu Valley. Snap a few photos of the stunning view, then take the 15-minute hike down (twice as long back up) to the beach. The trail is steep and rocky; it can also be muddy and slippery, so watch your step. The beach itself is a wide expanse of fine grey sand with piles of round boulders, surrounded by sheer green cliffs and backed by high dunes and ironwood trees. A gurgling stream leads from the beach to the back of the valley. ⚠ **This is not a safe swimming beach even though locals do swim, body board, and surf here. Dangerous rip currents and usually rough surf pose a real hazard.** Because this is a remote, isolated area far from emergency help, extreme caution is advised. **Amenities:** none. **Best for:** solitude. ⊠ *Hwy. 270, end of road, Kapaau.*

FAMILY **Spencer Park at Ohaiula Beach.** This white-sand beach is popular with local families because of its reef-protected waters. ■**TIP→ It's probably the safest beach in West Hawaii for young children.** It's also safe for swimming year-round, which makes it a reliable spot for a lazy day at the beach. There is a little shade, plus a volleyball court and pavilion, and the soft sand is perfect for sand castles. It does tend to get crowded with families and campers on weekends, but the beach is generally clean. Although you won't see a lot of fish if you're snorkeling here, in

HAWAII BEACH SAFETY

Hawaii's world-renowned, beautiful beaches can be extremely dangerous at times due to large swells and strong currents—so much so that the state rates wave hazards using three signs: a yellow square (caution), a red stop sign (high hazard), and a black diamond (extreme hazard). Signs are posted and updated three times daily or as conditions change.

Visiting beaches with lifeguards is strongly recommended, and you should swim only when there's a normal caution rating. Never swim alone or dive into unknown water or shallow breaking waves. If you're unable to swim out of a rip current by swimming sideways, tread water and wave your arms in the air to signal for help.

Even in calm conditions, this is still the ocean, and there are other dangerous things in the water to be aware of, including razor-sharp coral, jellyfish, eels, and sharks, to name a few.

Jellyfish cause frequent ocean injuries, and signs are posted along beaches when they're present. Box jellyfish swarm Hawaii's leeward shores 9 to 10 days after a full moon. Portuguese man-of-wars are usually found when winds blow from the ocean onto land. Reactions to a sting range from usually mild (burning sensation, redness, welts) to severe (breathing difficulties). If you are stung by a jellyfish, pick off the tentacles, rinse the affected area with rubbing alcohol or urine (really) and apply ice. Seek first aid from a lifeguard if you experience a severe reaction.

According to state sources, the chances of a shark bite in Hawaiian waters are very low; sharks attack swimmers or surfers three or four times per year. Of the 40 species of shark found near Hawaii, tigers are considered the most dangerous because of their size and indiscriminate feeding behavior (they eat just about anything at the water's surface). Tiger sharks are easily recognized by their blunt snouts and vertical bars on their sides.

To reduce your shark-attack risk, avoid swimming at dawn, dusk, and night, when some shark species may move inshore to feed. Steer clear of murky waters, harbor entrances, areas near stream mouths (especially after heavy rains), channels, or steep drop-offs.

The website ⊕ *oceansafety.soest. hawaii.edu* provides beach hazard maps for Oahu, Maui, Kauai, and the Big Island, as well as current weather and surf advisories, listings of closed beaches, and safety tips.

winter you can usually catch sight of a breaching whale or two. The beach park lies just below Puukohola Heiau National Historic Park, site of the historic war temple built by King Kamehameha the Great in 1810 after uniting the Islands. **Amenities:** lifeguards (weekends and holidays only); parking (no fee); showers; toilets. **Best for:** sunsets; swimming. ⊠ *Hwy. 270, Kawaihae* ✛ *Toward Kawaihae Harbor, just after road forks from Hwy. 19* ☎ *808/961–8311.*

THE HAMAKUA COAST

Although there are no actual beaches along the jagged cliffs of the Hamakua Coast, a few surf spots and swimming holes tucked into the lush landscape deserve an afternoon stop.

Kolekole Beach Park. This lush park is tucked away under a high bridge that crosses a gulch along Highway 19, between Akaka and Umauma falls. The beach is composed of large, smooth, waterworn stones, where the Kolekole stream meets the ocean. Although the shoreline is rocky and the ocean rough, the stream is usually calm and great for swimming, and the backdrop is stunning. There's even a rope swing tied to a banyan tree on the opposite side. The park is popular with locals, especially on weekends, when it can get rowdy. ■ TIP➜ **Where the stream meets the ocean, the surf is rough and the currents strong. Only very experienced swimmers should venture here. Amenities:** parking (no fee); showers; toilets. **Best for:** swimming. ⊠ *Hwy. 19, Honomu* ✢ *13 miles north of Hilo* ☎ *808/961–8311.*

HILO

Hilo isn't exactly known for tropical white-sand beaches, but there are a few nice ones in the area that offer good swimming and snorkeling opportunities, and some are surrounded by lush rain forest.

Honolii Beach Park. One of the most consistent places on the east side to catch a wave, Honolii is popular with the local surf crowd. The beach is a mix of black sand, coral, and sea glass, with plenty of rocks. A shady grassy area is great for picnics while you watch the surfers. ⚠ **The presence of surfers is not an indication that an area is safe for swimmers. Winter surf is very rough.** A pond just to the north is good for swimming, but it's deep and there is a drop-off. There's limited parking on the narrow roadside. Walk down the stairs and veer left over the rocks. **Amenities:** lifeguards; toilets. **Best for:** surfing. ⊠ *Hwy. 19, Hilo* ✢ *1½ miles north of Hilo* ☎ *808/961–8311.*

FAMILY **Onekahakaha Beach Park.** Shallow, rock-wall-enclosed tide pools and an adjacent grassy picnic area make this park a favorite among Hilo families with small children. The protected pools are great places to look for Hawaiian marine life like sea urchins and anemones. There isn't much white sand, but access to the water is easy. The water is usually rough beyond the line of large boulders protecting the inner tide pools, so be careful if the surf is high. This beach gets crowded on weekends. **Amenities:** lifeguards (weekends, holidays, and summer only); parking (no fee); showers; toilets. **Best for:** swimming. ⊠ *Onekahakaha Rd. and Kalanianaole Ave., via Kanoelehua St., Hilo* ✢ *3 miles east of Hilo* ☎ *808/961–8311.*

Reeds Bay Beach Park. Safe swimming, proximity to downtown Hilo, and a freshwater-fed swimming hole called the Ice Pond that flows into the backwaters of Hilo Bay are the enticements of this cove. No, there really isn't ice in the swimming hole; it just feels that way on a hot sultry day. The large pond, between Hilo Seaside Hotel and the

DID YOU KNOW?

You can see turtles at the Big Island's Punaluu Black Sand Beach Park, a popular resting and feeding spot for endangered Hawaiian green sea turtles. Absolutely no touching the animals—it's a hefty fine.

Ponds Hilo Restaurant, is a favorite of local kids, who enjoy jumping into and frolicking in the chilly fresh- and saltwater mix. The water is usually calm. **Amenities:** parking (no fee); showers. **Best for:** swimming. ⊠ *Banyan Dr. and Kalanianaole Ave., Hilo* ☎ *808/961–8311.*

FAMILY **Waiolena and Wailua Beach Parks and Richardson Ocean Center.** Just east of Hilo, almost at the end of the road, three adjacent parks make up one beautiful spot with a series of bays, protected inlets, lagoons, and pretty parks. This is one of the best snorkeling sites on this side of the island, as rocky outcrops provide shelter for schools of reef fish, sea turtles, and dolphins. Resist the urge to get too close to turtles or disturb them; they are protected from harassment by federal and state law. Local kids use the small black-sand pocket beach for body boarding. The shaded grassy areas are great for picnics. Be warned, this place is very crowded on weekends. **Amenities:** lifeguards (weekends, holidays, and summer only); parking (no fee); showers; toilets. **Best for:** snorkeling; walking. ⊠ *2349 Kalanianaole Ave., 4 miles east of Hilo, Hilo* ☎ *808/961–8311.*

PUNA

Puna's few beaches have some unusual attributes—swaths of new black sand, volcano-heated springs, and a coastline that is beyond dramatic—sheer walls of lava rock dropping into an electric blue ocean, surging with white water and ringed with coco palms. Ongoing eruptions of Kilauea have made parts of Puna inaccessible and closed some roads.

FAMILY **Ahalanui Park.** There's nothing like swimming in this natural, geothermally heated tide pool next to the ocean with palm fronds rustling lazily overhead. Popular with locals, this gorgeous, immaculate 3-acre beach park has a ½-acre pond of brackish water that's heated by volcanic steam. There's no sand, but there is smooth, rocky access to the ocean as well as the pond. Check with the lifeguard on duty, and heed all posted signs. The parking lot fills up quickly. **Amenities:** lifeguards; parking (no fee); showers; toilets. **Best for:** swimming. ⊠ *Hwy. 137, 2½ miles south of Hwy. 132, Pahoa* ☎ *808/961–8311.*

KAU

You shouldn't expect to find sparkling white-sand beaches on the rugged and rocky coasts of Kau, and you won't. What you will find is something a bit rarer and well worth the visit: black- and green-sand beaches. And there's the chance to see the endangered hawksbill or Hawaiian green sea turtles close up.

Papakolea Beach (*Green Sands Beach*). Tired of the same old gold-, white-, or black-sand beach? Then how about a green-sand beach? You'll need good hiking shoes or sneakers to get to this olive-green crescent, one of the most unusual beaches on the island. It lies at the base of Puu O Mahana, at Mahana Bay, where a cinder cone formed during an early eruption of Mauna Loa. The greenish tint is caused by an accumulation of olivine crystals that form in volcanic eruptions. The dry, barren landscape is totally surreal but stunning, as aquamarine waters lap on green sand against reddish cliffs. The surf is often rough, and swimming is hazardous due to strong currents, so caution is advised. Drive down to Ka Lae (South Point); at the end of the 12-mile paved road, take the road to the left and park at the end. Don't pay anyone for parking, but you may encounter some enterprising folks willing to take you to the beach in the back of their truck for a small fee. Of course, lock your car and don't leave valuables inside. To reach the beach, follow the 2¼-mile coastal trail, which ends in a steep and dangerous descent down the cliffside on an unimproved trail. The hike takes about two hours each way and it can get hot and windy, so bring lots of drinking water. Four-wheel-drive vehicles are no longer permitted on the trail. **Amenities:** none. **Best for:** solitude; walking. ⊠ *Hwy. 11, Naalehu* ✛ *2½ miles northeast of South Point.*

Fodor's Choice
★   **Punaluu Black Sand Beach Park.** A must-do on a south–southeast–bound trip to the volcano, this easily accessible black-sand beach is backed by low dunes, brackish ponds, and tall coco palms. The shoreline is jagged, reefed, and rocky. Most days, large groups of sea turtles nap on the sand—a stunning sight. Resist the urge to get too close or disturb them; they're protected by federal and state law, and fines for harassment can be hefty. Removing black sand is also prohibited. ⚠ **Extremely strong rip currents prevail, so only experienced ocean swimmers should consider getting in the water here.** Popular with locals and tour buses alike, this beach park can get very busy, especially on weekends (the north parking lot is usually quieter). Shade from palm trees provides an escape from the sun, and at the northern end of the beach, near the boat ramp, lie the ruins of Kaneeleele Heiau, an old Hawaiian temple. The area was a sugar port until the 1946 tsunami destroyed the buildings. Developers tried to bring a huge resort experience here in the early 1990s, but that has mostly failed. (You'll drive by a few abandoned resort buildings on your way to the beach.) ■ TIP➜ **Bring your camera and a picnic lunch. Amenities:** parking (no fee); showers; toilets. **Best for:** walking. ⊠ *Hwy. 11, between mile markers 55 and 56, Naalehu* ✛ *27 miles south of Hawaii Volcanoes National Park* ☎ *808/961–8311.*

4

WHERE TO EAT

Updated
by Karen
Anderson

Between star chefs and myriad local farms, the Big Island restaurant scene is becoming a destination for foodies. Food writers are praising the chefs of the Big Island for their ability to turn the local bounty into inventive blends inspired by the island's cultural heritage.

Resorts along the Kohala Coast have long invested in culinary programs offering memorable dining experiences that include inventive entrées, spot-on wine pairings, and customized chef's table options. But great food on the Big Island doesn't begin and end with the resorts. A handful of chefs have retired from the fast-paced hotel world and opened their own small bistros in upcountry Waimea, or other places off the beaten track. Unique and wonderful restaurants have cropped up in Hawi, Kainaliu, and Holualoa, and on the east side of the island in Hilo.

In addition to restaurants, festivals devoted to island products draw hundreds of attendees to learn about everything from breadfruit and mango to avocado, chocolate, and coffee. Agritourism has turned into a fruitful venture for farmers as farm tours afford the opportunity to meet with and learn from a variety of local producer. Some tours conclude with a meal of items sourced from the same farms. From goat farms churning creamy, savory goat cheese to Waimea farms planting row after row of bright tomatoes to high-tech aquaculture operations at NELHA (Natural Energy Lab of Hawaii Authority), visitors can see exactly where their next meal comes from.

BIG ISLAND DINING PLANNER

WITH KIDS
Keiki (kids) menus are offered at a majority of restaurants on the Big Island, the exceptions being a small handful of fine-dining restaurants that cater to adults.

SMOKING
Smoking is prohibited in all Hawaii restaurants and bars.

RESERVATIONS

Only a few restaurants on the Big Island require reservations. Nevertheless, always call ahead if you're bringing a large party or booking a special-occasion dinner.

WHAT TO WEAR

There isn't a single place on the Big Island that requires formal attire. There are a handful of restaurants (Ulu Ocean Grill and Sushi Lounge at the Four Seasons, the CanoeHouse at the Mauna Lani, and Merriman's) where you might feel out of place in your beach clothes, but resort wear is acceptable at even the most upscale restaurants.

HOURS AND PRICES

Though it might seem at first glance like the Big Island's dining scene consists of either high-end restaurants or hole-in-the-wall dives, there is in fact a fairly large middle ground of good restaurants that cater to both local and visiting families, with new places cropping up all the time. However, prices are generally higher than on the mainland. Tipping is similar to elsewhere in the country: 15%–20% of the bill or $1 per drink at a bar. Bills for large parties generally include an 18% tip, as do bills at some resort restaurants, so be sure to check before leaving extra.

WHAT IT COSTS				
	$	$$	$$$	$$$$
AT DINNER	under $17	$17–$26	$27–$35	over $35

Restaurant prices are for a main course at dinner, excluding 4.2% excise tax.

KAILUA-KONA

$ ✕ **Ba-Le.** Hidden away in a strip mall on Palani Road near KTA, Ba-Le
VIETNAMESE serves Vietnamese-influenced food such as pho, a soup laden with noo-
FAMILY dles, meat, and veggies. Sandwiches and cold rice noodle salads are also on the sizable menu. **Known for:** large portions at reasonable prices; great banh mi sandwiches; supercasual atmosphere. $ *Average main: $8* ⊠ *Kona Coast Shopping Center, 74-5588 Palani Rd., Kailua-Kona* ☎ *808/327–1212* ☉ *Sunday.*

$ ✕ **Bangkok House Thai Restaurant.** It may not look like much, with its
THAI small dark interior, but this is the local go-to for good Thai food. Tucked away in a small shopping center, Bangkok serves up tasty curries, satays, and soups, along with a random assortment of Chinese entrées. **Known for:** longtime, family-run business in Kona; crispy duck; homemade lychee ice cream. $ *Average main: $15* ⊠ *King Kamehameha Mall, 75-5626 Kuakini Hwy., Kailua-Kona* ☎ *808/329–7764* ☉ *No lunch weekends.*

$ ✕ **Bianelli's.** With indoor and outdoor seating, this easygoing Italian
ITALIAN restaurant serves up gourmet pizzas and a tasty selection of pasta
FAMILY dishes, calzones, sandwiches, and salads. For a couple of bucks, order a slice of pizza and pair it with an island-fresh dinner salad. **Known**

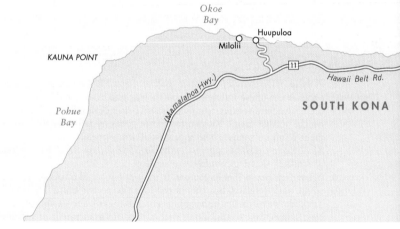

Where to Eat on the Kona Coast

0 ├───┼───┤ 2 miles
0 ├───┼───┤ 3 km

Okoe
Bay

Huupuloa

Milolii

KAUNA POINT

11

(Mamalahoa Hwy.)

Hawaii Belt Rd.

Pohue
Bay

SOUTH KONA

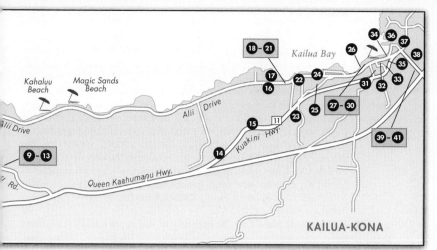

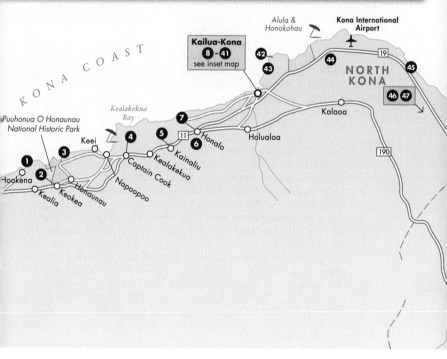

for: cozy dining room with quick service; patio seating inside upscale shopping center; pies you can take and bake at home. $ Average main: $12 ✉ Keauhou Shopping Center, 78-6831 Alii Dr., Kailua-Kona ☎ 808/322–0377 ⊕ www.bianellis.com ⊙ Closed Sun. No lunch.

$
HAWAIIAN
FAMILY

✕ **Big Island Grill.** This local-style Hawaiian restaurant looks like an old coffee shop—it's large and nondescript inside, with booths, basic tables, and bingo-hall chairs. Local families love it for the huge portions of pork chops, *loco moco* (local-style dish with meat, rice, and eggs smothered in gravy), and an assortment of fish specialties at very reasonable prices. "Biggie's" also serves a decent breakfast (the only meal it serves on Sunday). **Known for:** huge portions at relatively low prices; Sunday breakfast; popular with large groups and families. $ Average main: $12 ✉ 75-5702 Kuakini Hwy., Kailua-Kona ☎ 808/326–1153 ⊙ No lunch or dinner Sun.

$
AMERICAN
Fodor'sChoice
★

✕ **Bongo Ben's Island Café.** At the entry of this super-casual, oceanfront diner, menus printed on the giant bongos tell the story. Offering great deals on a plethora of breakfast, lunch, and dinner items, the open-air restaurant bakes its own breads, cinnamon rolls, desserts, pizza crust, and hamburger buns on-site. **Known for:** oceanfront views of Kailua Bay; prime rib night and other weekly specials; discounts on morning and happy hour cocktails. $ Average main: $15 ✉ 75-5819 Alii Dr., Kailua-Kona ☎ 808/329–9203 ⊕ www.bongobens.com.

$$
AMERICAN
FAMILY

✕ **Bubba Gump Shrimp Company.** This may be a chain named after an old Tom Hanks movie, but it has one of the nicest oceanfront patios in Historic Kailua Village, and the food's not bad, provided you know what to order. Anything with popcorn shrimp in it is a good bet, and the pear and berry salad (a combination of chicken, strawberries, pears, and glazed pecans) is the perfect size for lunch. **Known for:** hand-breaded coconut shrimp; front row seat to body boarders catching waves; kids' menu includes mini-corndogs and mac and cheese. $ Average main: $20 ✉ 75-5776 Alii Dr., Kailua-Kona ☎ 808/331–8442 ⊕ www.bubbagump.com.

$$
HAWAIIAN

✕ **Don the Beachcomber at Royal Kona Resort.** The "original home of the mai tai," Don the Beachcomber features a retro, tiki-bar setting with the absolute best view of Kailua Bay in town. Service can be slow, but the coconut prawns are worth the wait, as is the New York steak paired with bacon-wrapped shrimp. **Known for:** slow-roasted prime rib; dining on the water's edge; Don's Mai Tai Bar serves menu items and 10 types of mai tais. $ Average main: $20 ✉ Royal Kona Resort, 75-5852 Alii Dr., Kailua-Kona ☎ 808/329–3111 ⊕ www.royalkona.com/Dining.cfm ⊙ No lunch in main restaurant. No dinner in main restaurant Sun.–Wed.

$$
SEAFOOD
FAMILY

✕ **The Fish Hopper.** With a bayside view in the heart of Historic Kailua Village, the open-air Hawaii location of the popular Monterey, California, restaurant has an expansive menu for breakfast, lunch, and dinner. Inventive fresh-fish specials as well as simple fish-and-chips and clam chowder are what the original is known for. **Known for:** award-winning clam chowder; tropical oceanfront venue; signature Volcano flaming cocktail. $ Average main: $24 ✉ 75-5683 Alii Dr., Kailua-Kona ☎ 808/326–2002 ⊕ www.fishhopper.com/kona.

$$ ✗ **Foster's Kitchen.** Ocean breezes flow through this open-air, bay-front
AMERICAN restaurant on Alii Drive. Cajun and island influences can be found on
Fodor's Choice the quality menu, where almost all dishes are made to order and fea-
★ ture non-GMO, hormone-free, or USDA certified organic ingredients.
Known for: scratch-made food and cocktails; steak house pasta; two
happy hours daily. ⑤ *Average main: $23* ✉ *75-5805 Alii Dr., Kailua-
Kona* ☎ *808/326-1600* ⊕ *www.fosterskitchen.com.*

$ ✗ **Frenchman's Cafe.** A Parisian couple serves up authentic French crêpes,
FRENCH omelettes, galettes, and desserts at this hidden hideaway in Historic
Kailua Village. For lunch, the croque-monsieur is a good bet, while the
variety of savory or sweet crêpes include gluten-free options. **Known
for:** French owners; open early for breakfast; great croissants. ⑤ *Aver-
age main: $11* ✉ *Kona Marketplace, 75-5729 Alii Dr., Kailua-Kona*
☎ *808/365-2671* ☾ *Closed Tues.–Wed. No dinner.*

$ ✗ **Habanero's Grill.** Perched above Alii Drive near Royal Kona Resort,
MEXICAN this casually upscale restaurant with a view features traditional taque-
FAMILY ria-style offerings as well as more sophisticated, contemporary Mexican
cuisine. Gourmet entrées range from rib-eye steak served Veracruz style,
to seafood *relleno* (stuffing) brimming with shrimp, fish, scallops, and
jack cheese. **Known for:** contemporary Mexico City–style cuisine; full
cocktail bar and lounge; daily lunch specials. ⑤ *Average main: $15*
✉ *75-5864 Walua Rd., Kailua-Kona* ☎ *808/329-2814* ⊕ *habaneros-
grillhawaii.com* ☾ *Closed Sun.*

$ ✗ **Harbor House.** This open-air restaurant on the docks at Kona's sleepy
AMERICAN harbor is a fun place to grab a beer and a bite after a long day fishing,
beaching, or diving. The venue is nothing fancy, but Harbor House is a
local favorite for fresh-fish sandwiches and a variety of fried fish-and-
chip combos. **Known for:** chilled schooners of Kona Brewing Co. lager
at happy hour; waterfront dining; fun destination on the way to or
from Kona International Airport. ⑤ *Average main: $10* ✉ *Honokohau
Harbor, 74-425 Kealakehe Pkwy., Ste. 4, Kailua-Kona* ☎ *808/326-4166*
⊕ *harborhouserestaurantkona.com* ☾ *No dinner.*

$$ ✗ **Holuakoa Gardens and Cafe.** This respected slow-food restaurant in
HAWAIIAN Holualoa Village features fine dining in a lush, open-air setting beneath
the shade of an old monkeypod tree. The proprietors, top chefs from
the Bay Area, strive to use all local and organic ingredients for such
dinner entrées as handcrafted house gnocchi or Mediterranean seafood
stew. **Known for:** farm-to-table cuisine; adjacent coffeehouse lounge;
biodynamic and organic wines. ⑤ *Average main: $25* ✉ *76-5900 Old
Government Rd., Holualoa* ☎ *808/322-2233* ⊕ *www.holuakoacafe.
com* ☾ *No dinner Sun.*

$$$ ✗ **Honu's on the Beach.** Featuring al fresco dining near the sand, this
HAWAIIAN is one of the few truly beachfront restaurants in Historic Kailua Vil-
lage. Part of Courtyard by Marriott King Kamehameha's Kona Beach
Hotel, the venue offers prime views of Kailua Pier and the historic
grounds of Kamakahonu Bay. **Known for:** views of sacred temple;
magical beachside setting; tiki torches at night. ⑤ *Average main: $28*
✉ *Courtyard King Kamehameha's Kona Beach Hotel, 75-5660 Palani
Rd., Kailua-Kona* ☎ *808/329-2911* ⊕ *www.konabeachhotel.com/din-
ing.htm* ☾ *No lunch.*

4

$$$$
HAWAIIAN

✕ **Huggo's.** This is one of the few restaurants in town with prices and atmosphere comparable to the splurge restaurants at the Kohala Coast resorts. Dinner offerings sometimes fall short, considering the prices, but the *pupus* (appetizers) and small plates are usually a good bet. **Known for:** dining at the water's edge; landmark Kona restaurant; nightlife hot spot. ⑤ *Average main: $36* ✉ *75-5828 Kahakai Rd., off Alii Dr., Kailua-Kona* ☎ *808/329–1493* ⊕ *www.huggos.com* ☾ *No lunch.*

$
AMERICAN

✕ **Humpy's Big Island Alehouse.** This place is usually packed for a reason: the more than 36 craft brews on tap, plus an upstairs and downstairs bar with plenty of outdoor seating. Take in the oceanfront view while chowing down on stone-baked pizza, fresh salads, fish-and-chips, fish tacos, burgers, stone-baked subs, and lots of appetizers. **Known for:** largest selection of craft beer on the island; great crab cakes; monkey-pod cocktail bars. ⑤ *Average main: $15* ✉ *Coconut Grove MarketPlace, 75-5815 Alii Dr., Kailua-Kona* ☎ *808/324-2337* ⊕ *humpyskona.com.*

$$
AMERICAN

✕ **Island Lava Java.** Located just steps away from its previous landmark location, Island Lava Java is no longer just a colorful coffeeshop with sidewalk seating. With a cocktail bar upstairs and downstairs, the transformed restaurant has upped its food game, too, increasing the prices to boot. **Known for:** large portions using mostly local organic ingredients; new bar with extensive cocktail menu; 100% Kona coffee. ⑤ *Average main: $20* ✉ *Coconut Grove MarketPlace, 75-5801 Alii Dr., Kailua-Kona* ☎ *808/327–2161* ⊕ *www.islandlavajava.com.*

$$
AMERICAN
FAMILY
Fodor's Choice
★

✕ **Jackie Rey's Ohana Grill.** This brightly decorated, open-air restaurant is a favorite lunch and dinner destination of visitors and residents, thanks to generous portions and a nice variety of chef's specials, steaks, and seafood dishes. Meals pair well with selections from Jackie Rey's well-rounded wine list. **Known for:** strong local following; great value lunch menu with ribs and fish-and-chips; friendly servers and upbeat atmosphere. ⑤ *Average main: $23* ✉ *Pottery Terrace, 75-5995 Kuakini Hwy., Kailua-Kona* ☎ *808/327–0209* ⊕ *www.jackiereys.com* ☾ *No lunch weekends.*

$
HAWAIIAN

✕ **Kanaka Kava.** This is a popular local hangout, and not just because the kava makes you mellow. The Hawaiian proprietors also serve traditional Hawaiian food, including fresh poke, bowls of pulled kalua pork, and healthy organic greens, available in fairly large portions for less than you'll pay elsewhere. **Known for:** kava served in coconut cups; authentic Hawaiian food; Hawaiian specialties like fresh fish and laulau; colorful clientele. ⑤ *Average main: $12* ✉ *Coconut Grove Marketplace, 75-5803 Alii Dr., Space B6, Kailua-Kona* ☎ *808/327–1660* ⊕ *www.kanakakava.com.*

$$
JAPANESE
Fodor's Choice
★

✕ **Kenichi Pacific.** With black-lacquer tables and lipstick-red banquettes, Kenichi offers a more sophisticated dining atmosphere than what's normally found in Kona. This is where residents go when they feel like splurging on top-notch sushi, steak, and Asian-fusion cuisine. **Known for:** upscale dining at much less than resort prices; happy hour discounts on sushi; cheaper lounge menu of small plates. ⑤ *Average main: $25* ✉ *Keauhou Shopping Center, 78-6831 Alii Dr., D-125, Kailua-Kona* ☎ *808/322–6400* ⊕ *www.kenichirestaurants.com* ☾ *No lunch.*

$ ✗**Kona Brewing Co. Pub & Brewery.** This ultrapopular destination with
AMERICAN   an outdoor patio offers an excellent and varied menu, including famous
FAMILY   brews, pulled-pork quesadillas, gourmet pizzas, and a killer spinach
Fodor's Choice   salad with Gorgonzola cheese, macadamia nuts, and strawberries. The
★   most affordable option for lunch or dinner is the veggie slice and salad
—the garden salad is generous and the slice is moist and loaded with
toppings. **Known for:** Longboard Lager and other famous brews made
on-site; good pizza; money-saving beer sampler. $ *Average main: $12*
✉ *74-5612 Pawai Pl., off Kaiwi St. at end of Pawai Pl., Kailua-Kona*
☎ *808/329–2739* ⊕ *www.konabrewingco.com.*

$$ ✗**Kona Inn Restaurant.** This vintage open-air restaurant at the historic
AMERICAN   Kona Inn Shopping Village offers a beautiful oceanfront setting on
Kailua Bay. It's a great place to have a mai tai and some appetizers while
watching the sunset, or to enjoy a calamari sandwich, clam chowder, or
salad at lunch. **Known for:** sunset-watching spot; nice bar and lounge
at all times; inconsistent food at dinner. $ *Average main: $20* ✉ *Kona
Inn Shopping Village, 75-5744 Alii Dr., Kailua-Kona* ☎ *808/329–4455*
⊕ *www.windandsearestaurants.com.*

$$$$ ✗**La Bourgogne.** A genial husband-and-wife team owns this quiet, coun-
FRENCH   try-style bistro with dark-wood walls and private booths (no windows;
it's located in a nondescript office building). The traditional French
cuisine might not impress visitors from France, but this popular local
favorite offers such classics as escargots, beef with a Cabernet Sauvi-
gnon sauce, and rack of lamb with roasted garlic and rosemary. **Known
for:** nightly specials; great cassoulet; good wines by the glass. $ *Aver-
age main: $40* ✉ *77-6400 Nalani St., Kailua-Kona* ☎ *808/329–6711*
☽ *Closed Sun. and Mon. No lunch.*

$$ ✗**Lemongrass Bistro.** This well-kept secret occupies a small stylish venue
ASIAN   across from the Kailua-Kona public library. The Asian-fusion menu—
everything is made to order—includes Thai, Vietnamese, Japanese, Lao-
tian, and Filipino dishes. **Known for:** braised oxtail; $10 lunch special;
close to village shops. $ *Average main: $20* ✉ *75-5742 Kuakini Hwy.,
Suite 103, Kailua-Kona* ☎ *808/331–2708.*

$ ✗**Los Habaneros.** Hidden in the corner of Keauhou Shopping Center
MEXICAN   adjacent to the movie theater, Los Habaneros serves up fast, albeit aver-
FAMILY   age, Mexican food for low prices. Favorites are usually combos, which
can be anything from enchilada plates to homemade sopas and chiles
rellenos. **Known for:** before- or after-beach stop; margaritas, tequila
shots, and Mexican beer; take-out quality Mexican food. $ *Average
main: $7* ✉ *Keauhou Shopping Center, 78-631 Alii Dr., Kailua-Kona*
☎ *808/324–4688* ☽ *Closed Sun.*

$$ ✗**Mi's Waterfront Bistro.** Overlooking Kailua Bay at its new location in
ITALIAN   Waterfront Row, this steady presence in the Kona dining scene offers
a reliable, consistent menu. The restaurant's husband-and-wife owners
prepare homemade pastas and focaccia daily and also offer some deli-
cious pasta specials. **Known for:** waterfront views; consistent menu;
good desserts. $ *Average main: $18* ✉ *75-5770 Alii Drive, Kailua-Kona*
☎ *808/323–3880* ⊕ *www.miswaterfront.com.*

$ ✗**Pancho & Lefty's Cantina.** Across the street from the Kona Inn Shop-
MEXICAN   ping Village, in Kailua Village, this upstairs cantina is a nice perch for

enjoying nachos and margaritas (try the hibiscus margarita) on a lazy afternoon, or to watch the passersby below on Alii Drive. The main entrées are mediocre, but the chips, salsa, and ceviche might just hit the spot. **Known for:** popular happy hour hangout; better for snacks than a full meal; homemade salsa. $ *Average main: $15* ✉ *75-5719 Alii Dr., Kailua-Kona* ☎ *808/326–2171.*

$
CAFÉ
✕ **Peaberry & Galette.** The menu at this little crêperie includes Illy espresso, teas, excellent sweet and savory crêpes, sandwiches, soups, salads, and rich desserts like lemon cheesecake and chocolate mousse, all made fresh daily. The small venue has a relaxed, urban-café vibe. **Known for:** French crêpes; cushy seats; biweekly art exhibits. $ *Average main: $8* ✉ *Keauhou Shopping Center, 78-6831 Alii Dr., Kailua-Kona* ☎ *808/322–6020* ⊕ *www.peaberryandgalette.com* ☷ *No dinner.*

$
HAWAIIAN
FAMILY
✕ **Pine Tree Café.** Next to Matsuyama's market along Highway 11 on the way to the airport, the Pine Tree Café offers local classics such as loco moco, alongside new inventions like crab curry bisque. The fresh-fish plate is decent, and all meals are served with fries or rice and macaroni salad. **Known for:** early morning breakfast; fresh fish; last stop heading north toward the airport. $ *Average main: $12* ✉ *Kohanaiki Plaza, 73-4354 Mamalahoa Hwy. (Hwy. 11), Kailua-Kona* ☎ *808/327–1234.*

$
AMERICAN
FAMILY
Fodor's Choice
★
✕ **Quinn's Almost by the Sea.** With the bar in the front and the dining patio in the back, Quinn's may seem like a bit of a dive at first glance, but this venerable restaurant serves up the best darn cheeseburger and fries in town. Appropriate for families, the restaurant stays busy for lunch and dinner, while the bar attracts a cast of colorful regulars. **Known for:** strong cocktails; comfort food like meatballs; open late (until 11 pm). $ *Average main: $15* ✉ *75-5655 Palani Rd., Kailua-Kona* ☎ *808/329–3822* ⊕ *www.quinnsalmostbythesea.com.*

$$
SOUTH PACIFIC
Fodor's Choice
★
✕ **Rays on the Bay.** The Sheraton Kona's signature restaurant overlooks Keauhou Bay, offering nighttime views of native manta rays that appear nightly beneath the balcony. The stellar dinner menu includes fresh-catch seafood, island-raised beef, and farm-fresh salads, plus tantalizing appetizers like kampachi sashimi, pork potstickers and poke. **Known for:** spectacular bay-front location; late-night dining; spotlights attract manta rays below the restaurant after dark. $ *Average main: $25* ✉ *Sheraton Kona Resort & Spa, 78-128 Ehukai St., Keauhou* ☎ *808/930–4949* ⊕ *www.sheratonkona.com/dining/rays-on-the-bay-kona* ☷ *No lunch.*

$
JAPANESE
✕ **Restaurant Hayama.** Tucked into Kopiko Plaza, just below Long's, this local favorite for Japanese fare goes beyond sushi. Hayama serves traditional Japanese specialties like tempura, unagi, broiled fish, teriyaki, and udon noodles, all made from fresh local ingredients. **Known for:** affordable lunch options; friendly service; three-course meal for two. $ *Average main: $15* ✉ *75-5660 Kopiko St., Kailua-Kona* ☎ *808/331–8888* ☷ *Closed Sun. and Mon.*

$$
HAWAIIAN
FAMILY
✕ **Sam Choy's Kai Lanai.** Perched above a shopping center with a coastline view, celebrity chef Sam Choy's namesake restaurant includes a bar that looks like a charter-fishing boat and granite-topped tables with ocean views from every seat. Open for breakfast, lunch, and dinner daily, the restaurant has reasonably priced entrées, highlighted by

Sam's trio of fish served with shiitake-mushroom cream sauce. **Known for:** limited parking for such a popular place; family-friendly with a kid's menu; happy hour at the Short Bait Bar. $ *Average main: $22* ⊠ *Keauhou Shopping Center, 78-6831 Alii Dr., Suite 1000, Kailua-Kona* ☎ *808/333–3434* ⊕ *www.samchoyskailanai.com.*

$$ ╳ **Thai Rin Restaurant.** This dependable oceanfront restaurant near Island
THAI   Lava Java on Alii Drive offers an excellent selection of Thai food at decent prices. Everything is cooked to order, and the menu is brimming with choices, including five curries, a green-papaya salad, and deep-fried fish. **Known for:** great views with both indoor and outdoor seating; appetizer platters for sharing; convenient to village shops. $ *Average main: $18* ⊠ *75-5799 Alii Dr., Kailua-Kona* ☎ *808/329–2929* ⊕ *www. aliisunsetplaza.com.*

$ ╳ **TK Noodle House.** Former resort chef TK Keosavang serves up inven-
ASIAN FUSION   tive Asian-fusion cuisine with the emphasis on noodles. Generous portions are beautifully plated, like the crispy pork belly sauté with Chinese greens and garlic sauce. **Known for:** ample parking; noodle soups and salads; shabu shabu. $ *Average main: $12* ⊠ *75 Hanama Pl., Kailua-Kona* ✛ *Near Big Island Grill* ☎ *808/327–0070* ⊕ *www.cheftk.com.*

$ ╳ **Tunaichi Sushi.** This hidden gem behind Gertrude's Jazz Bar serves
JAPANESE   excellent sushi at affordable prices. Presenting an authentic vibe of Japan, this restaurant serves up such offerings as six-piece rolls for under $4. **Known for:** authentic Japanese experience; inexpensive sushi combos for two; BYOB welcome. $ *Average main: $12* ⊠ *75-5766 Alii Dr., Kailua-Kona* ☎ *808/747–2204* ⊗ *Closed Tues.–Wed.*

$ ╳ **Ultimate Burger.** Located in the Office Max shopping complex in
DINER   Kailua-Kona, this excellent burger joint may look like a chain, but it's
FAMILY   an independent, locally owned and operated eatery that serves 100%
Fodor's Choice   organic, grass-fed Big Island beef on buns locally made. Be sure to order
★   a side of seasoned Big Daddy fries served with house-made aioli dipping sauce. **Known for:** organic, hormone-free ingredients; supporting local farmers and ranchers; excellent French fries. $ *Average main: $8* ⊠ *Kona Commons Shopping Center, 74-5450 Makala Blvd., Kailua-Kona* ☎ *808/329–2326* ⊕ *www.ultimateburger.net.*

$$ ╳ **Umekes Fishmarket Bar and Grill.** Locals flock to this downtown Kailua-
HAWAIIAN   Kona restaurant for good reason: the poke is the most *onolicious* (super-
FAMILY   delicious) in town, and the many other seafood offerings are just as
Fodor's Choice   stellar. Sandwiches, burgers, desserts and salads round out the gourmet
★   menu. **Known for:** daily specials using the freshest fish; locally sourced ingredients; authentic Kona experience. $ *Average main: 12* ⊠ *74-5563 Kaiwi St., Kailua-Kona* ✛ *Old Industrial Park at intersection of Kuakini across from West Hawaii Today* ☎ *808/238-0571* ⊕ *www.umekesfishmarketbarandgrill.com.*

THE KONA COAST

SOUTH KONA

$
MODERN
AMERICAN
FAMILY

✗ Annie's Island Fresh Burgers. At this upcountry burger restaurant in Kona, the burgers are made of succulent, 100% island-raised beef, while the hand-cut garlic-basil French fries are a highlight. Leather couches, hardwood floors, artwork, and live palm trees growing through the floor up through the roof create a casual yet well-appointed feel. **Known for:** local, grass-fed beef burgers; stylish interior; lilikoi (passion fruit) spritzer with rum. $ *Average main: $13* ✉ *Mango Court, 79-7460 Hawaii Belt Rd., #105, Kainaliu* ☎ *808/324–6000* ⊕ *www.anniesislandfreshburgers.com.*

$
AMERICAN

✗ The Coffee Shack. Visitors enjoy stopping here for breakfast or lunch after a morning of snorkeling at Kealakekua Bay, and for good reason: the views of the Honaunau coast from this roadside restaurant are stunning. Breads are all homemade, and you get to choose your favorite when ordering a generously sized sandwich brimming with Black Forest ham and the like. **Known for:** scenic views of South Kona coastline; house-baked bread; its own brand of Kona coffee. $ *Average main: $12* ✉ *83-5799 Mamalahoa Hwy., Captain Cook* ☎ *808/328–9555* ⊕ *www.coffeeshack.com* ☼ *No dinner.*

$
HAWAIIAN
Fodor's Choice
★

✗ Kaaloa's Super Js Authentic Hawaiian Food. It figures that the best laulau in West Hawaii can be found at a roadside hole-in-the-wall rather than at an expensive resort luau. In fact, this humble family-run eatery was featured on the Food Network's *The Best Thing I Ever Ate.* **Known for:** authentic Hawaiian food; friendly and welcoming proprietors; plate lunches with chicken or pork laulau. $ *Average main: $9* ✉ *83-5409 Mamalahoa Hwy., between mile markers 106 and 107, Honaunau* ☎ *808/328–9566* ☼ *Closed Sun.*

$$
ECLECTIC

✗ Keei Café at Hokukano. This nicely appointed restaurant, perched above the highway just 15 minutes south of Kailua-Kona, serves delicious dinners with Brazilian, Asian, and European flavors highlighting fresh ingredients from local farmers. Favorites are the Brazilian seafood chowder or peanut-miso salad, followed by pasta primavera smothered with a basil-pesto sauce. **Known for:** most upscale restaurant in South Kona; live music; cash only. $ *Average main: $20* ✉ *79-7511 Mamalahoa Hwy., Kealakekua* ✛ *½ mile south of Kainaliu* ☎ *808/322–9992* ⊕ *www.keeicafe.net* ▭ *No credit cards* ☼ *Closed Sun. and Mon. No lunch.*

$
HAWAIIAN
FAMILY

✗ Manago Hotel. About 20 minutes upcountry of Kailua-Kona, the historic Manago Hotel is like a time warp; a vintage neon sign identifies the hotel, while Formica tables and old photos add to the authentically retro flavor. T-shirts brag that the restaurant has the best grilled pork chops in town, and it's not false advertising. **Known for:** excellent grilled pork chops; one of the only places in Kona serving opelu, a local fish; local hospitality. $ *Average main: $10* ✉ *82-6155 Mamalahoa Hwy., Captain Cook* ☎ *808/323–2642* ⊕ *www.managohotel.com* ☼ *Closed Mon.*

$ ✕ **Teshima's.** Teshima's doesn't look like much, either inside or out, but
JAPANESE it's been a *kamaaina* (local) favorite since 1929 for a reason. Locals
FAMILY gather at this small landmark restaurant 15 minutes south of Kailua-
Kona whenever they're in the mood for fresh sashimi, puffy shrimp
tempura, or *hekka* (beef and vegetables cooked in an iron pot) at a
reasonable price. **Known for:** excellent tempura combos; long-standing
family-owned establishment; local flavor. $ *Average main: $15* ✉ *79-
7251 Mamalahoa Hwy., Honalo* ☎ *808/322–9140* ⊕ *www.teshimares-
taurant.com.*

NORTH KONA

$$$ ✕ **Beach Tree at the Four Seasons Resort Hualalai.** This beautifully designed
MODERN ITALIAN venue provides a relaxed and elegant setting for alfresco dining near
FAMILY the sand, with its boardwalk-style deck, outdoor seating under the
Fodor's Choice trellis, and enormous vaulted ceiling. The menu features brick-oven
★ pizzas, grilled fresh catch of the day, pasta, risotto, seafood entrées,
steak, and an array of farm-fresh salads. **Known for:** special Ohana
Table four-course dinner; 60 wines by the glass; elegant resort
atmosphere. $ *Average main: $35* ✉ *Four Seasons Resort Huala-
lai, 72-100 Kaupulehu Dr., Kailua-Kona* ☎ *808/325–8000* ⊕ *www.
fourseasons.com/hualalai.*

$$$$ ✕ **Ulu Ocean Grill and Sushi Lounge at the Four Seasons Resort Hualalai.**
MODERN Casual elegance takes center stage at the resort's flagship oceanfront res-
HAWAIIAN taurant, one of the most upscale restaurants on the Big Island. Breakfast
Fodor's Choice can be à la carte or buffet, but nighttime is when the magic happens,
★ starting with an impressive wine program that includes boutique wines
and world-class imports. **Known for:** sushi lounge; sources ingredients
from 160 local purveyors; oceanfront dining. $ *Average main: $45*
✉ *Four Seasons Resort Hualalai, 72-100 Kaupulehu Dr., Kailua-Kona*
☎ *808/325–8000* ⊕ *www.uluoceangrill.com* ⊗ *No lunch.*

THE KOHALA COAST

$ ✕ **A-Bay's Island Grill.** This casual yet upscale restaurant and sports bar
MEDITERRANEAN offers a 24-tap digital beer tower, 10 TV screens, a Cruvinet wine pres-
Fodor's Choice ervation/dispensing system, and an innovative frost rail that spans the
★ length of the cocktail bar to keep your drinks cool. Patio seating outside
offers additional dining options. **Known for:** beer sommelier to help
with pairings; late-night dining; great tapas menu. $ *Average main: $14*
✉ *Kings' Shops, 250 Waikoloa Beach Dr., Waikoloa* ☎ *808/209-8494*
⊕ *www.a-bays.com.*

$$ ✕ **Bamboo Restaurant & Gallery.** This popular restaurant in the heart of
ASIAN Hawi provides a historical setting in which to enjoy a menu brimming
with Hawaiian country flair. Most of the creative entrées feature fresh
island fish prepared several ways. **Known for:** Pacific Rim menu; colorful plantation-style interiors; weekend entertainment. $ *Average main:
$25* ✉ *55-3415 Akoni Pule Hwy. (Hwy. 270), Hawi* ☎ *808/889–5555*
⊕ *www.bamboorestaurant.info* ⊗ *Closed Mon. No dinner Sun.*

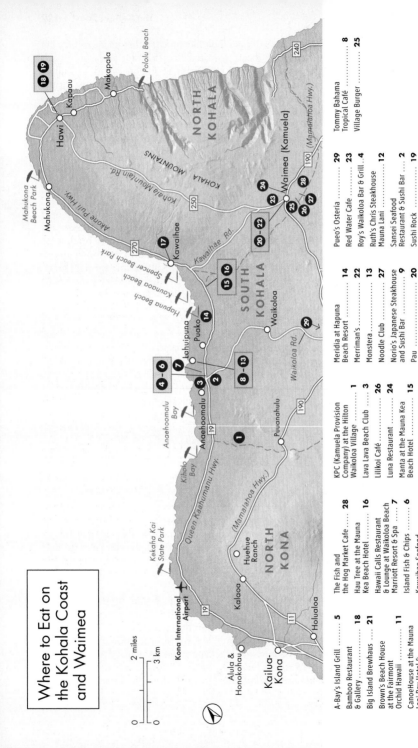

Where to Eat on the Kohala Coast and Waimea

2 miles

3 km

Kona International Airport

Kekaha Kai State Park

Kailua-Kona

Alula & Honokohau

Holualoa

NORTH KONA

Huehue Ranch

Kalaoa

Queen Kaahumanu Hwy.

Kihalo Bay

Mamalahoa Hwy.

Puuanahulu

Anaehoomalu Bay

Anaehoomalu

SOUTH KOHALA

Waikoloa

Waikoloa Rd.

Lahuipuaa

Puako

Hapuna Beach

Kaunaoa Beach

Spencer Beach Park

Kawaihae

Kawaihae Rd.

Akoni Pull Hwy.

Kohala Mountain Rd.

KOHALA MOUNTAINS

NORTH KOHALA

Waimea (Kamuela)

(Mamalahoa Hwy.)

Mahukona

Mahukona Beach Park

Hawi

Kapaau

Makapala

Pololu Beach

$$$$
MODERN
HAWAIIAN
Fodor's Choice
★

✕ **Brown's Beach House at the Fairmont Orchid Hawaii.** Sitting right on the resort's sandy bay, Brown's Beach House offers beautiful sunset dining and innovative cuisine. Attention to detail is evident in the sophisticated menu, which may include crab-crusted Kona kampachi, roasted duck breast, or Kona Coffee-crusted venison. **Known for:** equally good for seafood and non-seafood entrees; tiki torches beneath starry skies; dietary accommodations. ⑤ *Average main: $40* ⊠ *Fairmont Orchid Hawaii, 1 N. Kaniku Dr.* ☎ *808/885–2000* ⊕ *www.fairmont.com/ orchid-hawaii* ⊘ *No lunch.*

$$$$
ECLECTIC
Fodor's Choice
★

✕ **CanoeHouse at the Mauna Lani Bay Hotel & Bungalows.** One of the most romantic settings on the Kohala Coast, this landmark restaurant on the oceanfront showcases traditional Hawaiian flavors, artful presentations, and locally grown or raised products. The progressive menu spotlights grass-fed beef, lamb, fresh fish caught locally, shellfish, island-fresh greens, local goat cheese, and farm-to-table ingredients. **Known for:** memorable sunsets with tiki torches; good choice of wines by the glass; elaborate tasting menu at the Captain's table. ⑤ *Average main: $42* ⊠ *Mauna Lani Bay Hotel & Bungalows, 68-1400 Mauna Lani Dr.* ☎ *808/885–6622* ⊕ *www.maunalani.com* ⊘ *No lunch.*

$$
MODERN
HAWAIIAN

✕ **Hau Tree at the Mauna Kea Beach Hotel.** Though it sits on a patio by the pool, this beachside restaurant and beach bar is not just for pupus and cocktails. The island-infused dinner menu features excellent entrées such as the grass-fed Kulana beef tenderloin brochettes, plus plentiful seafood dishes and greens from local farms. **Known for:** famous Fredrico cocktail; great sunset views; Saturday clambake. ⑤ *Average main: $18* ⊠ *Mauna Kea Beach Hotel, 62-100 Mauna Kea Beach Dr., Kawaihae* ⊹ *Between Puako and Kawaihae* ☎ *808/882–5707* ⊕ *www. maunakeabeachhotel.com.*

$$
HAWAIIAN
FAMILY

✕ **Hawaii Calls Restaurant & Lounge at Waikoloa Beach Marriott Resort & Spa.** The only restaurant at the Waikoloa Beach Marriott, Hawaii Calls offers a contemporary and fresh menu. The real draw here are the weekly special nights, including Keahole Lobster Night on Wednesdays, and a prime rib and crab *paina* (feast) on Friday and Saturday. **Known for:** Sunday brunch; good breakfast buffet; reasonable prices for the resort area. ⑤ *Average main: $25* ⊠ *Waikoloa Beach Marriott, 69-275 Waikoloa Beach Dr., Waikoloa* ☎ *808/886–6789* ⊕ *www.waikoloabeachmarriott.com.*

$
AMERICAN
FAMILY
Fodor's Choice
★

✕ **Island Fish and Chips.** Hidden lakeside at the Kings' Shop, this little take-out place is a best-kept secret in the Waikoloa Beach Resort. The combo baskets brim with tempura fresh-catch fish, chicken, shrimp, and more, while breakfast options include loco moco laden with tempura fish fillet. **Known for:** open early for breakfast; locally owned since 2000; great fish-and-chips to go. ⑤ *Average main: $8* ⊠ *Kings' Shops, 69-250 Waikoloa Beach Dr., #D3, Waikoloa* ☎ *808/886–0005.*

$$
SEAFOOD

✕ **Kawaihae Seafood Bar & Grill.** Upstairs in a historical building, this seafood bar has been a hot spot for years, serving up a dynamite and well-priced bar menu with tasty pupus, and an always-expanding dinner menu that includes at least four fresh-fish specials daily. There's fare for landlubbers, too, including boneless braised short ribs, rib-eye steak, specialty pizza, and lots of salad options. **Known for:** affordable prices; kitchen open late; two nightly happy hours. ⑤ *Average main:*

4

$19 ✉ *61-3642 Kawaihae Harbor, Hwy. 270, Kawaihae* ☎ *808/880–9393* ⊕ *www.seafoodbargrill.com.*

$$$$ ✕ **KPC (Kamuela Provision Company) at the Hilton Waikoloa Village.** The
MODERN breezy lanai has the most spectacular view of the leeward coast of any
HAWAIIAN restaurant on the Big Island. It's the perfect accompaniment to the
elegant yet down-to-earth Hawaii Regional Cuisine and specialty cocktails, like the Island Passion mango martini. **Known for:** tapas menu;
the island's best sunset drinks spot; excellent desserts. ⑤ *Average main:*
$36 ✉ *Hilton Waikoloa Village, 69-425 Waikoloa Beach Dr., Waikoloa*
☎ *808/886–1234* ⊕ *www.hiltonwaikoloavillage.com* ☾ *No lunch.*

$$ ✕ **Lava Lava Beach Club.** Dig your toes into the sand at Anaehoomalu
HAWAIIAN Bay and enjoy one of the most happening, entertaining, and memo-
FAMILY rable bar/restaurants on the Kohala Coast. The atmosphere is super-
Fodor's Choice casual—you can dine in your beach togs. **Known for:** dining in the
★ sand; great Parmesan lava tots and coconut shrimp; signature Sandy
Toes cocktail. ⑤ *Average main: $20* ✉ *69-1081 Kuualii Pl., Waikoloa*
☎ *808/769–5282* ⊕ *lavalavabeachclub.com/bigisland.*

$$$$ ✕ **Manta at the Mauna Kea Beach Hotel.** Perched on the edge of a bluff
MODERN overlooking the sparkling waters of Kaunaoa Beach, the resort's flagship
HAWAIIAN restaurant is a compelling spot for a romantic meal at sunset, espe-
Fodor's Choice cially at one of the outside tables. The culinary team's take on Hawaii
★ regional cuisine highlights locally sourced, sustainable fish, chicken, and
beef. **Known for:** beachfront balcony dining; exhibition kitchen; Sun-
day brunch. ⑤ *Average main: $40* ✉ *Mauna Kea Beach Hotel, 62-100*
Mauna Kea Beach Dr., Kawaihae ☎ *808/882–5707* ⊕ *www.maunak-
eabeachhotel.com* ☾ *No lunch.*

$$$ ✕ **Meridia at Hapuna Beach Resort.** This open-air restaurant has high ceil-
MODERN ings and a lanai that overlooks the pool and the sandy-white shores of
HAWAIIAN Hapuna Beach. Small plate appetizers and main course entrée options
showcase a bounty of Big Island ingredients infused with Mediterranean
influences. **Known for:** friendly wait staff; signature seafood; interesting
architecture. ⑤ *Average main: $30* ✉ *The Westin Hapuna Beach Resort,*
62-100 Kaunaoa Dr. ☎ *808/880–1111* ⊕ *www.princeresortshawaii.com.*

$$ ✕ **Monstera.** It may not be beachfront with a view of the sunset, but
JAPANESE this eatery is worth a visit for its sophisticated *izakaya* (Japanese
FAMILY pub) food with a touch of local inspiration. Executive Chef Anthony
Gonzales's dinner menu includes Norio's Original 69 Roll with
Dungeness crab. **Known for:** sushi bar; sizable noodle dishes and
small plates to share; late-night dining. ⑤ *Average main: $20* ✉ *The*
Shops at Mauna Lani, 68-1330 Mauna Lani Dr. ☎ *808/887–2711*
⊕ *www.monterasushi.com* ☾ *No lunch.*

$$$$ ✕ **Norio's Japanese Steakhouse and Sushi Bar.** On the garden level of the
JAPANESE Fairmont Orchid, this classy restaurant appeals to both steak and sea-
food lovers. The star attraction is the signature Australian A6 Wagyu rib
eye, seasoned with five different kinds of Hawaiian sea salt. **Known for:**
sushi bar and lounge; extensive wine and sake roster; options for gluten-
and soy-free diners. ⑤ *Average main: $42* ✉ *Fairmont Orchid Hawaii,*
1 N. Kaniku Dr. ☎ *808/885–2000* ⊕ *www.fairmont.com/orchid-hawaii*
☾ *Closed Tues.–Wed. No lunch.*

$$
ITALIAN

✕ **Pueo's Osteria.** Hidden in a shopping center in residential Waikoloa Village, this late-night destination serves dinner from 5 until midnight (*pueo* means "owl" in Hawaiian, and refers to the restaurant's "night owl" concept). Renowned executive chef James Babian (Four Seasons Hualalai, Fairmont Orchid) serves up offerings that combine farm-fresh ingredients with fine imported Italian products like prosciutto from Parma. **Known for:** premium ingredients from Italy; lively atmosphere; Tuscan-inspired dining room. $ *Average main: $20* ✉ *Waikoloa Village Highlands Center, 68-1845 Waikoloa Rd., Waikoloa* ⊹ *Near Subway* ☎ *808/339–7566* ⊕ *www.pueososteria.com* ☾ *No lunch.*

$$$$
MODERN
HAWAIIAN
FAMILY

✕ **Roy's Waikoloa Bar & Grill.** Overlooking the lake at the Kings' Shops is, granted, not an oceanfront setting, but if you're staying nearby and are looking for reliable, albeit pricey, cuisine, this place fits the bill. The three-course, prix fixe meal is a good bet, as is blackened ahi, and the macadamia nut–crusted Hawaiian fish with Kona lobster cream sauce is a melt-in-your-mouth encounter. **Known for:** great appetizers to share; extensive list of wines by the glass; outstanding kid's menu. $ *Average main: $40* ✉ *Kings' Shops at Waikoloa Village, 250 Waikoloa Beach Dr., Waikoloa* ☎ *808/886–4321* ⊕ *www. roysrestaurant.com* ☾ *No lunch.*

$$$$
STEAKHOUSE
Fodor'sChoice
★

✕ **Ruth's Chris Steakhouse Mauna Lani.** The Big Island location of the popular upscale Louisiana steak-house franchise serves the sizzling steaks (yes, they do sizzle on the plate) and heaping sides the restaurant is known for. Early-evening Prime Time specials consist of a salad, entrée, side, and dessert for a fraction of the price. **Known for:** good happy hour food specials; winemaker dinners; great cocktails. $ *Average main: $40* ✉ *The Shops at Mauna Lani, 68-1330 Mauna Lani Dr., Waikoloa* ☎ *808/887–0800* ⊕ *www.ruthschris.com* ☾ *No lunch.*

$$
JAPANESE
FAMILY

✕ **Sansei Seafood Restaurant & Sushi Bar.** Creative sushi and contemporary Asian cuisine take center stage at this entertaining restaurant at Queens' MarketPlace. The lauded menu includes shrimp dynamite in a creamy garlic masago aioli and unagi glaze, and panko-crusted ahi sashimi sushi roll. **Known for:** early-bird 50% discount Sun. and Mon.; private dining room; karaoke on the weekends. $ *Average main: $20* ✉ *Queens' MarketPlace, 201 Waikoloa Beach Dr., Ste. 801, Waikoloa* ☎ *808/886–6286* ⊕ *www.sanseihawaii.com* ☾ *No lunch.*

$$
JAPANESE
Fodor'sChoice
★

✕ **Sushi Rock.** Located in historic Hawi Town, Sushi Rock isn't big on size—its narrow dining room is brightly painted and casually decorated with Hawaiian and Japanese knickknacks—but discerning locals and *akamai* (in-the-know) visitors come here for some of the island's best sushi. The restaurant prides itself on using local ingredients like grass-fed beef tenderloin, goat cheese, macadamia nuts, and mango in the Islands-inspired sushi rolls. **Known for:** well-priced trios; cone sushi; extensive salad menu. $ *Average main: $23* ✉ *55-3435 Akoni Pule Hwy., Hawi* ☎ *808/889–5900* ⊕ *sushirockrestaurant.net.*

$$$
MODERN
HAWAIIAN
FAMILY

✕ **Tommy Bahama Tropical Café.** This breezy, open-air restaurant, located upstairs at the Shops at Mauna Lani, offers an excellent roster of appetizers, including seared-scallop sliders and coconut-crusted crab cakes. The chef here has freedom to cook up his own daily specials, and the seared ahi is a standout. **Known for:** reliable cuisine and relaxed vibe; popular

4

cocktail bar and lounge; house-baked breads and specialty butters. ⓢ *Average main: $34* ✉ *The Shops at Mauna Lani, 68-1330 Mauna Lani Dr., No. 102* ☎ *808/881–8686* ⊕ *www.tommybahama.com.*

WAIMEA

$ ✕ **Big Island Brewhaus.** Owner Tom Kerns is a veteran brewer who's now
AMERICAN churning out premium ales, lagers, and specialty beers from his on-site brewery in Waimea. With a focus on fresh ingredients, the brewpub's menu includes burgers, poke, fish tacos, burritos, rellenos, and quesadillas fresh to order. **Known for:** pioneering local brewmaster; outdoor lanai seating; reliable pub menu. ⓢ *Average main: $11* ✉ *64-1066A Mamalahoa Hwy., Waimea (Hawaii County)* ☎ *808/887–1717* ⊕ *www. bigislandbrewhaus.com.*

$ ✕ **The Fish and the Hog Market Cafe.** This casual little restaurant along
ECLECTIC the highway serves up generous sandwiches, salads, and melt-in-your-mouth barbecue items, including kiawe-smoked meat like pulled pork, ribs, pork ribs, and brisket. Additional options range from pupu platters and gumbo to salads made with produce grown in Waimea. **Known for:** roadhouse vibe; slow-food creds; fresh seafood caught by the owners. ⓢ *Average main: $15* ✉ *64-957 Mamalahoa Hwy. (Hwy. 11), Waimea (Hawaii County)* ☎ *808/885–6268.*

$ ✕ **Lilikoi Café.** This gem of a café is tucked away in the back of the Parker
EUROPEAN Ranch Center. Locals love that it's hard to find because they want to
FAMILY keep its delicious breakfast crepes, freshly made soups, and croissants Waimea's little secret. **Known for:** handpainted murals; large variety of salads; creative sandwiches and hot lunch entrees. ⓢ *Average main: $9* ✉ *Parker Ranch Center, 67-1185 Mamalahoa Hwy. (Hwy. 11), Waimea (Hawaii County)* ☎ *808/887–1400* ⊗ *Closed Sun. No dinner.*

$ ✕ **Luna Restaurant.** Tucked away in a strip mall near KTA, this little restau-
ITALIAN rant makes some of the best pizza on the Big Island. Check out the Isola
FAMILY Grande laden with braised pork belly, caramelized onion, fresh pineapple,
Fodor's Choice and mozzarella. **Known for:** excellent pizza; friendly proprietor; Ital-
★ ian specialties like caprese and mushroom risotto. ⓢ *Average main: $12* ✉ *Waimea (KTA) Center, 65-1158 Mamalahoa Hwy., Waimea (Hawaii County)* ☎ *808/887–1313* ⊕ *www.lunawaimea.com* ⊗ *Closed Tues.*

$$$$ ✕ **Merriman's.** Located in upcountry Waimea, this signature restaurant
MODERN of Peter Merriman, one of the pioneers of Hawaii Regional Cuisine,
HAWAIIAN is the home of the original wok-charred ahi: it's seared on the outside and sashimi on the inside. If you prefer meat, try the Kahua Ranch braised lamb, raised locally to the restaurant's specifications, or the prime bone-in New York steak, grilled to order. **Known for:** great lunch specials; extensive wine list; chocolate oblivion torte. ⓢ *Average main: $45* ✉ *Opelo Plaza, 65-1227 Opelo Rd., Waimea (Hawaii County)* ☎ *808/885–6822* ⊕ *www.merrimanshawaii.com.*

$ ✕ **Noodle Club.** Star Wars toys and action figures line the shelves of Noo-
JAPANESE dle Club, a fun destination with serious food in Parker Ranch Center.
FUSION Veteran resort chef Edwin Goto simmers his broths for up to 36 hours
FAMILY to create the noodle or saimin dishes such as the savory Bowl of Seoul, or the All Things Pork Ramen. **Known for:** homemade pork, beef,

CLOSE UP

Big Island Farm Tours

As local ingredients continue to play a prominent role on Big Island menus, chefs and farmers are working together to support a burgeoning agritourism industry in Hawaii. Several local farms make specialty items that cater to the island's gourmet restaurants. The **Hawaii Island Goat Dairy** (⊕ *www.hawaiiislandgoatdairy.com*) produces specialty cheese; **Big Island Bees** (⊕ *www.bigislandbees.com*) boasts its own beekeeping museum and tasting room above Kealakekua

Bay; and **Hamakua Mushrooms** (⊕ *www.fungaljungle.com*) has turned harvested koa forests into a safe haven for gourmet mushrooms. Many farms—like **Greenwell Farms** (⊕ *www.mountainthunder.com*), which produces 100% organic Kona coffee, and **Hawaiian Vanilla Company** (⊕ *www.hawaiianvanilla.com*), which is cultivating vanilla from orchids on the Hamakua Coast—are open to the public and offer free tours.

and vegetable broths; bao buns with Hamakua Alii mushrooms; delicious desserts. $ *Average main: $14* ⊠ *Parker Ranch Center, 67-1185 Mamalahoa Hwy A106, Waimea (Hawaii County)* ☎ *808/885-8825* ⊕ *www.noodleclubwaimea.com* ⊗ *Closed Mon.*

$
ITALIAN
FAMILY
✕ **Pau.** Its name is Hawaiian for "done," perhaps an allusion to how eagerly the pizzas are gobbled up. On offer is a wide selection of appetizers, salads, sandwiches, pastas, and pizzas loaded with lots of local fresh ingredients. **Known for:** cool artwork and relaxed vibe; homemade sauces and dressings; triple slice lunch special. $ *Average main: $12* ⊠ *65-1227 Opelo Rd., Waimea (Hawaii County)* ☎ *808/885-6325* ⊕ *www.paupizza.com.*

$$$
ECLECTIC
FAMILY
✕ **Red Water Cafe.** Chef David Abraham serves Hawaiian café food with a twist and a side of aloha. The specialty is multicultural cuisine, like a Thai Caesar salad with crispy calamari croutons that is big enough to share. **Known for:** entrées served in half or full portions; sushi bar; good kids' menu. $ *Average main: $30* ⊠ *65-1299 Kawaihae Rd., Waimea (Hawaii County)* ☎ *808/885-9299* ⊕ *www.redwater-cafe.com* ⊗ *No lunch.*

$
AMERICAN
FAMILY
✕ **Village Burger.** This little eatery brings a whole new meaning to gourmet hamburgers. Locally raised, grass-fed, hormone-free beef is ground fresh, hand-shaped daily on-site, and grilled to perfection right before your eyes. **Known for:** great local brioche buns; lots of toppings for burgers; locally made ice cream. $ *Average main: $10* ⊠ *Parker Ranch Center, 67-1185 Mamalahoa Hwy., Waimea (Hawaii County)* ☎ *808/885-7319* ⊕ *www.villageburgerwaimea.com.*

HILO

$
DINER
FAMILY
Fodor's Choice
★
✕ **Bears' Coffee.** This favorite, cozy breakfast spot, a fixture downtown since the late 1980s, is much loved for its fresh-fruit waffles and tasty morning coffee. For lunch the little diner serves up huge deli sandwiches and decent entrée-size salads, plus specials like hearty meat loaf, roasted chicken, and pot roast. **Known for:** reliable breakfasts; local landmark; friendly atmosphere. $ *Average main: $10* ⊠ *106 Keawe St., Hilo* ☎ *808/935-0708* ⊗ *No dinner.*

$ ✗**Blane's Drive Inn.** At one point this was a real drive-in with car service.
HAWAIIAN   Now, customers park, order at the window, and eat at one of the few
FAMILY   picnic tables or take their food to go. **Known for:** plate lunches; afford-
able prices; local vibes. $ *Average main: $8* ✉ *217 Wainuenue Ave.,*
Hilo ☎ *808/969–9494.*

$ ✗**Café 100.** Established in 1948, this family-owned restaurant is famous
HAWAIIAN   for its tasty loco moco, prepared in more than three dozen ways, and
FAMILY   its low-priced breakfast and lunch specials. (You can stuff yourself
for $5 if you order right.) The word "restaurant," or even "café," is
used loosely here—you order at a window and eat on one of the outdoor benches provided—but you come here for the food, prices, and
authentic, old-Hilo experience. **Known for:** local flavor; Super Loco
Moco; generous portions. $ *Average main: $6* ✉ *969 Kilauea Ave.,*
Hilo ☎ *808/935–8683* ⊕ *www.cafe100.com* ⊙ *Closed Sun.*

$$ ✗**Café Pesto.** Located in a beautiful and historical venue, Café Pesto
ITALIAN   offers exotic pizzas (with fresh Hamakua mushrooms, artichokes, and
rosemary Gorgonzola sauce, for example). You can make a meal of
the Asian-inspired pastas and risottos, fresh seafood, delicious salads,
and appetizers. **Known for:** historic interiors; wood-fired pizza; happy
hour from 2 pm. $ *Average main: $20* ✉ *308 Kamehameha Ave., Hilo*
☎ *808/969–6640* ⊕ *www.cafepesto.com.*

$ ✗**Happy Valley Seafood Restaurant.** Don't let the name fool you. Though
CHINESE   Hilo's best Chinese restaurant does specialize in seafood (the salt-and-
pepper prawns are fantastic), it also offers a wide range of other Can-
tonese treats, including a sizzling lamb platter, salt-and-pepper pork,
Mongolian lamb, and vegetarian specialties like garlic eggplant and
crispy green beans. **Known for:** authentic Cantonese Chinese food; easy
parking; good soups. $ *Average main: $12* ✉ *1263 Kilauea Ave., Suite*
320, Hilo ☎ *808/933–1083.*

$$ ✗**Hilo Bay Café.** This popular upscale restaurant overlooks Hilo Bay
AMERICAN   from its towering perch on the waterfront; the sophisticated second-
Fodor's Choice   floor dining room looks like it's straight out of Manhattan. A sushi
★   bar complements the excellent selection of fresh fish, pork, beef, vegan
options; premium wines and sake are featured. **Known for:** excellent
bayside views; Blue Bay burger with shoestring fries; most upscale
restaurant in Hilo. $ *Average main: $20* ✉ *123 Lihiwai St., Hilo*
☎ *808/935–4939* ⊕ *www.hilobaycafe.com* ⊙ *Closed Sun.*

$ ✗**Ken's House of Pancakes.** For years, this 24-hour diner on Banyan Drive
DINER   between the airport and the hotels has been a gathering place for Hilo
FAMILY   residents and visitors. Breakfast is the main attraction: Ken's serves 11 types
Fodor's Choice   of pancakes, plus all kinds of fruit waffles (banana, peach) and popular
★   omelets, like Da Bradda, teeming with meats. **Known for:** local landmark
with old-fashioned vibe; extensive menu; weekly special nights like Sunday
spaghetti and Tuesday tacos. $ *Average main: $10* ✉ *1730 Kamehameha*
Ave., Hilo ☎ *808/935–8711* ⊕ *www.kenshouseofpancakes.com.*

$ ✗**Kuhio Grille.** There's no atmosphere to speak of, and water is served in
HAWAIIAN   unbreakable plastic tumblers, but if you're searching for local fare—that
undefinable fusion of ethnic cuisines—this is the place. Sam Araki serves
a 1-pound laulau that is worth the trip. **Known for:** authentic Hawaiian experience; good plate lunches; award-winning laulau. $ *Average*

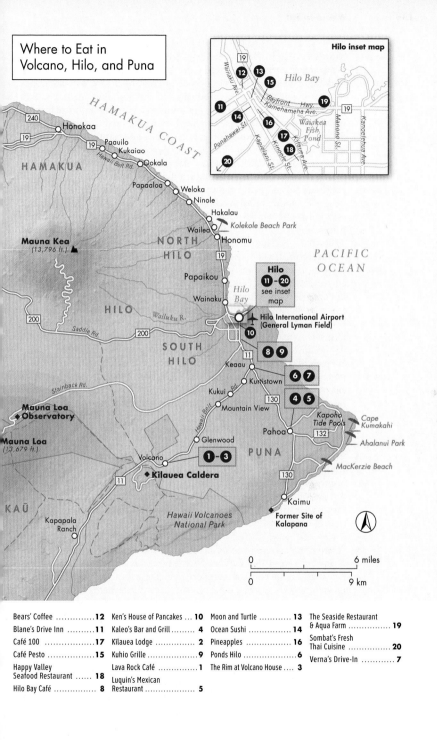

Where to Eat in Volcano, Hilo, and Puna

Hilo inset map

19

12 13

15

Hilo Bay

Wainaku Ave.

Bayfront Hwy.
Kamehameha Ave.

11

14

16

Waiakea
Fish
Pond

19

Ponahawai St.

Kapiolani St.

17

Kilauea Ave.

18

Manono St.

Kanoelehua Ave.

20

HAMAKUA COAST

240

Honokaa

19

Paauilo

19

Kukaiao

Hawaii Belt Rd.

Ookala

HAMAKUA

Papaaloa

Weloka

Ninole

Hakalau

Wailea

Kolekole Beach Park

Mauna Kea
(13,796 ft.)

NORTH
HILO

Honomu

19

Papaikou

PACIFIC
OCEAN

Wainaku

Hilo
Bay

200

Saddle Rd.

HILO

Wailuku R.

200

SOUTH
HILO

Hilo
11 - 20
see inset
map

Hilo International Airport
(General Lyman Field)

10

8 9

Keaau

11

Mauna Loa
Observatory

Stainback Rd.

Kurtistown

Kukui Rd.

6 7

Mauna Loa
(13,679 ft.)

Hawaii Belt Rd.

Mountain View

130

4 5

Glenwood

Kapoho
Tide Pools

Cape
Kumakahi

Volcano

1 - 3

Pahoa

132

Ahalanui Park

Kilauea Caldera

PUNA

MacKerzie Beach

11

130

Hawaii Volcanoes
National Park

Kaimu

KAŪ

Kapapala
Ranch

Former Site of
Kalapana

0   6 miles
0   9 km

Bears' Coffee **12**

Blane's Drive Inn **11**

Café 100 ....**17**

Café Pesto **15**

Happy Valley
Seafood Restaurant **18**

Hilo Bay Café **8**

Ken's House of Pancakes ...**10**

Kaleo's Bar and Grill **4**

Kīlauea Lodge **2**

Kuhio Grille **9**

Lava Rock Café **1**

Luquin's Mexican
Restaurant **5**

Moon and Turtle **13**

Ocean Sushi **14**

Pineapples **16**

Ponds Hilo **6**

The Rim at Volcano House **3**

The Seaside Restaurant
& Aqua Farm **19**

Sombat's Fresh
Thai Cuisine **20**

Verna's Drive-In **7**

main: $9 ⊠ *Prince Kuhio Plaza, 111 E. Puainako St., at Hwy. 11, Hilo* ☎ *808/959–2336* ⊕ *www.kuhiogrill.com.*

$$$
INTERNATIONAL

✕ **Moon and Turtle.** This sophisticated intimate restaurant in a bayfront building offers a classy selection of international fare with the focus on locally sourced meats, produce, and seafood. The menu changes daily—mushroom pappardelle and smoky sashimi are highlights, along with seafood chowder, spicy Kajiki Tartare and crispy moi whole-fried Pacific Threadfin. **Known for:** ever-changing international menu; lychee martinis; high prices for Hilo. Ⓢ *Average main: $25* ⊠ *51 Kalakaua St., Hilo* ☎ *808/961–0599* ⊙ *Closed Sun. and Mon.*

$
JAPANESE
FAMILY

✕ **Ocean Sushi.** What this restaurant lacks in ambience it certainly makes up for in quality and value. We're talking about light and crispy tempura; tender, moist teriyaki chicken; and about 25 specialty sushi rolls, all at unbeatable prices. **Known for:** family restaurant; reasonable prices; good kid's menu. Ⓢ *Average main: $12* ⊠ *235 Keawe St., Hilo* ☎ *808/961–6625* ⊙ *Closed Sun.*

$
AMERICAN
FAMILY

✕ **Pineapples.** If you expect that a restaurant named Pineapples would serve tropical libations in hollowed-out pineapples, you'd be exactly correct. Always packed, this open-air bistro looks like a tourist trap, but there is a fine-dining component to the menu, which includes fresh catch, kalbi ribs, teriyaki flank steak, burgers, wraps, and sandwiches. **Known for:** surprisingly inventive island cuisine; great pineapple salsa; delicous tropical drinks. Ⓢ *Average main: $14* ⊠ *332 Keawe St, Hilo* ☎ *808/238-5324* ⊕ *www.pineappleshilo.com* ⊙ *Closed Mon.*

$$
HAWAIIAN
FAMILY

✕ **Ponds Hilo.** Perched on the waterfront overlooking a scenic and serene pond, this restaurant has the look and feel of an old-fashioned, harborside steak house and bar. The menu features a good range of burgers and salads, steak and seafood—but the fish-and-chips are the star attraction. **Known for:** scenic location; difficult parking; popular Sunday brunch. Ⓢ *Average main: $20* ⊠ *135 Kalanianaole Ave., Hilo* ☎ *808/934–7663* ⊕ *www.pondshilo.com.*

$$
SEAFOOD
FAMILY

✕ **The Seaside Restaurant & Aqua Farm.** The Nakagawa family has been running this eatery since the early 1920s. The latest son to manage it has transformed both the menu and the decor, and that, paired with the setting (on a 30-acre natural, brackish fishpond) makes this one of the most interesting places to eat in Hilo. **Known for:** authentic local experience; ocean and pond views at sunset; mullet from their aqua farm. Ⓢ *Average main: $23* ⊠ *1790 Kalanianaole Ave., Hilo* ☎ *808/935–8825* ⊕ *www.seasiderestauranthilo.com* ⊙ *Closed Mon. No lunch.*

$
THAI
Fodor's Choice
★

✕ **Sombat's Fresh Thai Cuisine.** There's a reason why locals flock to this hideaway for the best Thai cuisine in Hilo. Fresh local ingredients highlight proprietor Sombat Saenguthai's menu (many of the herbs come from her own garden) to create authentic and tasty Thai treats like coconut curries, fresh basil rolls, eggplant stir-fry, and green papaya salad. **Known for:** special seasonings; friendly service; excellent pad Thai. Ⓢ *Average main: $13* ⊠ *Waiakea Kai Plaza, 88 Kanoelehue Ave., Hilo* ⊹ *Close to Ken's Pancakes* ☎ *808/969–9336* ⊕ *www.sombats.com* ⊙ *Closed Sun. No lunch.*

$
HAWAIIAN

✕ **Verna's Drive-In.** Verna's is tried and true among locals, who come for the juicy homemade burgers and filling plate lunches. The price is right with a burger combo that includes fries and a drink. **Known for:** local grindz; plate lunches; superlow prices. $ *Average main: $6* ⊠ *1765 Kamehameha Ave., Hilo* ☎ *808/935–2776.*

PUNA

$$
AMERICAN

✕ **Kaleo's Bar and Grill.** Pahoa Town isn't necessarily known for gourmet dining choices, but that's all changed with the arrival of Kaleo's. Hawaiian-inspired fare blends the gamut of island ethnic influences with such choices as kalua pork won tons, tempura ahi rolls, grilled burgers, and banana spring rolls. **Known for:** sophisticated menu; nightly entertainment; full bar. $ *Average main: $20* ⊠ *15-2969 Pahoa Village Road, Pahoa* ☎ *808/965–5600* ⊕ *www.kaleoshawaii.com.*

$
MEXICAN

✕ **Luquin's Mexican Restaurant.** Long an island favorite for tasty, albeit greasy, Mexican grub, this landmark is making a comeback in the funky town of Pahoa after a tragic fire burned the original restaurant to the ground in 2017. Breakfast is popular and includes delicious huevos rancheros. **Known for:** longtime Pahoa restaurant; affordable fare; community gathering spot. $ *Average main: $9* ⊠ *15-2942 Pahoa Village Rd., Pahoa* ☎ *808/965–9990* ⊕ *www.luquins.com.*

HAWAII VOLCANOES NATIONAL PARK AND VICINITY

VOLCANO

$$$
EUROPEAN

✕ **Kilauea Lodge.** The roaring fire, koa-wood tables, and intimate lighting are in keeping with this cozy lodge in the heart of Volcano Village. The dinner menu changes daily and features such entrées as venison, duck à l'orange with an apricot-mustard glaze, and lamb provençal garnished with papaya-apple-mint sauce. **Known for:** landmark location; fine dining with prices to match; popular Sunday brunch. $ *Average main: $30* ⊠ *19-3948 Old Volcano Rd., Volcano* ☎ *808/967–7366* ⊕ *www. kilauealodge.com.*

$
DINER
FAMILY

✕ **Lava Rock Café.** This is an affordable place to grab a sandwich or a coffee and check your email (Wi-Fi is free with purchase of a meal) before heading to Hawaii Volcanoes National Park. The homey, sit-down diner caters to families, serving up heaping plates of pancakes and French toast for breakfast. **Known for:** roadhouse atmosphere; family-friendly atmosphere; diner-style comfort food. $ *Average main: $10* ⊠ *19-3972 Old Volcano Hwy., Volcano* ✛ *Next to Kilauea General Store* ☎ *808/967–8526* ⊗ *No dinner Sun. and Mon.*

$$
HAWAIIAN
FAMILY

✕ **The Rim at Volcano House.** This fine-dining restaurant overlooks the rim of Kilauea caldera and its fiery glow. Featuring two bars, a lounge, and live entertainment, it highlights island-inspired cuisine and incorporates locally sourced produce and other ingredients. **Known for:** views of Halemaumau Crater; hot-buttered rum; well-priced Taste of Hawaii lunch special. $ *Average main: $25* ⊠ *Volcano House Hotel, Crater Rim Dr., Volcano* ☎ *808/756–9625* ⊕ *www.hawaiivolcanohouse.com.*

WHERE TO STAY

Updated
by Karen
Anderson

Even among locals, there is an ongoing debate about which side of the Big Island is "better," so don't worry if you're having a tough time deciding where to stay. Our recommendation? Do both. Each side offers a different range of accommodations, restaurants, and activities.

Consider staying at one of the upscale resorts along the Kohala Coast or in a condo in Kailua-Kona for half of your trip. Then, shift gears and check into a romantic bed-and-breakfast on the Hamakua Coast, South Kona, Hilo, or near the volcano. If you've got children in tow, opt for a vacation home or a stay at one of the island's many family-friendly hotels. On the west side, explore the island's most pristine beaches or try some of the fine-dining restaurants; on the east side, hike through rain forests, witness majestic waterfalls, or go for a plate lunch.

Some locals like to say that the east is "more Hawaiian," but we argue that King Kamehameha himself made Kailua-Kona his final home during his sunset years. Another reason to try a bit of both: your budget. You can justify splurging on a stay at a Kohala Coast resort for a few nights because you'll spend the rest of your time paying one-third that rate at a cozy cottage in Volcano or a vacation rental on Alii Drive. And although food at the resorts is very expensive, you don't have to eat every meal there. Condos and vacation homes can be ideal for a family trip or for a group of friends looking to save money and live like *kamaainas* (local residents) for a week or two. Many of the homes also have private pools and hot tubs, lanai, ocean views, and more—you can go as budget or as high-end as you like.

If you choose a bed-and-breakfast, inn, or an out-of-the-way hotel, explain your expectations fully to the proprietor and ask plenty of questions before booking. Be clear about your travel and location needs. Some places require stays of two or three days.

BIG ISLAND LODGING PLANNER

HOTELS AND RESORTS

The resorts—most clustered on the Kohala Coast—are expensive, no two ways about it. That said, many offer free nights with longer stays (fifth or seventh night free) and sometimes team with airlines or consolidators to offer package deals that may include a rental car, spa treatments, golf, and other activities. Some hotels allow children under 17 to stay for free. Ask about specials when you book, and check websites as well—many resorts have Internet-only deals.

CONDOS AND VACATION RENTALS

Renting a condo or vacation house gives you much more living space than the average hotel, plus the chance to meet more people (neighbors are usually friendly), lower nightly rates, and the option of cooking or barbecuing rather than eating out. When booking, remember that most properties are individually owned, with rates and amenities that differ substantially depending on the place. Some properties are handled by rental agents or agencies, while many are handled directly through the owner. The following is a list of our favorite booking agencies for various lodging types throughout the island. Be sure to call and ask questions before booking.

Contacts Abbey Vacation Rentals. ☎ 886/456–4252 ⊕ www.konarentals. com. **Big Island Villas.** ☎ 808/936–3870, 808/443–6991 ⊕ www.bigislandvillas.com. **CJ Kimberly Realtors.** ☎ 808/329–7000 ⊕ www.cjkimberly.com. **Hawaiian Beach Rentals.** ☎ 844/261–0464 ⊕ www.hawaiianbeachrentals.com. **Hawaii Vacation Rentals.** ☎ 808/882–7000 ⊕ www.vacationbigisland.com. **Keauhou Property Management.** ☎ 808/326–7053 ⊕ www.konacondo.net. **Kolea Vacations.** ☎ 888/565–3244 ⊕ www.koleavacations.com. **Kona Coast Vacations.** ☎ 808/329–2140 ⊕ www.konacoastvacations.com. **Kona Hawaii Vacation Rentals.** ☎ 808/329–3333 ⊕ www.konahawaii.com. **Knutson and Associates.** ☎ 808/329–1010 ⊕ www.konahawaiirentals.com. **South Kohala Management.** ☎ 808/883–8500 ⊕ www.southkohala.com.

B&BS AND INNS

Bed-and-breakfasts and locally run inns offer a nice alternative to hotels or resorts in terms of privacy and location. Guests enjoy the perks of a hotel (breakfast and maid service), but without the extras that drive up rates.

Be sure to check industry association websites as well as property websites, and call to ask questions. There are still a few "B&Bs" that are really just dumpy rooms in someone's house, and you don't want to end up there. Members of the Big Island–based **Hawaii Island Bed & Breakfast Association** (⊕ www.stayhawaii.com) are listed with phone numbers and rates in a comprehensive online brochure. In order to join this network, bed-and-breakfasts must be evaluated and meet fairly stringent minimum requirements, including a yearly walk-through by association officers, to maintain their membership. Another bed-and-breakfast association includes **Hawaii's Best Bed & Breakfasts** (808/885–4550 ⊕ www.bestbnb.com).

RESERVATIONS

You'll almost always be able to find a room on the Big Island, but you might not get your first choice if you wait until the last minute. Make reservations six months to a year in advance if you're visiting during the peak seasons (summer, Christmas holiday, and spring break). During the week after Easter Sunday, for example, the Merrie Monarch Festival is in full swing, and most of Hilo's rooms are booked. Kailua-Kona is packed in mid-October during the Ironman World Championship triathlon. ■TIP➔ **September and February are great months to visit Hawaii; fares are lower, crowds are less, and accommodation prices are reduced.**

PRICES

Keep in mind that many of the resorts charge "resort fees" for things like parking, Internet, daily newspaper service, beach gear, and activities. Most condos and vacation rental owners charge an additional cleaning fee. Always ask about hidden fees as well as specials and discounts when you book. Look online for great package deals.

OUR REVIEWS

Prices in the hotel reviews are the lowest cost of a standard double room in high season, which generally include taxes and service charges but not any optional meal plans. Prices for rentals are the lowest per-night cost for a one-bedroom unit in high season.

For expanded lodging reviews visit Fodors.com.

WHAT IT COSTS			
$	$$	$$$	$$$$
For Two People under $180	$180–$260	$261–$340	over $340

KAILUA-KONA

The bustling historic village full of restaurants, shops, and entertainment also offers tons of lodging options. In addition to a half-dozen hotels, oceanfront Alii Drive is lined with condos and vacation homes. All the conveniences are here, and there are several grocery stores and big-box retailers nearby for those who need to stock up on supplies. Kailua-Kona has a handful of beaches—Magic Sands, Kahaluu, and Kamakahonu (at the pier) among them. The downside to staying here is that you'll have to drive 30 to 45 minutes up the road to the Kohala Coast to visit Hawaii's signature, long, white-sand beaches. However, you'll also pay about half what you would at any of the major resorts, not to mention that Kailua-Kona offers a bit more local charm.

$$ Aston Kona by the Sea. Complete modern kitchens, tiled lanais, and
RENTAL   washer-dryer units are found in every suite of this comfortable ocean-
FAMILY   front condo complex. **Pros:** oceanfront; lobby and activities desk; ocean-fed saltwater pool next to the property. **Cons:** no beach access

(2 miles away); not walking distance to Kailua Village; individually owned units, so prices may vary. $ *Rooms from: $200* ✉ *75-6106 Alii Dr., Kailua-Kona* ☎ *808/327–2300, 877/997–6667* ⊕ *www.astonhotels.com* ⟿ *86 units* ⦿ *No meals.*

$
RENTAL
⌂ **Casa de Emdeko.** A large and pretty complex on the *makai* (oceanfront) side of Alii Drive, Casa de Emdeko offers a few more amenities than most condo complexes, including a florist, hair salon, and an on-site convenience store that makes sandwiches. **Pros:** oceanfront fresh-and saltwater pools; hidden from the street; very private. **Cons:** quality and prices depend on owner; not kid-friendly; no restaurant. $ *Rooms from: $125* ✉ *75-6082 Alii Dr., Kailua-Kona* ☎ *808/329–2160* ⊕ *www.casadeemdeko.org* ⟿ *106 units* ⦿ *No meals.*

$$$
HOTEL
FAMILY
⌂ **Courtyard by Marriott King Kamehameha's Kona Beach Hotel.** This landmark hotel by Kailua Pier is located right in the heart of Historic Kailua Village and offers good vibrations and authentic local hospitality—all for less than the price of a Kohala Coast resort. **Pros:** central location; historical ambience; on-site restaurant and poolside bar. **Cons:** most rooms have partial ocean views; some rooms face the parking lot; pricey buffet. $ *Rooms from: $339* ✉ *75-5660 Palani Rd., Kailua-Kona* ☎ *808/329–2911* ⊕ *www.konabeachhotel.com* ⟿ *452 rooms* ⦿ *No meals.*

$$
B&B/INN
⌂ **Hale Hualalai.** Perfect for couples, Hale Hualalai offers two exceptionally large suites with exposed beams, whirlpool tubs, and private lanai, but perhaps most memorable is the food—owner Ricky Brewster was a chef at Four Season's Hualalai Resort's Beach Tree restaurant. **Pros:** gourmet breakfasts; tastefully decorated house; whirlpool tubs. **Cons:** not for kids; just two suites; frequently booked. $ *Rooms from: $181* ✉ *74-4968 Mamalahoa Hwy., Holualoa* ☎ *808/464–7074* ⊕ *www.halehualalai.com* ⟿ *2 suites* ⦿ *Breakfast.*

$$
HOTEL
FAMILY
⌂ **Holiday Inn Express and Suites Kailua-Kona.** While the unattractive setting feels more parking lot than island paradise, this practical and comfortable hotel, which opened in 2015, offers lots of pluses. **Pros:** convenient downtown location; 24-hour business center; free high-speed Wi-Fi. **Cons:** most rooms don't have views; no landscaping; parking lot views on lower level. $ *Rooms from: $200* ✉ *75-146 Sarona Rd., Kailua-Kona* ☎ *808/329–2599* ⊕ *www.ihg.com* ⟿ *75 rooms* ⦿ *Breakfast.*

$$$$
B&B/INN
Fodor's Choice
★
⌂ **Holualoa Inn.** Six spacious rooms and suites—plus a private, vintage, one-bedroom cottage that's perfect for honeymooners—are available at this 30-acre coffee-country estate, a few miles above Kailua Bay in the heart of the artists' village of Holualoa. **Pros:** within walking distance of art galleries and cafés; everything necessary for hosting a wedding or event; luxurious, Zen-like vibe. **Cons:** not kid-friendly; non-heated swimming pool; no dinners. $ *Rooms from: $365* ✉ *76-5932 Mamalahoa Hwy., Holualoa* ☎ *808/324–1121, 800/392–1812* ⊕ *www.holualoainn.com* ⟿ *7 rooms, 1 cottage* ⦿ *Breakfast.*

$$
RESORT
Fodor's Choice
★
⌂ **Holua Resort at Mauna Loa Village.** Tucked away by Keauhou Bay amid a plethora of coconut trees, this well-maintained enclave of blue-roofed villas offers lots of amenities, including an 11-court tennis center (with a center court, pro shop, and lights), swimming pools, hot tubs, fitness center, manicured gardens, waterfalls, and covered parking. **Pros:** tennis center; upscale feeling; walking distance to major

resort restaurants. **Cons:** no beach; partial ocean views; no on-site restaurant. $ *Rooms from: $199* ✉ *78-7190 Kaleiopapa St., Kailua-Kona* ☎ *808/324–1550* ⊕ *www.shellhospitality.com* ⇝ *73 units* ⦿ *No meals.*

$ 🏠 **Kona Bali Kai.** These slightly older

RENTAL condominium units, spread out
FAMILY among three low-rises on the ocean side of Alii Drive, are situated at Kona's most popular surfing spot, Banyans, and also just a couple of minutes' drive from Kailua Village and within walking distance of the popular Magic Sands beach. **Pros:** close to town and beaches; convenience mart and beach-gear rental nearby; views of surfers on the water. **Cons:** mountain-view rooms close to noisy street; ocean-

KONA CONDO COMFORTS

The **Safeway at Crossroads** Shopping Center (✉ *75-1000 Henry St., Kailua-Kona* ☎ *808/329–2207*) offers an excellent inventory of groceries and produce, although prices can be steep.

For pizza, **Kona Brewing Co. Pub & Brewery** (✉ *75-5629 Kuakini Hwy., accessed through the Kona Old Industrial Park, Kailua-Kona* ☎ *808/329–2739*) is the best bet, if you can pick it up. Otherwise, for delivery, try **Domino's** (☎ *808/329–9500*).

front rooms don't have A/C; older-looking concrete buildings. $ *Rooms from: $140* ✉ *76-6246 Alii Dr., Kailua-Kona* ☎ *808/329–9381, 800/535–0085* ⊕ *www.castleresorts.com* ⇝ *64 units* ⦿ *No meals.*

$$ 🏠 **Kona Coast Resort.** Just below Keauhou Shopping Center, this resort

RENTAL offers furnished condos on 21 acres with pleasant ocean views and a host
FAMILY of on-site amenities including two swimming pools, beach volleyball, a cocktail bar, BBQ grills, hot tub, tennis courts, fitness center, hula classes, equipment rentals, and children's activities. **Pros:** all rooms updated in January 2018; kid-friendly; away from the bustle of downtown Kailua-Kona. **Cons:** some units have parking lot views; not on the beach; time-share salespeople. $ *Rooms from: $230* ✉ *78-6842 Alii Dr., Keauhou* ☎ *808/324–1721* ⊕ *www.shellhospitality.com* ⇝ *268 units* ⦿ *No meals.*

$ 🏠 **Kona Magic Sands.** Cradled between a lovely grass park and Magic

RENTAL Sands Beach Park, this condo complex is great for swimmers, surfers, and sunbathers. **Pros:** next door to popular beach; affordable; oceanfront view from all units. **Cons:** studios only; some units are dated; no restaurant. $ *Rooms from: $150* ✉ *77-6452 Alii Dr., Kailua-Kona* ☎ *808/329–9393, 800/622–5348* ⊕ *www.konamagicsands.org* ⇝ *15 units* ⦿ *No meals.*

$ 🏠 **Kona Seaside Hotel.** Located right in the heart of the action across the

HOTEL street from Kailua Pier in Kailua-Kona, Kona Seaside Hotel offers stan-
FAMILY dard, relatively tasteful accommodations ideal for visitors on a budget. **Pros:** affordable; central location; lots of on-site amenities. **Cons:** limited parking; $10 daily fee for parking; slightly dated. $ *Rooms from: $139* ✉ *75-5646 Palani Rd., Kailua-Kona* ☎ *808/329–2455* ⊕ *www.konaseasidehotel.com* ⇝ *142 rooms* ⦿ *No meals.*

$ 🏠 **Kona Tiki Hotel.** This three-story walk-up budget hotel about a mile

HOTEL south of downtown Kailua Village, with modest, pleasantly decorated rooms—all of which have lanai right next to the ocean—is simply the best deal in town. **Pros:** friendly staff; oceanfront lanai and pool; free

WHERE TO STAY ON THE BIG ISLAND

	LOCAL VIBE	PROS	CONS
Kailua-Kona	A bustling little village; Alii Drive brims with hotels and condo complexes.	Plenty to do, day and night; everything within easy walking distance of most hotels; many grocery stores in the area.	More traffic than anywhere else on the island; limited number of beaches; traffic noise on Alii Drive.
South Kona and Kau	Popular Kealakekua Bay has plenty of B&Bs and vacation rentals; with a few more farther south in Kau.	Kealakekua Bay is popular for kayaking and snorkeling and has some good restaurants; Captain Cook and Kainaliu have coffee farms.	Vog (volcano fog) from Kilauea often settles here; few sandy beaches; Kau is quite remote.
The Kohala Coast	Home to most of the Big Island's major resorts. Blue sunny skies prevail here, along with the island's best beaches.	Beautiful beaches; high-end shopping and dining; lots of activities for adults and children.	Pricey; long driving distances to Volcano, Hilo, and Kailua-Kona.
Waimea	Though it seems a world away, Waimea is only about a 15- to 20-minute drive from the Kohala Coast.	Beautiful scenery, *paniolo* (cowboy) culture; home to some exceptional local restaurants.	Can be cool and rainy year-round; nearest beaches are a 20-minute drive away.
The Hamakua Coast	A nice spot for those seeking peace, tranquility, and an alternative to the tropical-beach-vacation experience.	Close to Waipio Valley; foodie and farm tours in the area; good spot for honeymooners.	Beaches are an hour's drive away; convenience shopping is limited.
Hilo	Hilo is the wet and lush, eastern side of the Big Island. It's less touristy than the west side but retains much local charm.	Proximity to waterfalls, rain-forest hikes, museums, and botanical gardens; good B&B options.	The best white-sand beaches are on the other side of the island; noise from coqui frogs can be distracting at night.
Puna	Puna doesn't attract as many visitors as other regions, so you'll find good deals on rentals and B&Bs here.	A few black-sand beaches; off the beaten path and fairly wild; hot ponds; lava has flowed into the sea here in years past.	Few dining and entertainment options; no resorts or resort amenities; noisy coqui frogs at night.
Hawaii Volcanoes National Park and Vicinity	There are any number of enchanting B&B inns in fern-shrouded Volcano Village, near the park.	Good location for nighttime lava-watching; great for hiking, nature tours, and bike riding; close to Hilo and Puna.	Just a few dining options; not much nightlife; can be cold and wet.

5

parking. **Cons:** only one studio has a kitchen (others have fridges only); no TV in rooms; parking can be a challenge. $ *Rooms from: $119* ✉ *75-5968 Alii Dr., Kailua-Kona* ☎ *808/329–1425* ⊕ *www.konatiki-hotel.com* ⇆ *16 rooms* �‖*Breakfast.*

$$$
RENTAL
❂ **Outrigger Kanaloa at Kona.** The 18-acre grounds provide a peaceful and verdant background for this low-rise condominium complex bordering the Keauhou-Kona Country Club and within a five-minute drive of the nearest beaches (Kahaluu and Magic Sands). **Pros:** within walking distance of Keauhou Bay; three pools with hot tubs; shopping center and restaurants nearby. **Cons:** no restaurant on property; mandatory cleaning fee at check-in; A/C available only by paying a daily fee. $ *Rooms from: $280* ✉ *78-261 Manukai St., Kailua-Kona* ☎ *808/322–9625, 808/322–7222, 800/688–7444* ⊕ *www.outrigger. com* ⇆ *63 units* �‖*No meals.*

$
RESORT
FAMILY
❂ **Royal Kona Resort.** This is a great option if you're on a budget—the location is central; the bar, lounge, pool, and restaurant are right on the water; and the rooms feature contemporary Hawaiian decor with Polynesian accents. **Pros:** convenient location; waterfront pool; low prices. **Cons:** can be crowded; parking is tight; in-room Internet is extra. $ *Rooms from: $149* ✉ *75-5852 Alii Dr., Kailua-Kona* ☎ *808/329–3111, 800/222–5642* ⊕ *www.royalkona.com* ⇆ *430 rooms* �‖*No meals.*

$$
RESORT
FAMILY
❂ **Sheraton Kona Resort & Spa at Keauhou Bay.** What this big concrete structure lacks in intimacy, it makes up for with its beautifully manicured grounds, historical sense of place, stylish interiors, and stunning location on Keauhou Bay. Many rooms have great views of the bay and feel like they're right on the water, and each is decorated in a modern Polynesian style. **Pros:** cool pool; manta rays on view nightly; resort style at lower price. **Cons:** no beach; long walk from parking area; Wi-Fi can be spotty. $ *Rooms from: $240* ✉ *78-128 Ehukai St., Keauhou* ☎ *808/930–4900* ⊕ *www.sheratonkona.com* ⇆ *509 rooms* �‖*No meals.*

$
RENTAL
FAMILY
❂ **Silver Oaks Guest Ranch.** Three private cottages set on a 10-acre working ranch afford total privacy, with a few more amenities than a vacation house or condo. **Pros:** very private; deck with ocean views; great for animal lovers. **Cons:** five-night minimum stay; not near the beach; dated decor. $ *Rooms from: $165* ✉ *73-4570 Mamalahoa Hwy., just north of Kaloko Dr., Kailua-Kona* ☎ *808/325–2000* ⊕ *www.silveroaksranch. com* ⇆ *3 cottages* �‖*No meals.*

THE KONA COAST

There are no resorts in this area, but there are plenty of fantastic B&Bs and vacation rental homes at Kealakekua Bay and in the hills above. The towns of Captain Cook and Kainaliu offer excellent dining and shopping options, and there are several coffee farms open for tours. You can get to the volcano in about 90 minutes, and you're also close to several less well-known but wonderful beaches, including Hookena and Honomolino. Kailua-Kona is a 30-minute drive from Captain Cook, while the great, sandy beaches of the Kohala Coast are an hour or more away.

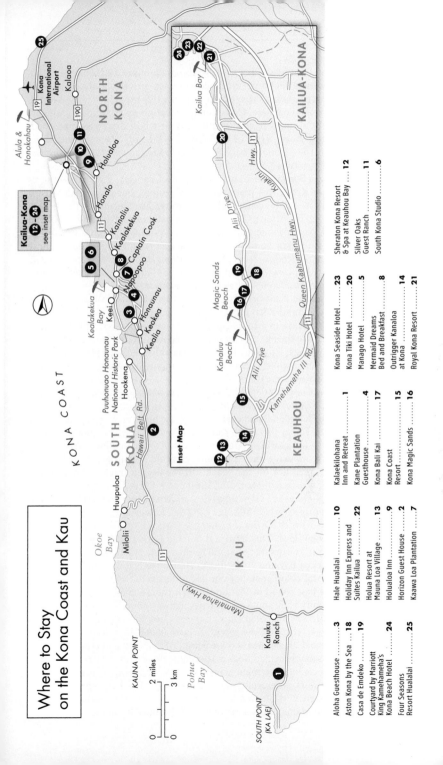

Where to Stay on the Kona Coast and Kau

KONA COAST

NORTH KONA

SOUTH KONA

KAU

KAILUA-KONA

KEAUHOU

Kailua-Kona
12–24
see inset map

Inset Map

Aloha Guesthouse **3**
Aston Kona by the Sea ... **18**
Casa de Emdeko **19**
Courtyard by Marriott
King Kamehameha's
Kona Beach Hotel **24**
Four Seasons
Resort Hualalai **25**

Hale Hualalai **10**
Holiday Inn Express and
Suites Kailua **22**
Holua Resort at
Mauna Loa Village **13**
Holualoa Inn **9**
Horizon Guest House **2**
Kaawa Loa Plantation ... **7**

Kalaekilohana
Inn and Retreat **1**
Kane Plantation
Guesthouse **4**
Kona Bali Kai **17**
Kona Coast
Resort **15**
Kona Magic Sands **16**

Kona Seaside Hotel **23**
Kona Tiki Hotel **20**
Manago Hotel **5**
Mermaid Dreams
Bed and Breakfast **8**
Outrigger Kanaloa
at Kona **14**
Royal Kona Resort **21**

Sheraton Kona Resort
& Spa at Keauhou Bay **12**
Silver Oaks
Guest Ranch **11**
South Kona Studio **6**

SOUTH KONA

$
B&B/INN

🍸**Aloha Guesthouse.** In the hills above Puuhonu O Honaunau, this guesthouse offers quiet elegance, complete privacy, and ocean views from every room. **Pros:** eco-conscious; full breakfast; views of the South Kona coastline. **Cons:** remote location up a bumpy 1-mile dirt road; 40 minutes from downtown; four-wheel drive recommended. ⑤ *Rooms from: $125* ✉ *Old Tobacco Rd., off Hwy. 11 near mile marker 104, Honaunau* ☎ *808/328–8955* ⊕ *www.alohaguesthouse. com* ⇆ *5 rooms* ⍟*Breakfast.*

$$
B&B/INN

🍸**Horizon Guest House.** Surrounded by McCandeless Ranch on 40 acres in South Kona, this place may seem remote, but it's actually just a short drive from some of the best water attractions on the island, including Puuhonua O Honaunau, Kealakekua Bay, and Hookena Beach. **Pros:** private and quiet; heated pool with Jacuzzi; beautiful views. **Cons:** not on the beach; 40 minutes from Kailua-Kona; remote location. ⑤ *Rooms from: $250* ✉ *Mamalahoa Hwy., between mile markers 101 and 100, Captain Cook* ☎ *808/938–7822* ⊕ *www.horizonguesthouse.com* ⇆ *4 suites* ⍟*Breakfast.*

$
B&B/INN

🍸**Kaawa Loa Plantation.** Proprietors Mike Martinage and Greg Nunn operate a grand B&B on a 5-acre coffee farm above Kealakekua Bay. The home features a 2,000-square-foot wraparound veranda with excellent views of the bay and the entire Honaunau coast. **Pros:** gracious and friendly hosts; excellent breakfast; Hawaiian steam room. **Cons:** not within walking distance of bay; some rooms share a bath; 20 minutes from downtown. ⑤ *Rooms from: $154* ✉ *82-5990 Napoopoo Rd., Captain Cook* ☎ *808/323–2686* ⊕ *www.kaawaloaplantation.com* ⇆ *4 rooms, 1 cottage* ⍟*Breakfast.*

$$
B&B/INN
Fodor's Choice
★

🍸**Kane Plantation Guesthouse.** The former home of late legendary artist Herb Kane, this luxury boutique guesthouse occupies a 16-acre avocado farm overlooking the South Kona coastline. **Pros:** sauna, hot tub, massage therapy room; upscale amenities; beautiful artwork. **Cons:** not on the beach; off the beaten track; 25 minutes to downtown. ⑤ *Rooms from: $260* ✉ *84-1120 Telephone Exchange Rd., off Hwy. 11, Honaunau* ✛ *¼ mile past mile marker 105, south of Captain Cook* ☎ *808/328–2416* ⊕ *www.kaneplantationhawaii. com* ⇆ *3 suites* ⍟*Breakfast.*

$
HOTEL

🍸**Manago Hotel.** This historical hotel is a good option if you want to escape the touristy thing but still be close to the water and attractions like Kealakekua Bay and Puuhonua O Honaunau National Historical Park. **Pros:** local color; rock-bottom prices; terrific on-site restaurant. **Cons:** not the best sound insulation between rooms; cheapest rooms share a community bath; some rooms have highway noise. ⑤ *Rooms from: $72* ✉ *81-6155 Mamalahoa Hwy., Captain Cook* ☎ *808/323–2642* ⊕ *www. managohotel.com* ⇆ *64 rooms, 42 with bath* ⍟*No meals.*

$$
B&B/INN

🍸**Mermaid Dreams Bed and Breakfast.** "Aloha" is the operative word at this mermaid-themed B&B a 10-minute drive from Kealakekua Bay. A self-proclaimed mermaid herself, hostess/proprietor Heather Reynolds takes guests on morning mermaid swims in the bay, where they can learn to swim while wearing a tail (she even has mermaid tails for rent if you need one). **Pros:** gracious hosts; beautifully landscaped grounds;

fireside lounge outside for evening cocktails. **Cons:** not on the beach; no children under age 13; two-night minimum stay. $ *Rooms from: $177* ✉ *81-1031 Keopuka Mauka Rd., Kealakekua* ☎ *808/649–9911* ⊕ *www.mermaiddreamsbedandbreakfast.com* ↪ *5 rooms* ⦿| *Breakfast.*

$ ⛺ **South Kona Studio.** This little studio is a great find for travelers on a
RENTAL budget: not only does it offer a kitchenette and private barbecue area, but it's just up the hill from a secluded beach with great snorkeling. **Pros:** budget friendly; cozy interior; ocean views. **Cons:** rural location; two guests max; steep hill to beach. $ *Rooms from: $120* ✉ *Kaohe Rd. and Hwy. 11, Captain Cook* ☎ *808/938–1172* ⊕ *southkonastudio.com* ↪ *1 room* ⦿| *No meals.*

NORTH KONA

$$$$ ⛺ **Four Seasons Resort Hualalai.** Beautiful views everywhere, polished
RESORT wood floors, custom furnishings and linens in warm earth and cool
FAMILY white tones, and Hawaiian fine artwork make this resort a peaceful
Fodor's Choice retreat. **Pros:** beautiful location; gourmet restaurants; renowned service.
★ **Cons:** not the best beach among the resorts; quite pricey; 20-minute drive to Kailua-Kona. $ *Rooms from: $889* ✉ *72-100 Kaupulehu Dr., Kailua-Kona* ☎ *808/325–8000, 888/340–5662* ⊕ *www.fourseasons. com/hualalai* ↪ *243 rooms* ⦿| *No meals.*

THE KOHALA COAST

The Kohala Coast is home to most all of the Big Island's megaresorts. Dotting the coastline, manicured lawns and golf courses, luxurious hotels, and white-sand beaches break up the long expanse of black lava rock along Queen Kaahumanu Highway. Many visitors to the Big Island check in here and rarely leave the area. If you're looking to be pampered and lounge on the beach or by the pool all day with an umbrella drink in hand, this is where you need to be. You can still see the rest of the island since most of the hiking and adventure-tour companies offer pick-ups at the Kohala Coast resorts, and many of the hotels have connections to car-rental agencies (though the number of cars is limited, and you will need to book ahead). Housing developments in Waikoloa and the Kawaihae area have vacation homes for rent, primarily through local property management companies. However, some owners prefer to handle rentals themselves, through websites like ⊕ *www.vrbo.com* and ⊕ *airbnb.com*. Nothing in this area will be far from beaches, restaurants, airport, and good weather, but double-check that the home is located on the coast and not in North Kohala (which is beautiful but a bit of a drive to the beach). Be sure to ask about parking, pools, and cleaning deposits.

$$ ⛺ **Aston Shores at Waikoloa.** Villas with terra-cotta–tile roofs are set amid
RENTAL landscaped lagoons and waterfalls at the edge of the championship Waiko-
FAMILY loa Village Golf Course. **Pros:** good prices for the area; great location; kid-friendly. **Cons:** no restaurants; daily resort fee; older decor in some rooms. $ *Rooms from: $189* ✉ *69-1035 Keana Pl., Waikoloa* ☎ *808/886–5001, 800/922–7866* ⊕ *www.astonhotels.com* ↪ *120 rooms* ⦿| *No meals.*

Where to Stay on the Kohala Coast and Waimea

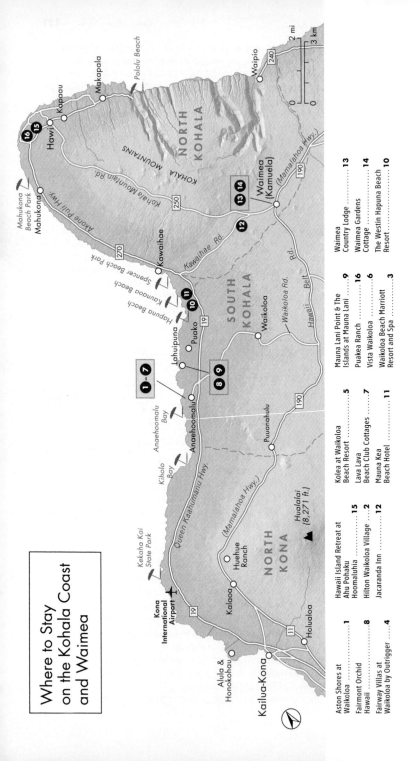

$$$$
RESORT
FAMILY
Fodor's Choice
★
⌂ **Fairmont Orchid Hawaii.** This first-rate resort overflows with tropical gardens, cascading waterfalls, sandy beach cove, beautiful wings with "open sesame" doors, a meandering pool, and renovated rooms with all the amenities. **Pros:** oceanfront location; excellent pool; aloha hospitality. **Cons:** top resort features come at a high price; 40-minute drive to Kailua-Kona; not the best beach among Kohala Coast resorts. ⑤ *Rooms from: $499* ✉ *1 N. Kaniku Dr.* ☎ *808/885–2000, 800/845–9905* ⊕ *www.fairmont. com* ⥥ *540 rooms* ⦵ *No meals.*

$$
RENTAL
⌂ **Fairway Villas at Waikoloa by Outrigger.** These large and comfy town houses and condominiums are located just off the fairway of the Waikoloa Beach Course and are a short walk from Anaehoomalu Bay. Designed in the style of plantation-era homes, these villas are decorated with rattan furniture and tropical themes, and come complete with top-notch appliances in fully equipped kitchens. **Pros:** good location for beach, shopping, dining, and golf; infinity pool; kid-friendly. **Cons:** no ocean views; lots of guest rules and regulations; expensive cleaning fees. ⑤ *Rooms from: $159* ✉ *Waikoloa Beach Resort, 69-200 Pohakulana Pl., Waikoloa* ☎ *808/886–0036* ⊕ *www.outrigger.com* ⥥ *70 units* ⦵ *No meals.*

$$$
B&B/INN
⌂ **Hawaii Island Retreat at Ahu Pohaku Hoomaluhia.** Here, above the sea cliffs in North Kohala's Hawi, sustainability meets luxury without sacrificing comfort: the resort generates its own solar and wind-turbine power, harnesses its own water, and grows much of its own food. **Pros:** stunning location; ancient Hawaiian spiritual sites; eco-friendly. **Cons:** somewhat isolated and not within walking distance of restaurants; yurts don't have in-unit showers; some luxury details are lacking. ⑤ *Rooms from: $298* ✉ *250 Maluhia Rd., off Hwy. 270 in Hawi, Kapaau* ☎ *808/889–6336* ⊕ *www.hawaiiislandretreat.com* ⥥ *20 rooms* ⦵ *Breakfast.*

$$
RESORT
FAMILY
⌂ **Hilton Waikoloa Village.** Dolphins swim in the lagoon; pint-size guests zoom down the 175-foot waterslide; a bride poses on the grand staircase; a fire-bearing runner lights the torches along the seaside path at sunset—these are some of the typical scenes at this 62-acre megaresort. **Pros:** family-friendly; lots of restaurant and activity options, including 2 golf courses; close to retail shopping. **Cons:** gigantic and crowded; lots of kids; restaurants are pricey. ⑤ *Rooms from: $301* ✉ *69-425 Waikoloa Beach Dr., Waikoloa* ☎ *808/886–1234, 800/445–8667* ⊕ *www. hiltonwaikoloavillage.com* ⥥ *1,241 rooms* ⦵ *No meals.*

KOHALA CONDO COMFORTS

If you require anything not provided by the management, both the **Kings' Shops** (✉ *250 Waikoloa Beach Dr., Waikoloa* ☎ *808/886–8811*) and the **Queens' MarketPlace** (✉ *201 Waikoloa Beach Dr., Waikoloa* ☎ *808/886–8822*) in the Waikoloa Beach Resort are good places to go. There is a small general store with liquor department and several nice restaurants at the Kings' Shops. Across the street, Queens' MarketPlace also has a food court and sit-down restaurants, as well as a gourmet market where you can get pizza baked to order.

5

$$$ ☷ **Kolea at Waikoloa Beach Resort.** These modern, impeccably furnished
RENTAL   condos appeal to the high-end visitor typically associated with the
FAMILY   Mauna Lani Bay Hotel & Bungalows, with far more amenities than
Fodor's Choice   the average condo complex, including both an infinity pool and a sand-
★   bottom children's pool at its oceanside Beach Club; a fitness center;
and a hot tub. **Pros:** high design; close to beach and activities; resort
amenities of nearby Hilton. **Cons:** pricey; no on-property restaurants;
limited view from some units. ⑤ *Rooms from: $375* ⊠ *Waikoloa Beach
Resort, 69-1000 Kolea Kai Circle, Waikoloa* ☎ *808/987–4519* ⊕ *www.
kolea.com* ⇌ *53 units* ❍| *No meals.*

$$$$ ☷ **Lava Lava Beach Club Cottages.** Spend the day swimming at the beach
RENTAL   just steps away from your private lanai and fall asleep to the sound of the
FAMILY   ocean at these four artfully decorated one-room cottages, located right on
Fodor's Choice   the sandy beach at Anaehoomalu Bay. It's a short stroll to the adjacent Lava
★   Lava Beach Club bar/restaurant, which serves lunch and dinner daily. **Pros:**
on the beach; fully air-conditioned; free Wi-Fi. **Cons:** beach is public, so
there will be people on it in front of cottage; quite expensive; often booked.
⑤ *Rooms from: $500* ⊠ *69-1081 Kuualii Pl., Waikoloa* ☎ *808/769–5282*
⊕ *www.lavalavabeachclub.com* ⇌ *4 cottages* ❍| *No meals.*

$$$$ ☷ **Mauna Kea Beach Hotel.** The grande dame of the Kohala Coast has long
RESORT   been regarded as one of the state's premier vacation resort hotels, and it
borders one of the island's finest white-sand beaches, Kaunaoa. **Pros:** beau-
tiful beach; premier tennis center; extra-large contemporary rooms. **Cons:**
small swimming pool; pricey; 27 miles from airport. ⑤ *Rooms from: $625*
⊠ *62-100 Mauna Kea Beach Dr., Kawaihae* ☎ *808/882–7222, 866/977–
4589* ⊕ *www.maunakeabeachhotel.com* ⇌ *252 rooms* ❍| *No meals.*

$$$$ ☷ **Mauna Lani Bay Hotel & Bungalows.** Popular with honeymooners and
RESORT   anniversary couples for decades, this elegant Kohala Coast classic is
FAMILY   still one of the most beautiful resorts on the island, highlighted by a
Fodor's Choice   breathtaking, open-air lobby with cathedral-like ceilings, Zen-like koi
★   ponds, and illuminated sheets of cascading water. **Pros:** beautiful design;
award-winning spa; many cultural programs. **Cons:** no luau; on-going
renovations; 26 miles from airport. ⑤ *Rooms from: $429* ⊠ *68-1400
Mauna Lani Dr.* ☎ *808/885–6622, 800/367–2323* ⊕ *www.maunalani.
com* ⇌ *336 rooms, 5 bungalows* ❍| *No meals.*

$$$$ ☷ **Mauna Lani Point and the Islands at Mauna Lani.** Surrounded by the emer-
RENTAL   ald greens of a world-class oceanside golf course, private, independent,
luxury condominiums at Islands at Mauna Lani offer spacious two-story
suites, while Mauna Lani Point's villas are closer to the beach. **Pros:**
friendly front desk; stellar views; extra-large units. **Cons:** quite pricey;
individually owned units vary in decor and amenities; some units are
a distance from the BBQ/pool area. ⑤ *Rooms from: $400* ⊠ *68-1050
Mauna Lani Point Dr., Waimea (Hawaii County)* ☎ *808/885–5022,
800/642–6284* ⊕ *www.classicresorts.com* ⇌ *66 units* ❍| *No meals.*

$$$ ☷ **Puakea Ranch.** Four beautifully restored ranch houses and bun-
RENTAL   galows occupy this historic country estate in Hawi, where guests
FAMILY   enjoy their own private swimming pools, horseback riding, round-
Fodor's Choice   the-clock concierge availability, and plenty of fresh fruit from the
★   orchards. **Pros:** charmingly decorated; beautiful bathrooms; private
swimming pools. **Cons:** 15 minutes to the beach; spotty cellphone

coverage; sometimes windy. $ *Rooms from: $289* ✉ *56-2864 Akoni Pule Hwy., Hawi* ☎ *808/315–0805* ⊕ *www.puakearanch.com* ↩*4 bungalows* ⦿*No meals.*

$ | 🏨 **Vista Waikoloa.** Older and more reasonably priced than most of the
RENTAL | condo complexes along the Kohala Coast, the well-appointed, two-bed-
FAMILY | room, two-bath Vista condos have ocean views and two lanai per unit. **Pros:** reasonably priced; very large units; 75-foot lap pool. **Cons:** hit or miss on decor because each unit is individually owned; somewhat dated; some units don't allow children. $ *Rooms from: $180* ✉ *Waikoloa Beach Resort, 69-1010 Keana Pl., Waikoloa* ☎ *808/886–3594* ⊕ *www. waikoloabeachresort.com* ↩ *122 units* ⦿*No meals.*

$$$$ | 🏨 **Waikoloa Beach Marriott Resort and Spa.** Covering 15 acres with
RESORT | ancient fishponds, historic trails, and petroglyph fields, the Marriott
FAMILY | has rooms with sleek modern beds, bright white linens, Hawaiian art, and private lanai. **Pros:** more low-key than the Hilton Waikoloa; sunset luau Wednesday and Saturday; sand-bottom pool for kids. **Cons:** some rooms lack views; expensive daily parking charge; Wi-Fi is not free (and expensive). $ *Rooms from: $400* ✉ *69-275 Waikoloa Beach Dr., Waikoloa* ☎ *808/886–6789, 800/228–9290* ⊕ *www.marriott.com* ↩ *297 rooms* ⦿*No meals.*

$$ | 🏨 **The Westin Hapuna Beach Resort.** More reasonably priced than its
RESORT | neighbor resorts and with direct access to the Big Island's largest sandy
FAMILY | beach, this massive hotel has enormous columns and a terraced, open-air lobby with rotunda ceiling, curved staircases, and skylights. **Pros:** extra-large rooms, all ocean-facing; direct access to one of island's best beaches; resort has 18-hole championship golf course. **Cons:** fitness center a five-minute walk from the hotel; expensive daily resort fee; 27 miles from airport. $ *Rooms from: $425* ✉ *62-100 Kaunaoa Dr.* ☎ *808/880–1111, 866/774–6236* ⊕ *wwwhapunabeachresort.com* ↩ *349 rooms* ⦿*No meals.*

WAIMEA

Though it seems a world away, Waimea is only about a 15- to 20-minute drive from the Kohala Coast resorts, which places it considerably closer to the island's best beaches than Kailua-Kona. Yet few visitors think to book lodging in this pleasant upcountry ranching community, where you can enjoy cool mornings and evenings after a day spent basking in the sun. To the delight of residents and visitors, there are some very good restaurants. Sightseeing is easy from here, too: Mauna Kea is a short drive away, and Hilo and Kailua-Kona are about an hour away. There aren't as many condos and hotels here, but there are some surprisingly good B&B and cottage options—as well as some great deals, especially considering their vantage point. Many have spectacular views of Maunakea, the ocean, and the beautiful green hills of Waimea.

$ | 🏨 **Jacaranda Inn.** While the historical Jacaranda Inn may not always
B&B/INN | live up to its potential, this sprawling estate, built in 1897 and once the home of the manager of Parker Ranch, provides a unique lodging option for visitors who appreciate history. **Pros:** historical charm; hot tubs in most rooms; walking distance to Waimea restaurants. **Cons:** service not

always reliable; no pool; can be rainy and windy. ⑤ *Rooms from: $149* ✉ *65-1444 Kawaihae Rd., Waimea (Hawaii County)* ☎ *808/557–5068* ⊕ *www.jacarandainn.com* ⇆ *8 suites, 1 cottage* ꤫ *No meals.*

$ ꤫ **Waimea Country Lodge.** In the heart of cowboy country, this modest
HOTEL ranch house–style lodge offers views of the green, rolling slopes of Maunakea. **Pros:** affordable; kitchenettes in some rooms; free coffee in morning. **Cons:** not near the beach; no pool; no breakfast. ⑤ *Rooms from: $116* ✉ *65-1210 Lindsey Rd., Waimea (Hawaii County)* ☎ *808/885–4100, 800/367–5004* ⊕ *www.waimeacountrylodge.com* ⇆ *21 rooms* ꤫ *No meals.*

$ ꤫ **Waimea Gardens Cottage.** Surprisingly luxe yet cozy and quaint,
RENTAL the three charming country cottages and one suite at this histori-cal Hawaiian homestead are surrounded by flowering private gar-dens and a backyard stream. **Pros:** charming self-contained units; manicured gardens; cascading stream. **Cons:** requires 50% deposit within two weeks of booking and payment in full six weeks prior to arrival; cash only; three-night minimum stay. ⑤ *Rooms from: $170* ✉ *Waimea (Hawaii County)* ✣ *Located off Kawaihae Rd., 2 miles from Waimea town* ☎ *808/885–8550* ⊕ *www.waimeagardens.com* ▭ *No credit cards* ⇆ *4 units* ꤫ *Breakfast* ☞ *Physical address given out only after a confirmed reservation.*

THE HAMAKUA COAST

A stretch of coastline between Waimea and Hilo is an ideal spot for those seeking peace, tranquility, and beautiful views, which makes it a favorite with honeymooners avoiding the big resorts. Several über-romantic B&Bs dot the coast, each with its own personality and views. As with Hilo, the beaches are an hour's drive away or more, so most visitors spend a few nights here and a few closer to the beaches on the west side. A handful of vacation homes provide an extra level of privacy for couples, groups, or families. Honokaa Town is a charming area with a couple of restaurants, banks, and convenience stores.

$$ ꤫ **The Palms Cliff House Inn.** This handsome Victorian-style mansion,
B&B/INN 15 minutes north of downtown Hilo and a few minutes from Akaka Falls, is perched on the sea cliffs 100 feet above the crashing surf of the tropical coast. **Pros:** stunning views; terrific breakfast; all rooms have private outdoor entrances. **Cons:** no pool; remote location means you have to drive 13 miles to Hilo for dinner; 50% booking deposit required. ⑤ *Rooms from: $299* ✉ *28-3514 Mamalahoa Hwy., Honomu* ☎ *866/963–6076, 808/963–6076* ⊕ *www.palmscliffhouse.com* ⇆ *8 rooms* ꤫ *Breakfast.*

$ ꤫ **Waipio Wayside.** Nestled amid the avocado, mango, coffee, and kukui
B&B/INN trees of a historical plantation estate (circa 1932), this serene home provides a retreat close to the Waipio Valley. **Pros:** close to Waipio; gracious owner; full breakfast served in the dining room. **Cons:** remote location; close quarters; no lunch or dinner on property. ⑤ *Rooms from: $130* ✉ *42-4226 Waipio Rd. (Hwy. 240), Honokaa* ☎ *808/775–0275, 800/833–8849* ⊕ *www.waipiowayside.com* ⇆ *5 rooms* ꤫ *Breakfast.*

HILO

Hilo is the wettest part of the Big Island, full of waterfalls and rainforest hikes, a very different alternative to the warm, dry, white-sand beaches of the Kohala Coast. Locals have taken a greater interest in Hilo, signs showing in new restaurants, restored buildings, and a handful of clean and pleasant parks. Hilo has a few decent hotels, but no high-end resorts. Hilo's fantastic B&Bs have taken over lovely historical homes and serve breakfast comprising ingredients from backyard gardens. The volcano is only a 30-minute drive, as are the sights of the Puna region. There are also a number of nice beaches and surf spots, though nothing in the class of South Kohala.

$ **The Bay House.** Overlooking Hilo Bay and just steps away from the
B&B/INN Singing Bridge near Hilo's historical downtown area, this small, quiet B&B is vibrantly decorated, with Hawaiian-quilted beds and private lanai in each of the three rooms. **Pros:** every room has its own oceanfront lanai; cliffside hot tub; Hilo Bay views. **Cons:** only two people per room; occasional street noise; no twin beds. $ *Rooms from: $175* ⊠ *42 Pukihae St., Hilo* ☎ *888/235–8195, 808/961–6311* ⊕ *www.bayhousehawaii.com* ⤵ *3 rooms* ⦿ *Breakfast.*

$ **Dolphin Bay Hotel.** Units in this circa-1950s motor lodge are modest
HOTEL but charming, as well as clean and inexpensive; a glowing lava flow
FAMILY sign marks the office and bespeaks owner John Alexander's passion for the volcano. **Pros:** great value; full kitchens in all units; helpful and pleasant staff. **Cons:** no pool; no phones in the rooms; dated decor. $ *Rooms from: $109* ⊠ *333 Iliahi St., Hilo* ☎ *808/935–1466* ⊕ *www.dolphinbayhotel.com* ⤵ *24 rooms* ⦿ *No meals.*

$ **Grand Naniloa Hotel–A Doubletree by Hilton.** Hilo isn't known for its
HOTEL fancy resort hotels, but the recently renovated Grand Naniloa Hotel
FAMILY attempts to remedy that situation in grand fashion. **Pros:** within walking distance of botanical park and Coconut Island; rental kayaks, bikes, and SUPs; free golf at adjacent 9-hole course and driving range. **Cons:** some rooms don't have ocean views; limited parking spaces; small swimming pool. $ *Rooms from: $149* ⊠ *93 Banyan Dr., Hilo* ☎ *808/969–3333* ⊕ *www.grandnaniloahilo.com* ⤵ *388 rooms* ⦿ *No meals.*

$ **Hale Kai Bed & Breakfast.** On a bluff above Honolii surf beach, this
B&B/INN modern 5,400-square-foot home is 2 miles from downtown Hilo and features four rooms—each with patio, deluxe bedding, and grand ocean views within earshot of the surf. **Pros:** delicious hot breakfast; panoramic views of Hilo Bay; smoke-free property. **Cons:** no kids under 13; just outside walking distance to downtown Hilo; occasional coqui frog noise. $ *Rooms from: $170* ⊠ *111 Honolii Pl., Hilo* ☎ *808/935–6330* ⊕ *www.halekaihawaii.com* ⤵ *4 rooms* ⦿ *Breakfast.*

$ **Hilo Hawaiian Hotel.** This landmark hotel has large bayfront rooms
HOTEL offering spectacular views of Maunakea and Coconut Island on Hilo
FAMILY Bay. Street-side rooms overlook the golf course, and the hotel is within walking distance to the botanical park. **Pros:** Hilo Bay views; private lanai in most rooms; free parking. **Cons:** pricey breakfast buffet; older hotel; lacks amenities. $ *Rooms from: $169* ⊠ *71 Banyan Dr., Hilo*

☎ *808/935–9361, 800/367–5004 from mainland, 800/272–5275 inter-island ⊕ www.castleresorts.com ⟿ 286 rooms* ⊺⊙⊦ *No meals.*

$
B&B/INN
⌂ **Hilo Honu Inn.** A charming old Craftsman home lovingly restored by a friendly and hospitable couple from North Carolina, the Hilo Honu offers quite a bit of variety. **Pros:** spectacular Hilo Bay views; historical setting; free Wi-Fi. **Cons:** no toddlers in the upstairs suite; not on the beach; A/C in only two of the three rooms. ⑨ *Rooms from: $150* ⊠ *465 Haili St., Hilo* ☎ *808/935–4325* ⊕ *www.hilohonu.com* ⟿ *3 rooms* ⊺⊙⊦ *Breakfast.*

$
HOTEL
⌂ **Hilo Seaside Hotel.** Ten minutes from the airport, this local-flavor destination is a friendly, laid-back, and otherwise peaceful place, with tropical rooms that have private lanai. **Pros:** private lanai; friendly staff; budget friendly with frequent specials. **Cons:** not walking distance to historic bayfront; hotel is a little dated; no restaurant. ⑨ *Rooms from: $119* ⊠ *126 Banyan Way, Hilo* ☎ *808/935–0821, 800/560–5557* ⊕ *www.hiloseasidehotel.com* ⟿ *133 rooms* ⊺⊙⊦ *No meals.*

$
B&B/INN
⌂ **The Inn at Kulaniapia Falls.** Overlooking downtown Hilo and the ocean beyond, this inn sits next to a 120-foot waterfall that tumbles into a 300-foot-wide natural pond—ripe for swimming, conditions permitting. **Pros:** waterfalls on property; good value; eco-friendly. **Cons:** isolated; dark road challenging to navigate at night; no air-conditioning. ⑨ *Rooms from: $179* ⊠ *100 Kulaniapia Dr., Hilo* ☎ *808/935–6789* ⊕ *www.waterfall.net* ⟿ *11 rooms* ⊺⊙⊦ *Breakfast.*

PUNA

Puna is a world apart—wild jungles, volcanically heated hot springs, and not a resort for miles around. There are, however, a handful of well-priced vacation homes and B&Bs. It's not your typical vacation spot: there are a few black-sand beaches (some of them clothing-optional), few dining or entertainment options, and quite a few, er, interesting locals. That said, for those who want to have a unique experience, get away from everything, witness molten lava flowing into the ocean (depending on activity), and don't mind the sound of the chirping coqui frogs at night, this is the place to do it. The volcano and Hilo are both within easy driving distance. Ongoing eruptions of Kilauea have made some parts of Puna inaccessible and closed roads.

$
RENTAL
⌂ **Your Hawaiian Retreat.** A collection of three little rentals deep in the heart of Puna and well off the beaten path comprise this exotic destination on an organic farm. **Pros:** sustainable; breakfast items stocked for Mango and Avocado House; Ohana House good for groups. **Cons:** remote; not on the beach; three-night minimum stay. ⑨ *Rooms from: $100* ⊠ *13-809 Kamaili Rd., Pahoa* ✛ *6 miles south of Pahoa* ☎ *808/965–7088* ⊕ *www.yourhawaiianretreat.org* ⟿ *3 units* ⊺⊙⊦ *No meals.*

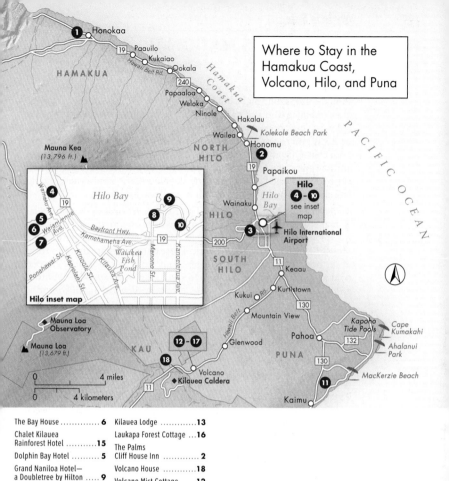

Where to Stay in the Hamakua Coast, Volcano, Hilo, and Puna

Honokaa **1**
Paauilo
Kukaiao
Ookala
Papaaloa
Weloka
Ninole
Hakalau
Wailea
Kolekole Beach Park
Honomu **2**
HAMAKUA
Hamakua Coast
Mauna Kea (13,796 ft.)
NORTH HILO
Papaikou
Hilo
4 - **10** see inset map
Wainaku
Hilo Bay
HILO
Hilo International Airport **3**
PACIFIC OCEAN
SOUTH HILO
Keaau **11**
Kurtistown
Kukui
Mountain View
130
Kapoho Tide Pools
Cape Kumakahi
Mauna Loa Observatory
Mauna Loa (13,679 ft.)
KAU
12 - **17**
Glenwood
Pahoa
132
Ahalanui Park
PUNA
18
Volcano
Kilauea Caldera
130
MacKerzie Beach
11
Kaimu

Hilo inset map
Hilo Bay
4
9
5
6
8
10
7
Wainaku Ave.
Waianuenue Ave.
Bayfront Hwy.
Kamehameha Ave.
Ponahawai St.
Kinoole St.
Kilauea Ave.
Manono St.
Kanoelehua Ave.
Kapiolani St.
Waiakea Fish Pond

0   4 miles
0   4 kilometers

HAWAII VOLCANOES NATIONAL PARK AND VICINITY

If you are going to visit Hawaii Volcanoes National Park—and you should—spend one night in Volcano Village. This allows you to see the glow of Halemaumau Crater at night—if there's activity, that is—without worrying about driving an hour or more back to your condo, hotel, or B&B. There are plenty of places to stay in the area, and many are both charming and reasonable. Volcano Village has just enough dining and shopping options to satisfy you for a day or two, and you're also close to Hilo, the Puna region, and Punaluu Black Sand Beach, should you decide to make Volcano your home base for longer.

$
HOTEL
FAMILY
Chalet Kilauea Rainforest Hotel. This quirky, yet upscale accommodation features four artistically distinctive rooms that unveil beautiful views of the rain forest from a great location five minutes from Hawaii Volcanoes National Park. **Pros:** unique decor; friendly front desk; hot tub. **Cons:** space heaters; not close to the beach; can get cold at night. $ *Rooms from: $165* ✉ *19-4178 Wright Rd., Volcano* ☎ *808/967–7786, 800/937–7786* ⊕ *www.volcano-hawaii.com* ➠ *4 rooms* ⊦○⊦ *No meals.*

$
RENTAL
FAMILY
Hale Ohia Cottages. A stately and comfortable Queen Anne–style mansion, Hale Ohia was built in the 1930s as a summer home for a wealthy Scotsman (the property is listed on the State Historic Register). **Pros:** unique architecture; free Wi-Fi and parking; privacy. **Cons:** no TVs; simple breakfast offerings; 30 minutes from downtown Hilo via car. $ *Rooms from: $149* ✉ *11-3968 Hale Ohia Rd., Volcano* ☎ *808/967–7986, 800/455–3803* ⊕ *www.haleohia.com* ➠ *15 rooms* ⊦○⊦ *Breakfast.*

$$
HOTEL
Fodor's Choice
★
Kilauea Lodge. A mile from the entrance of Hawaii Volcanoes National Park, this lodge was initially built as a YMCA camp in the 1930s; now it is a pleasant inn, tastefully furnished with European antiques, photographs, and authentic Hawaiian quilts. **Pros:** great restaurant; close to volcano; fireplaces. **Cons:** no TV or phone in lodge rooms; 45 minutes to downtown Hilo; few shopping options nearby. $ *Rooms from: $199* ✉ *19-3948 Old Volcano Rd., 1 mile northeast of national park, Volcano* ☎ *808/967–7366* ⊕ *www.kilauealodge.com* ➠ *12 rooms, 4 cottages* ⊦○⊦ *Breakfast.*

$
RENTAL
Fodor's Choice
★
Laukapa Forest Cottage. Outfitted in cedar with beautiful architectural accents, this upscale accommodation in Volcano Village offers a romantic retreat perfect for couples, with no details spared to create a comfortable hideaway. **Pros:** unique architecture; well-equipped kitchen; upscale amenities including bags of Hawaii-grown coffee. **Cons:** no nightlife nearby; two-night minimum; limited shopping nearby. $ *Rooms from: $150* ✉ *Volcano* ☎ *808/967–7990, 877/967–7990* ⊕ *www.volcanoplaces.com* ➠ *1* ⊦○⊦ *No meals* ☞ *Physical address given only upon a confirmed reservation.*

$$$
HOTEL
Fodor's Choice
★
Volcano House. Hawaii's oldest hotel—and the only one in Volcanoes National Park—is committed to sustainable practices and promoting local Hawaiian culture and history through its locally sourced restaurants, artisan-crafted decor, and eco-focused guest programs. **Pros:** unbeatable location; views of the lava lake; sense of place and history.

Cons: basic facilities; closes completely if there is a federal government shutdown; some rooms have parking lot views. $ *Rooms from: $285* ✉ *1 Crater Rim Dr., Hawaii Volcanoes National Park* ☎ *808/756–9625* ⊕ *www.hawaiivolcanohouse.com* ⤶ *33 rooms* ◎ *No meals.*

$$$
RENTAL
▣ **Volcano Mist Cottage.** Both rustic and Zen, this magical cottage in the rain forest features cathedral ceilings, spruce walls, cork flooring, and amenities not usually found at Volcano vacation rentals, like bathrobes, a Bose home theater system, and Trek mountain bikes. **Pros:** private; outdoor Jacuzzi tub; upscale amenities. **Cons:** not large enough for families; 45 minutes from downtown Hilo; limited shopping options nearby. $ *Rooms from: $300* ✉ *11-3932 9th St., Volcano* ☎ *808/895–8359* ⊕ *www.volcanomistcottage.com* ⤶ *1 cottage* ◎ *Some meals.*

$$
RENTAL
▣ **Volcano Teapot Cottage.** A near-perfect spot for couples seeking a romantic getaway in Volcano Village, this historical 1912 two-bedroom cottage evokes a vintage country feeling in keeping with the summer homes of the era. **Pros:** hot tub; fireplace; laundry facilities. **Cons:** not quite large enough to accommodate four people—three people max; can get cold at night; occasionally wet and rainy. $ *Rooms from: $225* ✉ *19-4041 Kilauea Rd., Volcano* ☎ *808/937–4976* ⊕ *www.volcanoteapot.com* ⤶ *1 cottage* ◎ *Breakfast.*

KAU

Far from the West Hawaii resorts, Kau is a good place for those looking to get away from it all. You won't find a lot in terms of amenities, but there are several nice options including vacation rental cottages, B&B inns, and a condo resort complex with golf course. The main visitor attraction is the beautiful Punaluu Black Sand Beach, home of the endangered hawksbill turtle.

$$$$
B&B/INN
▣ **Kalaekilohana Inn and Retreat.** You wouldn't really expect to find a top-notch B&B in Kau, but just up the road from South Point, this grand residence offers large private suites with locally harvested hardwood floors, private lanai with ocean and mountain views, and big, comfy beds with high-thread-count sheets and fluffy down comforters. **Pros:** luxurious beds; beautiful decor reminscent of Old Hawaii; delicious breakfast. **Cons:** not for children under 12; no pool; very limited nearby shopping. $ *Rooms from: $369* ✉ *94-2152 South Point Rd., Naalehu* ☎ *808/939–8052* ⊕ *www.kau-hawaii.com* ⤶ *4 rooms* ◎ *Breakfast.*

NIGHTLIFE AND PERFORMING ARTS

Updated
by Kristina
Anderson

If you're the sort of person who doesn't come alive until after dark, you might be a little lonely on the Big Island. Blame it on the sleepy plantation heritage. People did their cane raising in the morning, thus very limited late-night fun.

Still, there are a few lively bars on the island, a handful of great local playhouses, half a dozen or so movie houses (including those that play foreign and independent films), and plenty of musical entertainment to keep you happy.

Also, many resorts have bars and late-night activities and events, and keep pools and gyms open late so there's something to do after dinner.

And let's not forget the luau. These fantastic dance and musical performances are combined with some of the best local food on the island and are plenty of fun for the whole family.

NIGHTLIFE

KAILUA-KONA

BARS

Humpy's Big Island Alehouse. Beer lovers appreciate the 36 craft brews on tap at this oceanfront restaurant, with dining downstairs and another bar upstairs that features live music and dancing. It's always busy with young local revelers. Humpy's food can be hit or miss, but it's great for late-hour grill items. Happy-hour specials are available weekdays 3 to 6, and the bar stays open until 2 am. ⊠ *75-5815 Alii Dr., Kailua-Kona* ☎ *808/324–2337* ⊕ *www.humpyskona.com.*

Fodor'sChoice **Kona Brewing Co. Pub & Brewery.** The only genuine brewpub in Kona,
★ this spot is beloved by locals and visitors alike. Good pizzas and salads, excellent locally brewed beer (go for the sampler and try four of them), and an outdoor patio with live music on Sunday night means this place can get crowded, especially on weekends. The location isn't at all scenic, but that's not the draw of the brewpub. The main entrance is at the end of Pawai Street, in the Old Industrial area.

✉ *75-5629 Kuakini Hwy., Kailua-Kona* ☎ *808/334–2739* ⊕ *www.konabrewingco.com.*

Korner Pocket. A favored haunt of the South Kona crowd, Korner Pocket is tucked in the back of a strip mall. But don't let that deter you. It has fantastic affordable food, pool tables, and live music and dancing on the weekend with no cover. ✉ *81-970 Haleki'i St., Kealakekua* ☎ *808/322–2994.*

The Mask-querade Bar. Hidden away in an unassuming strip mall, this is one of the Big Island's most venerable gay bars. Drag shows, hot DJs, live music, karaoke, drink specials, fiestas, and Sunday barbecues are included in the roster of weekly events. All are welcome. ✉ *Kopiko Plaza, 75-5660 Kopiko St., behind Longs Drugs, Kailua-Kona* ☎ *808/329–8558* ⊕ *www.themask-queradebar.com.*

> ## BEST SUNSET MAI TAIS
>
> **Huggo's on the Rocks** (Kailua-Kona). Table dining in the sand, plus live music Friday and Saturday.
>
> **Kona Inn** (Kailua-Kona). Wide, unobstructed view of the Kailua-Kona coastline.
>
> **Rays on the Bay at the Sheraton Kona Resort** (Kailua-Kona). Fantastic sunset views from plush lounge chairs, followed by spotlighted glimpses of nearby manta rays.
>
> **Waioli Lounge in the Hilo Hawaiian Hotel** (Hilo). A nice view of Coconut Island, live music Friday and Saturday nights.

6

Oceans Sports Bar & Grill. A popular gathering place, this sports bar in the back of the Coconut Grove Marketplace has a pool table and an outdoor patio, along with dozens of TVs screening the big game (whatever it happens to be that day). It really gets hopping on the weekends and for karaoke on Tuesday and Thursday. There's good happy hour pricing and $3 Taco Tuesdays. ✉ *Coconut Grove Marketplace, 75-5811 Alii Dr., Kailua-Kona* ☎ *808/327–9494.*

CLUBS

Foster's Kitchen. With happy hour from 3 to 5 pm and then again from 9 to 10 pm, oceanfront Foster's Kitchen offers every reason to come and kick back and enjoy the sunset and evening Kailua Bay views. Craft beers, well drinks, and house wine are all priced under $4. There's also island-style music seven nights a week. ✉ *75-5805 Alii Dr., Kailua-Kona* ☎ *808/326–1600* ⊕ *www.fosterskitchen.com.*

Gertrude's Jazz Bar. You know you're in the right place when you climb the stairs to this little gem and notice that the steps are painted like piano keys. With a location in the heart of town, including a perfect view of Kailua Bay, this open-air club features an incredible variety of music (jazz, Latin, country, classical) and special events such as dance lessons, art nights, and themed dress-up parties. There's a small cover charge, but that helps pay the musicians a living wage. ✉ *75-5699 Alii Dr., Kailua-Kona* ☎ *808/327–5299* ⊕ *gertrudesjazzbar.com.*

Huggo's on the Rocks. Jazz, Island, and classic-rock bands perform here nightly, and outside you may see people dancing in the sand. The food can miss, but the location, on the waterfront by the Royal Kona Resort, doesn't get better. Happy hour is 3 to 6. ⊠ *75-5828 Kahakai Rd., at Alii Dr., Kailua-Kona* ☎ *808/329–1493* ⊕ *www.huggosontherocks.com.*

Laverne's Sports Bar. On weekends, live concerts are on tap. Sometimes Hawaiian and Island Music headliners perform here, like recording artist Anuhea and Rebel Souljahz. After 10, DJs spin on the ocean-breeze-cooled dance floor. ⊠ *Coconut Grove Marketplace, 75-5819 Alii Dr., Kailua-Kona* ☎ *808/331–2633* ⊕ *www.laverneskona.com.*

THE KOHALA COAST

BARS

Kona Tap Room. A favorite after-work spot for employees from the surrounding hotels, this lounge in the Hilton Waikoloa Village offers friendly bartenders, free Wi-Fi, and pool tables. Enjoy tropical cocktails, craft beers, light fare, and live music from 8 to 10 pm nightly. ⊠ *Hilton Waikoloa Village, 425 Waikoloa Beach Dr., Waikoloa* ☎ *808/886–1234* ⊕ *www.hiltonwaikoloavillage.com.*

Luana Lounge. This wood-paneled lounge in the Fairmont Orchid has a large terrace and an impressive view. The bartenders are skilled, service is impeccable. The crowd is subdued, so it's a nice place for an early evening cocktail or after-dinner liqueur. There's live music at sunset until 9 pm. ⊠ *Fairmont Orchid, 1 N. Kaniku Dr., Waimea (Hawaii County)* ☎ *808/885–2000* ⊕ *www.fairmont.com/orchid.*

HILO

BARS

Coqui's Hideaway Diner and Sports Bar. Whoever named this place has a real sense of humor as the shrieking invasive frogs you hear around the Big Island at night are a ubiquitous icon of the East side—you can't hide from them. Irregardless, this sports bar features pool and Ping-Pong tables and a great daily happy hour with free *pupus* (appetizers.) There's live music and dancing starting at 6 pm Wednesdays through Fridays and a DJ on Saturdays. ⊠ *1550 Kamehameha Ave., Hilo* ☎ *808/934–7288* ⊕ *coquishilo.com.*

Cronies Bar & Grill. A sports bar by night and hamburger joint by day, Cronies is a local favorite. When the lights go down, the bar gets packed. ⊠ *11 Waianuenue Ave., Hilo* ☎ *808/935–5158* ⊕ *www.cronieshawaii.com.*

PERFORMING ARTS

LUAU AND POLYNESIAN REVUES

KAILUA-KONA

Haleo Luau at the Sheraton Kona Resort & Spa at Keauhou Bay. On the graceful grounds of the Sheraton Kona Resort & Spa at Keauhou Bay, this popular luau (Monday and Friday evenings) takes you on a journey of song and dance, celebrating the historic Keauhou region, birthplace of King Kamehameha III. Before the show, you can participate in workshops on topics ranging from coconut-frond weaving to poi ball techniques. The excellent buffet is a feast of local favorites, including kalua pig, poi, ahi poke, chicken long rice, fish, and mango chutney. Generous mai tai refills are a plus, and a highlight is the dramatic fire-knife dance finale. ⊠ *Sheraton Kona Resort & Spa at Keauhou Bay, 78-128 Ehukai St., Kailua-Kona* ☎ *808/930–4900* ⊕ *www.sheratonkona.com* ⊠ *$125.*

Island Breeze Luau. With traditional dancing showcasing the interconnected Polynesian roots of Hawaii, Samoa, Tahiti, and New Zealand, the "We Are *Ohana* (family)" luau is not a hokey tourist-trap event. These performers take their art seriously. The historic oceanfront location at King Kamehameha's former royal compound near Ahuena Heiau adds to the authenticity, and the bounty of food includes kalua pig cooked in an underground *imu* (oven). Validated parking at the hotel. ⊠ *75-5660 Palani Rd., Kailua-Kona* ☎ *866/482–9775* ⊕ *www.islandbreezeluau.com* ⊠ *$101.77.*

Voyagers of the Pacific. The Royal Kona Resort lights its torches for a spectacular show and oceanfront buffet four times a week (Monday–Wednesday and Friday). The entire Polynesian Triangle is represented through song and dance by seasoned professional performers who love sharing their dance traditions with visitors. Traditional luau fare is served along with succulent pork cooked in an authentic underground *imu* (oven), and an open bar offers mai tais and other tropical concoctions. An exciting Samoan fire-knife dancer caps off the show. It may just be the best luau deal in town. ⊠ *Royal Kona Resort, 75-5852 Alii Dr., Kailua-Kona* ☎ *808/329–3111* ⊕ *www.royalkona.com* ⊠ *$70.*

THE KOHALA COAST

Hawaii Loa Luau. This gorgeous show is slickly produced and well choreographed, incorporating both traditional and contemporary music and dance, along with an array of beautiful costumes. It tells the tale of Hawaiiloa, the great navigator from Tahiti and of the celestial object— *Hokulea* , "Star of Gladness"—that guided him to the islands later named Hawaii. Presented under the stars at the Fairmont Orchid Hawaii on Saturdays, the meal offers several stations with a variety of Hawaiian and Hawaii regional dishes, and there's a full bar for mai tais and other tropical libations. ⊠ *Fairmont Orchid Hawaii, 1 N. Kaniku Dr., Waimea (Hawaii County)* ☎ *808/885–2000, 808/326–4969* ⊕ *www.gatheringofthekings.com* ⊠ *$115.*

FAMILY **Legends of Hawaii Luau at Hilton Waikoloa Village.** Presented outdoors at the Kamehameha Court, this show is aptly subtitled, "Our Big Island Story." A delicious buffet offers Big Island–grown luau choices as well as more familiar fare and an open tropical bar. Pay a small fee and upgrade to Alii seating for a front-row vantage and your own buffet station. A children's station has kid favorites. Delicious desserts such as haupia cream puffs and Kona-coffee cheesecake top it all off. ⊠ *Hilton Waikoloa Village, 69-425 Waikoloa Beach Dr., Waikoloa* ☎ *808/886–1234* ⊕ *www.hiltonwaikoloavillage.com/resort-experiences/legends-of-hawaii-luau* ⊠ *$135.*

CLOSE UP

Hawaiian Music on the Big Island

It's easy to forget that Hawaii has its own music until you step off a plane onto the Islands—and then there's no escaping it. It's a unique blend of the strings and percussion favored by the early settlers and the chants and rituals of the ancient Hawaiians, reflecting the unique mixed heritage of this special place. Hawaiian music today includes Island-born tunings of acoustic guitar—slack key and steel guitar—along with the ukulele and vocals.

This is one of the few folk music traditions in the United States that is fully embraced by the younger generation, with no prodding from their parents or grandparents. A good many radio stations on the Big Island play Hawaiian/"Island"/reggae music, and concerts performed by Island favorites

like Makana or L.T. Smooth are filled with fans of all ages.

The best introduction is one of the annual festivals: the free **Hawaiian Slack Key Guitar Festival** (Labor Day weekend), with a handful of greats performing at the Sheraton Keauhou Bay Resort and Spa; the **Great Waikoloa Ukulele Festival** (March), which features prominent players and everything ukulele; and the **KWXX Hoolaulea** (September), a popular Island Music jam with big names performing on four stages in downtown Hilo.

Or you can catch live performances most nights at a handful of local bars and clubs, including **Chillin' on the Bay, Huggo's on the Rocks, Island Lava Java,** and the **Kona Brewing Co.** in Kailua-Kona; and **Cronies Bar and Grill** in Hilo.

Mauna Kea Beach Hotel Clambake. The weekly clambake near the sand at Hau Tree beach restaurant features an extensive menu with oysters on the half shell, Manila clams, Dungeness crab legs, mussels, sashimi, and "all-you-can-eat" Keahole lobster. There's even prime rib and a dessert station. Live Hawaiian music is often accompanied by a graceful hula dancer. ⊠ *Mauna Kea Beach Hotel, 62-100 Mauna Kea Beach Dr., Waimea (Hawaii County)* ☎ *808/882–5707* ⊕ *maunakeabeachhotel.com* ⌘ *$122.*

FAMILY
Fodor's Choice
★
Mauna Kea Beach Hotel Oceanfront Luau. On the oceanfront North Pointe Luau Grounds, you can sample the best of island cuisine—a traditional feast of imu-roasted kalua pig, island fish, lomilomi salmon, and sashimi—while enjoying the music and hula of the renowned Lim family. The luau includes an amazing fire-knife dance, spirited chanting, and very traditional hula. *Keiki* (children) can learn the *hukilau* (a traditional song and dance), and you can relax right on the beach, under the stars. If you choose one luau during your visit to the Big Island, this should be the one. ■TIP➔ You can elect to see the show only for a reasonable fee. ⊠ *Mauna Kea Beach Hotel, 62-100 Mauna Kea Beach Dr., Waimea (Hawaii County)* ☎ *808/882–5810, 808/882-7222* ⊕ *maunakeabeachhotel.com* ⌘ *$117; show only, $52.*

Waikoloa Beach Marriott Resort & Spa Sunset Luau. Overlooking the white sands of Anaehoomalu Bay, this Polynesian luau includes a spectacular Samoan fire dance performance as well as cultural music and dances from various Pacific Island cultures. Traditional dishes are served alongside more familiar Western fare, and there's also an open bar. ✉ *Waikoloa Beach Marriott Resort & Spa, 69-275 Waikoloa Beach Dr., Waikoloa* ☎ *808/886–8111* ⊕ *www.waikoloabeachresort.com* 🍽 *$106.25.*

FESTIVALS

There is a festival dedicated to just about everything on the Big Island. Some of them are small community affairs, but a handful of film, food, and music festivals provide quality entertainment for visitors and locals alike. The following are our favorites.

Black and White Night. The signature event of the Downtown Hilo Improvement Association, this lovely annual street party takes place in and around downtown Hilo. Stores stay open late, sidewalks are dotted with live jazz bands, there are crafts and cultural info as well as a treasure hunt, and everyone dresses in black and white, some in shorts and tees and others in gowns and tuxes. (The town does the same thing for First Fridays of the month, only without the black and white.) ✉ *329 Kamehameha Ave., Hilo* ☎ *808/935–8850.*

King Kamehameha Day Celebration Parade. Each June on the Saturday following King Kamehameha Day, at least 100 regal riders on horseback parade through historic Kailua Village, showing off the colorful flora and aloha spirit of Hawaii. The traditional royal pau riders include a queen and princesses representing the major Hawaiian Islands. A cultural festival with live music always follows. ✉ *Historic Kailua Village, Alii Dr., Kailua-Kona* ☎ *808/322–9944* ⊕ *www.konaparade.org.*

Kona Brewers Festival. At this lively annual celebration in early March by Kailua Pier, 70 types of ales and lagers by Hawaii and mainland craft brewers are showcased, along with culinary contributions by Hawaii Island chefs. There's also live "Blues & Brews" music, an art auction, a home brewers competition, fashion shows, a fun run, and a golf tournament. The multiday event is a community fundraiser and local favorite, but you must be 21 to attend. ■TIP➔ **Get tickets early online as this event always sells out.** ✉ *Courtyard King Kamehameha's Kona Beach Hotel, 75-5660 Palani Rd., Kailua-Kona* ☎ *808/331–3033* ⊕ *www. konabrewersfestival.com.*

Kona Coffee Cultural Festival. Held over 10 days in early November, on the Kona side, the longest-running food festival in Hawaii celebrates world-renowned Kona coffee. The highly anticipated festival includes coffee contests, serious cupping competitions, a lecture series, label contests, farm tours, and a colorful community parade featuring the newly crowned Miss Kona Coffee. During the Holualoa Village Coffee and Art Stroll, you can meet artists and sample estate coffees. ✉ *Kailua-Kona* ☎ *808/323–2006* ⊕ *www.konacoffeefest.com.*

Kona Surf Film Festival. Attendees of this fun festival gather once a year to celebrate surfing as showcased by a variety of independent filmmakers. Proceeds benefit local surfing and community organizations. ✉ *Kailua-Kona* ☎ *808/936–0089* ⊕ *konasurffilmfestival.org.*

6

KWXX Hoolaulea. For more than two decades, a local radio station has sponsored the largest free concert on the island. This famous *hoolaulea* (party) takes place mid-September in downtown Hilo, attracting a bounty of Big Island musical talent featuring Hawaiian, reggae, and Island music styles. Some big names play here on four different stages, and there is dancing in the streets of Bayfront, rain or shine. ⊠ *257 Kamehameha Ave., Hilo* ☎ *808/935–5461* ⊕ *www.kwxx.com.*

Fodor'sChoice   **Merrie Monarch Festival.** The mother of all Hawaii festivals, the world-
★   class Merrie Monarch celebrates all things hula for one fantastic week every April in Hilo with competitions, activities, parades, and more. The esteemed event honors the legacy of King David Kalakaua, the man responsible for reviving fading Hawaiian cultural traditions including hula. The three-day hula competition is staged at the Edith Kanakaole Multi-Purpose Stadium during the first week following Easter Sunday. Hula *halau* (studios) worldwide come to perform both *kahiko* (ancient) and *auana* (modern) dance styles, both solo and in groups. ■TIP➔ You should reserve accommodations and rental cars up to a year in advance. Ticket requests must be mailed and postmarked after December 26 of the preceding year. ⊠ *Edith Kanakaole Multi-Purpose Stadium, 350 Kalanikoa St., Hilo* ☎ *808/935–9168* ⊕ *www.merriemonarch.com.*

Moku O Keawe International Hula Festival. This multiday hula extravaganza, held each November on the big stage at Waikoloa Bowl, features halau from Hawaii and Japan competing under the stars. During the day, workshops and cultural and crafts fairs take place at the Waikoloa Beach Marriott Resort. ⊠ *Waikoloa Bowl, 69-150 Waikoloa Beach Dr., Waikoloa* ⊕ *www.mokif.com.*

FILM

HILO

Fodor'sChoice   **Palace Theater.** After decades of neglect, this historic theater dating from
★   the silent-movie era (1925) survived Hilo's many tsunamis and has been beautifully restored through community support. Today, it showcases everything from film festivals and old movies to musical productions and holiday concerts. There's even $10 jazz nights in the lobby and performances by big-name artists. It's open during the day, so you can have a peek through the curtains at the lovely vintage details and feel like you stepped back in time. ⊠ *38 Haili St., Hilo* ☎ *808/934–7010* ⊕ *www.hilopalace.com.*

SHOPS AND SPAS

Updated
by Karen
Anderson

Residents like to complain that there isn't a lot of great shopping on the Big Island, but unless you're searching for winter coats, you can find plenty to deplete your pocketbook.

Dozens of shops in Kailua-Kona offer a range of souvenirs from far-flung corners of the globe and plenty of local coffee and foodstuffs to take home to everyone you left behind. Housewares and artworks made from local materials (lauhala, coconut, koa, and milo wood) fill the shelves of small boutiques and galleries throughout the island. Upscale shops in the resorts along the Kohala Coast carry high-end clothing and accessories, as do a few boutiques scattered around the island. Galleries and gift shops, many showcasing the work of local artists, fill historical buildings in Waimea, Kainaliu, Holualoa, and Hawi. Hotel shops generally offer the most attractive and original resort wear, but, as with everything else at resorts, the prices run higher than elsewhere on the island.

High prices are entirely too common at the island's resort spas, but a handful of unique experiences are worth every penny. Beyond the resorts, the Big Island is also home to independent massage therapists and day spas that offer similar treatments for lower prices, albeit usually in a slightly less luxurious atmosphere. In addition to the obvious relaxation benefits of any spa trip, the Big Island's spas have done a fantastic job incorporating local traditions and ingredients into their menus. Massage artists work with coconut or *kukui* (candlenut) oil, hot-stone massages are conducted with volcanic stones, and ancient healing techniques such as *lomilomi*—a massage technique with firm, constant movement—are staples at every island spa.

SHOPS

In general, stores on the Big Island open at 9 or 10 am and close by 6 pm. Hilo's Prince Kuhio Plaza stays open until 8 pm on weekdays and 9 pm on Friday and Saturday. In Historic Kona Village, most shopping plazas geared to tourists remain open until 9 pm. Grocery stores such as KTA Superstore are open until 11 pm.

KAILUA-KONA

SHOPPING CENTERS

Coconut Grove Marketplace. This meandering oceanfront marketplace includes gift shops, cafés, restaurants (Outback Steakhouse, Humpy's Big Island Alehouse, Bongo Ben's, Lava Java, Foster's Kitchen, Fumi's Kitchen), sports bars, sushi, boutiques, a frozen-yogurt shop, Jack's Diving Locker, and several art galleries. At night, locals gather to watch outdoor sand volleyball games held in the courtyard or grab a beer and enjoy live music. This place is always hopping, and it has the biggest free parking lot in downtown Kailua-Kona. ⊠ *75-5795–75-5825 Alii Dr., Kailua-Kona.*

Crossroads Shopping Center. This in-town shopping center includes a Safeway with an excellent deli section for on-the-go snacks, as well as a Walmart, where visitors can find affordable Hawaiian souvenirs, including discounted Kona coffee and macadamia nuts. For a quick meal, there's a Denny's, a Subway, and a Domino's, as well as a small sushi restaurant. Crystal Hair & Salon offers affordable hair and nail services, and accepts walk-ins. ⊠ *75-1000 Henry St., Kailua-Kona* ☎ *808/329–4822.*

Kaloko Light Industrial Park. This large retail complex near the airport includes Costco, the best place to stock up on food if you're staying at a vacation rental. Kona Wine Market and the Spoon Shop feature gourmet finds, and Mrs. Barry's Kona Cookies sells beautifully packaged, delicious "souvenirs." ⊠ *Off Hwy. 19 and Hina Lani St. , near Kona airport, Kailua-Kona.*

Keauhou Shopping Center. About 5 miles south of Kailua Village, this neighborhood shopping center includes KTA Superstore, Longs Drugs, Kona Stories bookstore, and a multiplex movie theater. Kenichi Pacific, an upscale sushi restaurant, and Peaberry & Galette, a café that serves excellent crepes, are favorite eateries joined by Bianelli's Pizza and Sam Choy's Kai Lanai, which is perched above the center. You can also grab a quick bite at Los Habaneros, Subway, or L&L Hawaiian Barbecue. ⊠ *78-6831 Alii Dr., Kailua-Kona* ☎ *808/322–3000* ⊕ *www.keauhoushoppingcenter.com.*

King Kamehameha Mall. Around the corner from Courtyard King Kamehameha's Kona Beach Hotel, this tiny neighborhood center includes Bangkok House Thai Restaurant, Ocean Seafood Chinese Restaurant, and a karaoke bar. Quilt Passions Quilt and Needlework Shop and the Music Exchange music store are also located in the center. ⊠ *75-5626 Kuakini Hwy., Kailua-Kona.*

Kona Commons. This downtown center features a Ross Dress for Less (for suitcases, shoes, swimsuits, and aloha wear), or Hawaiian Island Creations (for a great selection of surf gear, clothing, and accessories). Food and drink options include fast-food standbys like Dairy Queen, Subway, and Panda Express; as well as Ultimate Burger for local beef and delicious homemade fries, and Genki Sushi, where the goods are delivered via conveyer belt. ■TIP➔ **Target has fresh-flower leis for a fraction of the cost that local florists charge.** ⊠ *75-5450 Makala Blvd., Kailua-Kona* ⊕ *www.konacommons.com.*

Kona Inn Shopping Village. Originally a hotel, the Kona Inn was built in 1928 to woo a new wave of wealthy travelers. As newer condos and resorts opened along the Kona and Kohala coasts, it was transformed into a low-rise, outdoor shopping village with dozens of clothing boutiques, art galleries, gift shops, and island-style eateries. Broad lawns with coconut trees on the ocean side provide a lovely setting for an afternoon picnic. The open-air Kona Inn Restaurant is a local favorite for sunset mai tais. ⊠ *75-5744 Alii Dr., Kailua-Kona.*

Kona Marketplace. On the *mauka* (mountain) side of Alii Drive, near Hulihee Palace, this small retail enclave in Historic Kailua Village includes galleries, T-shirt/souvenir shops, a tattoo parlor, phone repair, a karaoke bar, Holy Donuts donut shop, Frenchman's Cafe, and Sam's Hideaway bar. Local favorite Hayashi's You Make the Roll offers shaded outdoor seating and affordable sushi to go. ⊠ *75-5744 Alii Dr., Kailua-Kona.*

Makalapua Center. On the *mauka* (moutain) side of the highway above Kona's Old Industrial area, this shopping center attracts visitors with great souvenir bargains at Kmart as well as island-influenced clothing, jewelry, and housewares at the upscale Macy's, the best place in Kona to find aloha shirts. The center also has one of the island's largest movie theaters. ⊠ *Kamakaeha Ave., at Hwy. 19, Kailua-Kona.*

ARTS AND CRAFTS

Fodor's Choice ★ **Hula Lamps of Hawaii.** Located near Costco in the Kaloko Light Industrial complex, this one-of-a-kind shop features the bronze creations of artist Charles Moore. Inspired by the vintage hula-girl lamps of the 1930s, Moore creates art pieces sought by visitors and residents alike. Mix and match with an array of hand-painted lamp shades. ⊠ *73-5613 Olowalu St., Suite 2, Kailua-Kona* ✛ *Near Costco on upper road* ☎ *808/326–9583* ⊕ *www.hulalamps.com* ☽ *Closed Sat.–Sun.*

Just Ukes. As the name suggests, this place is all about ukeleles—from music books to T-shirts to accessories like cases and bags. The independently owned shop carries a variety of ukuleles ranging from low-priced starter instruments to high-end models made of koa and mango. ⊠ *Kona Inn Shopping Village, 75-5744 Alii Dr., Kailua-Kona* ☎ *808/769–5101* ⊕ *justukes.com.*

BOOKSTORES

Kona Stories. With more than 10,000 titles, this bookstore also sells Hawaiiana, children's toys, and whimsical gifts. Special events, such as readings and book signings, are held weekly. ⊠ *Keauhou Shopping Center, 78-6831 Alii Dr., Kailua-Kona* ✛ *Located in Keahou Shopping Center near KTA* ☎ *808/324–0350* ⊕ *www.konastories.com.*

CLOTHING AND SHOES

Honolua Surf Company. Surfer chic, compliments of Roxy, Billabong, and the like, is for sale here for both men and women. This is a great place to shop for a bikini or board shorts, or to pick up a cool, retro-design T-shirt or Hawaii-style embroidered sweat jacket. Another location at the Waikoloa Kings' Shops focuses on *wahine* (women's) apparel. ⊠ *Kona Inn Shopping Village, 75-5744 Alii Dr., Kailua-Kona* ☎ *808/329–1001* ⊕ *www.honoluasurf.com.*

Mermaids Swimwear. Local residents know that Mermaids is the best place in Kona to buy fashion-forward ladies' swimwear, sandals, hats, and other stylish beach accessories. The owner's husband, Tony, is a famous surfboard maker whose World Core surf shop is just around the corner. ⌧ *Kona Inn Shopping Village, 75-5744 Alii Dr., Kailua-Kona* ☎ *808/329–6677.*

Paradise Found. Carrying contemporary silk and rayon clothing for adult women, this reputable shop is in the upcountry town of Kainaliu, near Aloha Theatre, but there's also a branch at Keauhou Shopping Center. ⌧ *79-7406 Mamalahoa Hwy., Kainaliu* ☎ *808/322–2111 Kainaliu location, 808/324–1177 Keauhou location.*

FOOD AND WINE

Kailua Candy Company. This chocolate company has been satisfying sweet tooths for more than three decades with decadent desserts and sinful bites of chocolate heaven. Many truffles and candies incorporate local ingredients (passion-fruit truffles and chocolate-covered mango—yum). Cheesecakes and mousse cakes melt in your mouth. Of course, tasting is part of the fun. ■TIP➔ Through a glass wall you can watch the chocolate artists at work Monday through Saturday from 9 to 5. ⌧ *Kaloko Light Industrial Park, 73-5612 Kauhola St., Kailua-Kona* ☎ *808/329–2522* ⊕ *www.kailuacandy.com* ☺ *Closed Sun.*

Fodor's Choice ★ **Keauhou Store.** This historical roadside store has been transformed into a combination convenience store, bakeshop, lunch stop, gift shop, and museum. When Kurt and Thea Brown purchased the property in 2010, they discovered a treasure trove of untouched inventory dating to the 1920s. These artifacts are on display, along with such gift items as koa bowls, cool retro T-shirts, and Kona coffee grown on-site. Stop by for fresh produce, beverages, spirits, ice cream, Thea's yummy fresh-baked cookies, or a burger or sandwich enjoyed on the outdoor lanai overlooking the coffee trees. ⌧ *78-7010 Mamalahoa Hwy., Holualoa* ☎ *808/322–5203* ⊕ *www.keauhoustore.com* ☺ *Closed Sun.*

Kona Coffee & Tea Company. This family-owned coffee company operates all of their businesses—growing, roasting, brewing, and serving their authentic Kona coffee—within a 10-mile radius of the farm. Stop by the café/outlet on Wednesdays (starting at 8:30 am) for a free curated tasting with the baristas, and shop for other Hawaiian-made treats, from honey and jams to chocolate-covered coffee beans. There's also free Wi-Fi. ■TIP➔ Tours of the farm are available. ⌧ *Kona Coast Shopping Center, 74-5588 Palani Rd, Kailua-Kona* ☎ *808/329–6577* ⊕ *www.konacoffeeandtea.com.*

Kona Wine Market. Near Costco, this longtime local wineshop carries both local and imported varietals (with more than 600 high-end wines), specialty liquors, 150 craft beers, gourmet foods, and even cigars. As a bonus, the market delivers wine and gift baskets to hotels and homes. ⌧ *73-5613 Olowalu St., Kailua-Kona* ☎ *808/329–9400* ⊕ *www.konawinemarket.com.*

Mrs. Barry's Kona Cookies. For 30 years, Mrs. Barry and her family have been serving yummy home-baked cookies, including macadamia nut, white chocolate–macadamia nut, oatmeal raisin, and coffee crunch.

Packaged in beautiful gift boxes or bags, the cookies make excellent gifts for family back home. Stop by on your way to Costco or the airport and pick up a bag or two or three. Ah heck, just ask Mrs. Barry to ship your stash instead. ✉ *73-5563 Maiau St., Kailua-Kona ⊹ Below Costco in the New Industrial.* ☎ *808/329–6055* ⊕ *www.konacookies.com.*

Fodor'sChoice
★
The Spoon Shop. Williams-Sonoma has nothing on this excellent gourmet kitchenware store that brims with every manner of accoutrement for the avid cook. There's a great selection of gourmet seasonings, olive oils, dressings, and condiments, and, if you're planning a party or reception during your stay in paradise, the Spoon Shop has items for every occasion. Cooking classes with guest chefs take place weekly in the store's high-end demo kitchen. ✉ *73-4976 Kamanu St. , #105, Kailua-Kona ⊹ Near Home Depot in New Industrial area* ☎ *808/887-7666* ⊕ *www. thespoonshopkona.com* ☾ *Closed Sun.*

Fodor'sChoice
★
Westside Wines. Tucked away in a small downtown Kona retail center below Longs, this nifty gourmet wine and spirits shop offers restaurant-quality "wine list" wines at affordable prices. It's also the place to find large-format craft beers, French Champagne, single-malt Scotches, organic vodka, small-batch bourbon, rye whiskey, fresh bread, and artisan cheese from around the world. George Clooney's Casamigos tequila is the store's house tequila. A certified wine specialist, proprietor Alex Thropp was one of the state's top wholesale wine reps for decades. Wine tastings take place Friday and Saturday afternoons from 3 to 6. ✉ *75-5660 Kopiko St. #4, Kailua-Kona ⊹ Below Longs Drugs in Lanihau Center* ☎ *808/329–1777.*

GALLERIES

Kona Art Gallery. Gary and Elizabeth Theriault showcase a variety of local art here, including Gary's Big Island life photos and Elizabeth's hand-painted drums and rattles. The gallery owners also feature work from other artists, including Hawaiian *ipus* (gourds used as instruments in hula dancing), exotic wood items, paper sculptures, quilts, and jewelry. ✉ *76-5938 Mamalahoa Hwy., Holualoa* ☎ *808/322–5125* ☾ *Closed Sun.–Mon.*

MARKETS

Alii Gardens Marketplace. This mellow, parklike market, open Tuesday through Sunday 10 to 5, features outdoor stalls offering tropical flowers, produce, soaps, kettle corn, coffee, coconut postcards, cookies, jewelry, koa wood, clothing, antiques and collectibles, handmade leis, silk flowers, and kitschy crafts. The homemade barbecue is a real hit. A food kiosk also serves shave ice, fish tacos, coconut water, fresh-fruit smoothies, and hamburgers. You can also book spearfishing excursions here. Free parking and Wi-Fi are available. ✉ *75-6129 Alii Dr., Kailua-Kona ⊹ 1½ miles south of Kona Inn Shopping Village* ⊕ *alii-gardens-marketplace.business.site* ☾ *Closed Sun.*

Keauhou Farmers Market. Held once a week in the parking lot at Keauhou Shopping Center, this cheerful market is the place to go on Saturday morning for live music, local produce (much of it organic), goat cheese, honey, island-raised meat, flowers, macadamia nuts, fresh-baked pastries,

Kona coffee, and plenty of local color. ✉ *Keauhou Shopping Center, 78-6831 Alii Dr., Kailua-Kona* ⊕ *www.keauhoufarmersmarket.com.*

Kona Inn Farmers' Market. An awesome florist creates custom arrangements while you wait at this touristy farmers' market near the ocean. There are more than 40 vendors with lots of crafts for sale as well as some of the best prices on fresh produce and orchids in Kona. The market is held in a parking lot at the corner of Hualalai Road and Alii Drive, Wednesday to Sunday 7 to 4. ✉ *75-7544 Alii Dr., Kailua-Kona.*

THE KONA COAST

ARTS AND CRAFTS

Kimura's Lauhala Shop. Originally a general store built in 1914, this shop features handmade products crafted by local lauhala weavers. Among the offerings are hats, baskets, containers, and mats, many of which are woven by the proprietors. Owner Alfreida Kimura-Fujita was born in the house behind the shop, and her daughter Renee is also an accomplished weaver. ✉ *77-996 Hualalai Rd., Holualoa* ☎ *808/324–0053* ⊕ *www.holualoahawaii.com/member_sites/kimura.html.*

GALLERIES

Cliff Johns Gallery. Under new ownership, this fine-art gallery still retains the name of local woodworker Cliff Johns, who had a knack for sourcing unique, handcrafted finds by Big Island artists. The gallery features wood sculptures, paintings, carvings, and other crafts different from the standard fare, not to mention jewelry and other finely crafted carvings and *netsuke* (small sculptures). ✉ *Mango Court, 76-7460 Mamalahoa Hwy., Kealakekua* ✛ *Next to Annie's Burgers* ☎ *808/322–0044.*

Holualoa Gallery. One of several excellent galleries along the narrow highway in this historic artists' village, this shop carries stunning contemporary *raku* pottery, original paintings by co-owner Mary Lovein and other local artists, and other collectibles, including gallery co-owner Matt Lovein's famous Wish Keepers ceramic sculptures. ✉ *76-5921 Mamalahoa Hwy., Holualoa* ☎ *808/322–8484* ⊕ *www.lovein.com.*

MARKET

Pure Kona Green Market. A favorite in Captain Cook, this Sunday farmers' market offers great hot breakfast and lunch items, produce from local farms, and artists selling their work. ✉ *Amy B.H. Greenwell Ethnobotanical Garden, 82-6160 Mamalahoa Hwy., Captain Cook.*

THE KOHALA COAST

SHOPPING CENTERS

Kawaihae Harbor Shopping Center. This almost-oceanfront shopping plaza houses the exquisite Harbor Gallery, which represents more than 200 Big Island artists. Stroll inside before or after your meal at the acclaimed Café Pesto, Kohala Burger and Taco, or Kawaihae Kitchen. Try the Big Island–made ice cream and shave ice (the best in North Hawaii) at local favorite Anuenue. Also here are Mountain Gold Jewelers and Kohala Divers. ✉ *61-3665 Akoni Pule Hwy. 270, Kawaihae.*

7

Kings' Shops at Waikoloa Beach Resort. Stores here include Martin & MacArthur, featuring koa furniture and accessories, and Tori Richard, which offers upscale resort wear, as well as a small Macy's and high-end chains Coach, Tiffany, L'Occitane, and Michael Kors. Gourmet offerings include Roy's Waikoloa Bar & Grill, A-Bay's Island Grill, Island Fish and Chips, and the Koa Table by Chef Ippy. Stock your hotel fridge with fresh local produce from the Kings' Shops Farmers Market, held Wednesday 8:30 to 2:30. ⊠ *Waikoloa Beach Resort, 250 Waikoloa Beach Dr., Waikoloa* ☎ *808/339–7145* ⊕ *www.kingsshops.com.*

Queens' MarketPlace. The largest shopping complex on the Kohala Coast, Queens' MarketPlace houses fashionable clothing stores, jewelry boutiques, galleries, gift shops, and restaurants, including Sansei Seafood, Steakhouse and Sushi Bar; Daylight Mind; and Romano's Macaroni Grill. Island Gourmet Markets and Starbucks are also here, as is an affordable food court. Waikoloa Luxury Cinemas offers the ultimate movie experience and includes a restaurant called Bistro at the Cinemas. ⊠ *Waikoloa Beach Resort, 201 Waikoloa Beach Dr., Waikoloa* ☎ *808/886–8822* ⊕ *www.queensmarketplace.net.*

The Shops at Mauna Lani. The best part about this complex is its roster of restaurants, which includes coffee, smoothies, and sandwich shops, Tommy Bahama Tropical Restaurant, Ruth's Chris Steakhouse, Under the Bodhi Tree café for gourmet vegetarian options, and Monstera for noodles and sushi. You can find tropical apparel at Jams World, high-end housewares at Oasis Lifestyle, and original art at a number of galleries. Kids love the "adventure ride" theater, boasting the only "4-D" screens in Hawaii. ⊠ *68-1330 Mauna Lani Dr., Waimea (Hawaii County)* ☎ *808/885–9501* ⊕ *www.shopsatmaunalani.com.*

ARTS AND CRAFTS

Elements Jewelry & Fine Crafts. The beautiful little shop carries lots of original handmade jewelry made by local artists as well as carefully chosen gifts, including unusual ceramics, paintings, prints, glass items, baskets, fabrics, bags, and toys. ⊠ *55-3413 Akoni Pule Hwy., next to Bamboo Restaurant, Hawi* ☎ *808/889–0760* ⊕ *www.elementsjewelryandcrafts.com.*

Hawaiian Quilt Collection. The Hawaiian quilt is a work of art that is prized and passed down through generations. At this store, you'll find everything from hand-quilted purses and bags to wall hangings and blankets. You can even get a take-home kit and sew your very own Hawaiian quilt. ⊠ *Queens' MarketPlace, 69-201 Waikoloa Beach Dr., #305, Waikoloa* ☎ *808/886–0494* ⊕ *www.hawaiian-quilts.com.*

Island Pearls by Maui Divers. Among the fine jewelry at this boutique is a wide selection of high-end pearl jewelry, including Tahitian black pearls, South Sea white and golden pearls, and chocolate Tahitian pearls. Also here are freshwater pearls in the shell, black coral (the Hawaii state gemstone), and diamonds. Prices are high but so is the quality. ⊠ *Queens' MarketPlace, 69-201 Waikoloa Beach Dr. , Space J11, Waikoloa* ☎ *808/886–4817* ⊕ *www.mauidivers.com.*

CLOTHING AND SHOES

As Hawi Turns. This landmark North Kohala shop, housed in the 1932 Toyama Building, brings sophisticated offerings in resort wear with items made of hand-painted silk in tropical designs by local artists. There are plentiful vintage treasures, jewelry, gifts, hats, bags, and toys, plus handmade ukuleles by local luthier David Gomes. ⊠ *55-3412 Akoni Pule Hwy., Hawi* ☎ *808/889–5023.*

Blue Ginger. The Waikoloa branch of this fashion veteran offers really sweet matching aloha outfits for the entire family. There are also handbags, shoes, robes, jewelry, and lotions. ⊠ *Queens' MarketPlace, 69-201 Waikoloa Beach Dr., Waikoloa* ☎ *808/886–0022* ⊕ *www.blueginger.com.*

Persimmon. This darling little boutique is stocked with trendy women's clothing from lines such as Michael Stars, Free People, Blu Moon, and Sky, plus local favorite Acacia swimwear. Gift items include stationery and cards, regional artwork, locally designed jewelry, and island-themed bath and body products. ⊠ *Queens' MarketPlace, 69-201 Waikoloa Beach Dr., #910, Waikoloa* ☎ *808/886–0303* ⊕ *www.persimmonboutique.com.*

Reyn's. Reyn Spooner's dressy clothing has been a tradition in Hawaii since 1959 and remains popular among locals and visitors alike. The store offers aloha shirts for both men and boys, men's shorts, and some dresses for women and girls. Prices may be high, but you're buying the best. ⊠ *Queens' MarketPlace, 69-201 Waikoloa Beach Dr., Waikoloa* ☎ *808/886–1162* ⊕ *www.reynspooner.com.*

GALLERIES

Ackerman Fine Art Gallery. This multiple-gallery/café is truly a family affair. Local artist Gary Ackerman's wife, Yesan, runs Ackerman Fine Art Gallery, featuring Gary's original oil paintings, fused glass art, and glass sculpture, plus works from other local artists. Down the street, Gary's daughter, Alyssa, and her husband, Ronnie, run Ackerman Gift Gallery, which showcases fine art, photography, and gifts, and their own King's View Cafe, located across from the historic King Kamehameha statue. ⊠ *54-3878 Akoni Pule Hwy., Kapaau* ☎ *808/889–5138 Ackerman Fine Art Gallery* ⊕ *www.ackermangalleries.com.*

Bamboo Restaurant & Gallery. Inside Bamboo Restaurant, this gallery seduces with elegant koa-wood furniture and an array of gift items, such as boxes, jewelry, and even aloha shirts. ⊠ *Bamboo Restaurant, 55-3415 Akoni Pule Hwy., Hawi* ☎ *808/889–1441* ⊕ *www.bamboorestaurant.info.*

Harbor Gallery. Since 1990, this gallery has been enticing visitors with a vast collection of paintings and sculptures by more than 200 Big Island artists. There are also antique maps and prints, wooden bowls, paddles, koa furniture, jewelry, and glasswork. The shop hosts two annual wood shows. ⊠ *Kawaihae Harbor Shopping Center, 61-3665 Akoni Pule Hwy., Kawaihae* ☎ *808/882–1510* ⊕ *www.harborgallery.biz.*

Rankin Gallery. Watercolorist and oil painter Patrick Louis Rankin showcases his own work at his shop in a restored plantation store next to the bright-green Chinese community and social hall, on the way to Pololu Valley. The building sits right at a curve in the road, in the Palawa *ahupuaa* (land division) past Kapaau. ✉ *53-4380 Akoni Pule Hwy., Kapaau* 🕿 *808/889–6849* ⊕ *www.patricklouisrankin.net.*

WAIMEA

SHOPPING CENTERS

Parker Ranch Center. With a snazzy ranch-style motif, this shopping hub includes a supermarket, some great local eateries (Village Burger, Noodle Club, and Lilikoi Café), a coffee shop, natural foods store, galleries, and clothing boutiques. The Parker Ranch Store and Parker Ranch Visitors Center and Museum are also here. ✉ *67-1185 Mamalahoa Hwy., Waimea (Hawaii County)* ⊕ *www.parkerranchcenterads.com.*

Parker Square. Although the Gallery of Great Things is this center's star attraction, it's also worth looking in at the Waimea General Store; Sweet Wind, for books, chimes, and beads; and Sassafras, which sells locally crafted Hawaiian jewelry. Waimea Coffee Company satisfies with salads, sandwiches, and Kona coffee. ✉ *65-1279 Kawaihae Rd., Waimea (Hawaii County).*

FOOD AND WINE

Fodor's Choice ★ **Kamuela Liquor Store.** From the outside it doesn't look like much, but this store sells the best selection of premium spirits, wines, and gourmet items on the island. Alvin, the owner, is a collector of fine wines, as evidenced by his multiple cellars. Wine-and-cheese tastings take place Friday afternoon from 3 to 6 and Saturday at noon—the store offers an extensive selection of artisanal cheeses from around the world. Favorites like duck mousse round out the inventory. ✉ *64-1010 Mamalahoa Hwy., Waimea (Hawaii County)* 🕿 *808/885–4674.*

Fodor's Choice ★ **Waimea General Store.** Since 1970, this Waimea landmark at Parker Square has been a favorite of locals and visitors alike. Although specialty kitchenware takes center stage, the shop brims with local gourmet items, books, kimonos, and Hawaiian gifts and souvenirs. ✉ *Parker Square, 65-1279 Kawaihae Rd., Suite 112, Waimea (Hawaii County)* 🕿 *808/885–4479* ⊕ *www.waimeageneralstore.com.*

GALLERIES

Fodor's Choice ★ **Gallery of Great Things.** You might lose yourself exploring the trove of fine art and collectibles in every price range at this gallery, which represents hundreds of local artists and has a low-key, unhurried atmosphere. The "things" include hand-stitched quilts, ceramic sculptures, vintage kimonos, original paintings, koa-wood bowls and furniture, etched glassware, Niihau shell lei, and feather art by local artist Beth McCormick. ✉ *Parker Square, 65-1279 Kawaihae Rd., Waimea (Hawaii County)* 🕿 *808/885–7706* ⊕ *www.galleryofgreatthingshawaii.com.*

Wishard Gallery. A Big Island–born artist whose verdant landscapes and *paniolo* (cowboy)-themed paintings have become iconic throughout the Islands, Harry Wishard showcases his original oils at this Parker Ranch Center gallery, along with works by other renowned local artists like Kathy Long, Edward Kayton, and Lynn Capell. ✉ *Parker Ranch Center, 67-1185 Mamalahoa Hwy., D103, Waimea (Hawaii County)* 🕿 *808/887–2278* ⊕ *www.wishardgallery.com.*

THE HAMAKUA COAST

ARTS AND CRAFTS

Glass from the Past. Near Akaka Falls, this is a fun place to shop for a quirky gift or just to poke around. The store is chock-full of old Hawaiian bottles, antiques, vintage clothing, Japanese collectibles, and interesting ephemera. There's often even a "free" table out front to add to the discovery. ⊠ *28-1672 Old Mamalahoa Hwy., Honomu* ☎ *808/963–6449.*

GALLERIES

Waipio Valley Artworks. In this quaint gallery in a vintage home, you can find finely crafted wooden bowls, koa furniture, paintings, and jewelry—all made by local artists. There's also a great little café where you can pick up a sandwich or ice cream before descending into Waipio Valley. ⊠ *485416 Kukuihaele Rd., Kukuihaele* ☎ *808/775–0958* ⊕ *www.waipiovalleyartworks.com.*

Woodshop Gallery. Run by local artists Peter and Jeanette McLaren, this Honomu gallery showcases their woodwork and photography collections along with beautiful ceramics, photography, glass, and paintings from other Big Island artists. The McLarens also serve up plate lunches, shave ice, homemade ice cream, and espresso to hungry tourists in the adjoining café. The historical building still has a working soda fountain dating from 1935. ⊠ *28-1690 Old Government Rd., Honomu* ✛ *2 miles from Akaka Falls, 13 miles north of Hilo* ☎ *808/963–6363* ⊕ *www.woodshopgallery.com.*

HILO

SHOPPING CENTERS

Prince Kuhio Plaza. The Big Island's most comprehensive mall has indoor shopping, entertainment (a multiplex), and dining, including KFC, Hot Dog on a Stick, Cinnabon, Genki Sushi, the island's only IHOP, and Maui Tacos. The kids might like the arcade (near the food court), while you enjoy the stores, anchored by Macy's and Sears. ⊠ *111 E. Puainako St., Hilo* ☎ *808/959–3555* ⊕ *www.princekuhioplaza.com.*

ARTS AND CRAFTS

Most Irresistible Shop in Hilo. This place lives up to its name by stocking unique gifts from around the Pacific, be it pure Hawaiian ohia lehua honey, ka'u coffee, aloha wear, or tinkling wind chimes. ⊠ *256 Kamehameha Ave., Hilo* ☎ *808/935–9644.*

BOOKSTORES

Fodor's Choice ★ **Basically Books.** Boasting a new location, this legendary shop stocks one of Hawaii's largest selections of maps, including topographical and relief maps, and Hilo's largest selection of Hawaiian music. Of course, it also has a wealth of books about Hawaii, including great choices for children. If you're in need of an umbrella on a rainy Hilo day, this bookstore has plenty of them. Open seven days a week. ⊠ *1672 Kamehameha Ave., Hilo* ✛ *Near Ken's House of Pancakes* ☎ *808/961–0144,* ⊕ *www.basicallybooks.com.*

CLOTHING AND SHOES

Sig Zane Designs. This acclaimed boutique sells distinctive island wearables with bold colors and motifs designed by the legendary Sig Zane, known for his artwork honoring native flora and fauna. All apparel is handcrafted in Hawaii, and is often worn by local celebrities and businesspeople. ✉ *122 Kamehameha Ave., Hilo* ☎ *808/935–7077* ⊕ *www.sigzane.com.*

FOOD

Fodor'sChoice
★

Big Island Candies. A local legend in the cookie- and chocolate-making business, Big Island Candies is a must-see for connoisseurs of fine chocolates. The packaging is first-rate, which makes these world-class confections the ideal gift or souvenir. Enjoy a free cookie sample and a cup of Kona coffee as you watch through a window as sweets are being made. The store has a long list of interesting and tasty products, but it is best known for its chocolate-dipped shortbread cookies. ✉ *585 Hinano St., Hilo* ☎ *808/935–8890* ⊕ *www.bigislandcandies.com.*

Hilo Coffee Mill. In addition to a fantastic coffee-farm tour, the Hilo Coffee Mill sells coffee from a variety of local producers, along with locally made baked goods, candies, artwork, and gifts. Free coffee samples are offered. The mill is closed Sunday and hosts a farmers' market Saturday 8 to 1. ✉ *17-995 Volcano Rd., Mountain View* ⊹ *Between mile markers 12 and 13* ☎ *808/968–1333* ⊕ *www.hilocoffeemill.com* ⊗ *Closed Sun. and Mon.*

Fodor'sChoice
★

Sugar Coast Candy. Located on the bayfront in downtown Hilo, this beautifully decorated candy boutique, owned by interior decorator Carolyn Arashiro, is a blast from the past, featuring an amazing array of nostalgic candies, artisan chocolates, and wooden barrels overflowing with saltwater taffy and other delights. ✉ *274 Kamehameha Ave., Hilo* ☎ *808/935–6960.*

Two Ladies Kitchen. This hole-in-the-wall confections shop has made a name for itself thanks to its pillowy *mochi* (Japanese rice pounded into a sticky paste and molded into shapes). The proprietors are best known for their huge ripe strawberries wrapped in a white mochi covering, which won't last as long as a box of chocolates—most mochi items are good for only two or three days. To guarantee you get your fill, call and place your order ahead of time. ✉ *274 Kilauea Ave., Hilo* ☎ *808/961–4766* ⊗ *Closed Sun. and Mon.*

HOME DECOR

Dragon Mama. Step into this hip downtown Hilo spot to find authentic Japanese fabrics, futons, and gifts along with an elegant selection of clothing, sleepwear, and tea-service accoutrements. Handmade comforters, pillows, and futon pads are sewn of natural fibers on-site. ✉ *266 Kamehameha Ave., Hilo* ☎ *808/934–9081* ⊕ *www.dragonmama.com.*

HAWAII VOLCANOES NATIONAL PARK AND VICINITY

ARTS AND CRAFTS

Fodor'sChoice
★
Kilauea Kreations. Beautiful hand-stitched Hawaiian quilts grace the walls here, quilting kits and books abound, and the vast inventory of tropical fabrics is amazing. The friendly proprietors also offer fine art, photography, cards, and cool souvenirs you won't find anywhere else. A second location, Kilauea Kreations II, recently opened in downtown Hilo, features a larger store and collection of fabrics as well as classroom space. ⊠ *19-3972 Volcano Rd., Volcano* ✛ *Next to Lava Rock Cafe* ☎ *808/967–8090, 808/961–1100 Kilauea Kreations II* ⊕ *www.kilaueakreations.com* ☾ *Closed Sun.*

2400 Fahrenheit. At the end of Old Volcano Road near Volcano Village, this small gallery and studio has hand-blown glass inspired by the eruption of Kilauea and the colors of the tropics. You can see the artists in action Thursday through Monday from 10 to 4, and Tuesday and Wednesday by appointment. ⊠ *Old Volcano Rd., off Hwy. 11, Volcano* ✛ *Between mile markers 23 and 24* ☎ *808/985–8667* ⊕ *www.2400f.com.*

SPAS

Most of the full-service spas on the Big Island are at the resorts. With the exception of the Four Seasons Spa at Hualalai, these spas are open to anyone. In fact, many of the hotels outsource spa management, and there is no price difference for guests and nonguests, although guests can receive in-room services.

KAILUA-KONA

A Ala Hawaii Massage and Spa. With oceanfront views of Kailua Bay, this spa offers a full menu of massage treatments as well as wraps, facials, and waxing. It's a convenient place to get pampered before hitting the village shops. ⊠ *Kona Inn Shopping Village, 75-5744 Alii Dr., #245, Kailua-Kona* ☎ *808/937–9707* ⊕ *www.oceanfrontmassage.com.*

Hoola Spa at the Sheraton Kona Resort & Spa at Keauhou Bay. The hotel's oceanfront spa offers a menu of tropical delights with combination options that let you mix and match for a super-heavenly—and affordable—treatment. The private outdoor lanai lets you melt into dreamland as you listen to waves lapping at the rocks inches away. After your treatment, rinse off with hot steam and cool water in the complimentary shower/steam room. The spa has Hawaii's first Himalayan Salt Room, a natural therapy for spa-going guests. Couples' treatments take place outside on the secluded balcony and start with a private whirlpool bath followed by a side-by-side massage. ⊠ *Sheraton Kona Resort & Spa, 78-128 Ehukai St., Kailua-Kona* ☎ *808/930–4848* ⊕ *www.hoolaspa.com.*

The Lotus Center. Tucked away on the first floor of the Royal Kona Resort, the Lotus Center provides a convenient option for massage treatments, facials, and waxing. There's also a chiropractor on the premises. Oceanside massage is available on a private patio outside the treatment rooms.

7

Alternative offerings include acupuncture, yoga, Reiki, crystal-energy sessions, and biofeedback. ⊠ *Royal Kona Resort, 75-5852 Alii Dr., Kailua-Kona* ☎ *808/334–0445* ⊕ *www.konaspa.com.*

The Spa at Hualalai. For the exclusive use of Four Seasons Resort guests and members, this spa features 28 massage treatment areas. Tropical breezes waft through 14 outdoor massage *hales* (huts), situated in beautiful garden settings. The therapists are top-notch, and a real effort is made to incorporate local traditions. Apothecary services allow you to customize your treatment with almost 40 ingredients like kukui nuts, Hawaiian salts, and coconut. Massage options range from traditional lomilomi to Thai. ⊠ *Four Seasons Resort Hualalai, 72-100 Kaupulehu Dr., Kailua-Kona* ☎ *808/325–8000* ⊕ *www.fourseasons.com/hualalai/spa.*

THE KONA COAST

Kona Shiatsu Clinic. Tucked away in a vintage bungalow near Manago Hotel, this peaceful little clinic offers deep-tissue shiatsu massage, Japanese style. A master of shiatsu with more than 35 years' experience, Tom Langenstein helps clients work out the kinks or recover from injuries. ⊠ *82-6161 Mamalahoa Hwy., Captain Cook* ☎ *808/323–3111* ⊕ *www.konashiatsu.com* ⊗ *Closed Sun.*

Mamalahoa Hot Tubs and Massage. Tucked into a residential neighborhood above Kealakekua, this is a welcome alternative to the large Kohala Coast resort spas. It feels like a secret hideaway aglow with tiki torches, and offers Hawaiian lomilomi and hot-stone massages at affordable prices. ■ TIP→ **Soaking tubs, enclosed in their own thatched gazebos with roof portholes for stargazing, are great for a couple's soak.** ⊠ *81-1016 St. John's Rd., Kealakekua* ☎ *808/323–2288* ⊕ *www.mamalahoa-hottubs.com* ⊗ *Closed Sun.–Tues.*

THE KOHALA COAST

Hapuna Spa at the Hapuna Beach Prince Hotel. Locals and visitors come to the contemporary salon at Hapuna Spa for the latest haircuts and styling. The adjoining full-service spa offers a menu of facials, body treatments, and massages, the most popular being the traditional Hawaiian lomilomi massage. An outdoor, covered treatment lanai is the spot for couples to enjoy fresh tropical breezes and ocean sounds. ⊠ *Hapuna Beach Prince Hotel, 62-100 Kaunaoa Dr., Waimea (Hawaii County)* ☎ *808/880–3335* ⊕ *www.princeresortshawaii.com.*

Hawaii Island Retreat Maluhia Spa. This remote and elegant sanctuary in North Kohala offers three artfully appointed indoor treatment rooms and two outdoor massage platforms that overlook the valley. The spa is first-rate, with handcrafted wooden lockers, rain-style showerheads, and a signature line of lotions and scrubs that's made locally. The owners also create their own scrubs and wraps from ingredients grown on the property. The Papaya Delight lives up to its name and features roasted ground papaya seeds mixed with goat yogurt and geranium. The slate of massages includes lomilomi, Thai, and deep tissue. ⊠ *250 Maluhia Rd., Kapaau* ☎ *808/889–6336* ⊕ *www.hawaiiislandretreat.com.*

Kohala Spa at the Hilton Waikoloa Village. Naupaka grows in abundance along the shores of Hawaii Island, and Kohala Spa pays it tribute with the 80-minute Signature Naupaka White Flower Ritual. The feast for the senses incorporates a foot massage with awa root and Hawaiian ginger, followed by warmed body compressions with healing herbs and a full-body massage blending essential oils. The island's volcanic character is expressed in lava rock soaking tubs and in treatments including the Pohaku hot-stone massage and reflexology with healing stones. Locker rooms are outfitted with a wealth of beauty and bath products, and the spa's retail facility offers signature Coco-Mango lotions, body washes, and shampoos. An open-air, seaside cabana provides a tropical spot for a massage overlooking the Pacific, while the fitness center has the latest machines and plentiful classes. ✉ *Hilton Waikoloa Village, 69-425 Waikoloa Beach Dr., Hilo* ☎ *808/886–2828* ⊕ *www.kohalaspa.com.*

Mandara Spa at the Waikoloa Beach Marriott Resort. Overlooking the hotel's main pool with a distant view of the ocean, Mandara offers a complete, if not unique, spa menu, with lomilomi, scrubs, wraps, and more facial options than at the island's other spas. Mandara, which operates spas all over the world, uses Elemis products and incorporates local ingredients (lime and ginger in the scrubs, warm coconut milk in the wraps). The facility, which fuses contemporary and traditional Asian motifs, is beautiful. A glam squad awaits you at the full-service salon. ✉ *Waikoloa Beach Marriott, 69-275 Waikoloa Beach Dr., Waikoloa* ☎ *808/886–8191* ⊕ *www.mandaraspa.com.*

Fodor's Choice ★ **Mauna Lani Spa.** This is a one-of-a-kind experience with a mix of traditional standbys (lomilomi massage, moisturizing facials) and innovative treatments influenced by ancient traditions and incorporating local products. Most treatments take place in outdoor thatched hales surrounded by lava rock. An exception is Watsu therapy, in which clients are cradled in the arms of a certified therapist in warm saltwater in a 1,000-square-foot grotto between two lava tubes. (It's great for people with disabilities who can't enjoy traditional massage.) Black volcanic clay applications are offered in a natural lava sauna. Aesthetic treatments incorporate high-end products from Epicuran and Emminence, so facials have lasting therapeutic effects. The spa also offers a full regimen of fitness and yoga classes. ✉ *Mauna Lani Bay Hotel & Bungalows, 68-1365 Pauoa Rd., Waimea (Hawaii County)* ☎ *808/881–7922* ⊕ *www.maunalani.com.*

Fodor's Choice ★ **Spa Without Walls at the Fairmont Orchid Hawaii.** This ranks among the best massage facilities on the island, partially due to the superlative setting—private massage areas are situated amid the waterfalls, saltwater pools, and meandering gardens, as well as right on the beach. ■TIP→ **The Fairmont Orchid is one of the few resorts on the island to offer beachside massage.** Splurge on the 110-minute Alii Experience, with hot coconut oil treatments, lomilomi, and hot-stone massage. Other great treatments include caviar facials, fragrant herbal wraps, and coffee-and-vanilla scrubs. Where else can you relax to the sounds of cascading waterfalls while watching tropical yellow tang swim beneath you through windows in the floor? ✉ *Fairmont Orchid Hawaii, 1 N. Kaniku Dr., Waimea (Hawaii County)* ☎ *808/887–7540* ⊕ *www.fairmont.com/orchid-hawaii/spa/.*

HAWAII VOLCANOES NATIONAL PARK AND VICINITY

Hale Hoola Spa in Volcano. Although this spa is located in a private home, those staying in Volcano have easy access to body treatments, massages, and facials at far more reasonable prices than on the other side of the island. Hale Hoola's menu features a bounty of local ingredients and traditional Hawaiian treatments, including *lomi hula*, which is lomilomi massage choreographed to hula music, and *laau hamo*, which blends lomilomi with traditional Hawaiian and Asian healing herbs and plant extracts. *Popo kapai* is a divine blend of hot-stone massage and laau hamo, incorporating lomilomi with warm compresses filled with healing herbs. Facials and body scrubs use traditional ginger, coconut, and macadamia nuts, but also some surprises, including taro, vanilla, and volcanic clay. ■TIP➔ Call ahead of time, as they don't accept walk-ins. ⊠ *Mauna Loa Estates, 11-3913 7th St., Volcano* ☏ *808/756–2421* ⊕ *www.halehoola.net.*

HILO

Spa Vive. Occupying a circa-1897 house just above Hilo Town on the way to Rainbow Falls, this charming day spa and salon features 10 treatment rooms, a nail and hair salon, a hot tub, a dry sauna, and aesthetician services. Body scrubs and waxings are also available upon request. ⊠ *306 Lehua St., Hilo* ✛ *Drive up Waianuenue Ave., turn right at Keawe, and proceed across small bridge into a residential neighborhood* ☏ *808/930–3830* ⊕ *www.spavive.com.*

WATER SPORTS AND TOURS

Updated by Kristina Anderson

The ancient Hawaiians, who took much of their daily sustenance from the ocean, also enjoyed playing in the water. In fact, surfing was the sport of kings. Though it's easy to be lulled into whiling away the day baking in the sun on a white-, gold-, black-, or green-sand beach, getting into or onto the water is a highlight of most trips.

All of the Hawaiian Islands are surrounded by the Pacific Ocean, and blessed with a temperate latitude, making them some of the world's greatest natural playgrounds. But certain experiences are even better on the Big Island: nighttime diving trips to see manta rays; deep-sea fishing in Kona's fabled waters, where dozens of Pacific blue marlin of 1,000 pounds or more have been caught; and kayaking among the dolphins in Kealakekua Bay, to name a few.

From almost any point on the Big Island, the ocean is nearby. Whether it's body boarding and snorkeling or kayaking and surfing, there is a water sport for everyone. For most activities, you can rent gear and go it alone. Or book a group excursion with an experienced guide, who offers convenience and security, as well as special insights into Hawaiian marine life and culture. Want to try surfing? Contrary to what you may have heard, there *are* waves on the Big Island. You can take lessons that promise to have you standing the first day out.

The Kona and Kohala coasts of West Hawaii boast the largest number of ocean sports outfitters and tour operators. They operate from the small-boat harbors and piers in Kailua-Kona, Keauhou, Kawaihae, and at the Kohala Coast resorts. There are also several outfitters in the East Hawaii and Hilo areas.

As a general rule, the waves are gentler here than on the other Islands, but there are a few things to be aware of. First, don't turn your back on the ocean. It's unlikely, but if conditions are right, a wave could come along and push you face-first into the sand or drag you out to sea. Second, when the Big Island does experience high surf, dangerous conditions prevail and can change rapidly. Watch the ocean for a few minutes before going out. If it looks rough, don't chance it. Third, realize that ultimately you must keep yourself safe. We strongly encourage you to obey lifeguards and weather advisories, and heed the advice of outfitters from whom you rent equipment, and even from locals on shore. It could save your trip, or even your life.

ADVENTURE CRUISES

Lava Ocean Tours. The best lava boat operator on the island, Captain Shane Turpin takes visitors out on the brand-new, 39-passenger *Lava-One* for a thrilling, up-close view of live lava flows spilling out of Kilauea's southeast vent into the ocean. If the lava's not flowing, you can take an incredible boat tour of the Hamakua Coast in search of otherwise inaccessible waterfalls and pods of dolphins. Captain Turpin visits every scenic spot, getting close enough for you to feel the spray of the waterfalls, and is the only boat operator on the east side currently doing a waterfall tour. Tours include drinks and snacks and leave from Hilo. ✉ *Hilo* ☎ *808/966–4200* ⊕ *www.seelava.com* 💲 *From $75.*

BODY BOARDING AND BODYSURFING

According to the movies, in the Old West there was always friction between cattle ranchers and sheep ranchers. A somewhat similar situation exists between surfers and body boarders (and between surfers and stand-up paddleboarders). That's why they generally keep to their own separate areas. Often the body boarders, who lie on their stomachs on shorter boards, stay closer to shore and leave the outside breaks to the board surfers. Or the board surfers may stick to one side of the beach and the body boarders to the other. The truth is, body boarding (often called "boogie boarding," in homage to the first commercial manufacturer of this slick, little, flexible-foam board) is a blast. Most surfers also sometimes carve waves on a body board, no matter how much of a purist they claim to be. ■TIP➡ Novice body boarders should catch shore-break waves only. Ask lifeguards or locals for the best spots. You'll need a pair of short fins to get out to the bigger waves offshore (not recommended for newbies). As for bodysurfing, just catch a wave and make like Superman going faster than a speeding bullet.

BEST SPOTS

Hapuna Beach State Recreation Area. Often considered one of the top 10 beaches in the world, Hapuna Beach State Recreation Area offers fine white sand, turquoise water, and easy rolling surf on most days, making it great for bodysurfing and body boarding at all levels. Ask the lifeguards—who only cover areas south of the rocky cliff that juts out near the middle of the beach—about conditions before heading into the water, especially in winter. Sometimes northwest swells create a dangerous undertow. ✉ *Hwy. 19, near mile marker 69, just south of Mauna Kea Hotel, Kohala Coast* ⊕ *dlnr.hawaii.gov/dsp/parks/hawaii/ hapuna-beach-state-recreation-area.*

Honolii Cove. North of Hilo, this is the best body-boarding spot on the east side of the island. ✉ *Off Hwy. 19, near mile marker 4, Hilo.*

Magic Sands Beach Park (White Sands Beach). This white-sand, shore-break cove is great for beginning to intermediate bodysurfing and body boarding. Sometimes in winter, much of the sand here washes out to sea and forms a sandbar just offshore, creating fun wave conditions. Also known as White Sands, it's popular and can get crowded with locals, especially when school is out. Watch for nasty rip currents at high tide. ■TIP→ If you're not using fins, wear reef shoes for protection against sharp rocks. ✉ *Alii Dr., just north of mile marker 4, Kailua-Kona.*

EQUIPMENT

Equipment-rental shacks are located at many beaches and boat harbors, along the highway, and at most resorts. Body-board rental rates are around $12–$15 per day and around $60 per week. Ask the vendor to throw in a pair of fins—some will for no extra charge.

Honolua Surf Company. Surfboards, apparel, gear, and logowear are available at these moderately priced surf shops. There are several locations statewide. ✉ *Kona Shopping Village, 75-5744 Alii Dr., Kailua-Kona* ☎ *808/329–1001* ⊕ *www.honoluasurf.com.*

Orchidland Surfboards & Surf Shop. This venerable shop—in business more than 40 years—carries a wide variety of surf and other water sports equipment for sale or rent. They stock professional custom surfboards, body boards, and surf apparel. Owner Stan Lawrence, famous for his "Drainpipe" legacy, was probably the last person to surf that famous break before lava flows claimed the Kalapana area (the rubber slippers he left on the beach burned up before he got out of the water). Old photos, surf posters, and memorabilia on the walls add to the nostalgia. Through the shop, he hosts surf contests here and on Oahu, and does the daily surf report for local radio stations. Located in the heart of historic downtown Hilo, this surf shop is as authentic as they get. ✉ *262 Kamehameha Ave., Hilo* ☎ *808/935–1533* ⊕ *www.orchidlandsurf.com* ✍ *From $15 body board; $25 surfboard.*

Fodor's Choice ★ **Pacific Vibrations.** This family-owned surf shop—in business more than 35 years—holds the distinction of being the oldest, smallest surf shop in the world. Even at a compact 400 square feet, this place stocks tons of equipment, surf wear and gear, sunglasses, and GoPro cameras. You can rent a surfboard, stand-up paddleboard, or a body board, but you have to buy or bring your own fins. Located oceanfront in downtown Kailua Town, it is tucked away fronting a vintage cul de sac, and is worth a stop just for the cool Hawaii surf vibe. ✉ *75-5702 Likana La., #B, at Alii Dr., Kailua-Kona* ☎ *808/329–4140* ✍ *$15/day, surfboard; $15/hr., paddleboard; $5/day, body board.*

DID YOU KNOW?

Kealakekua Bay, with its calm waters and spinner dolphins, is an excellent spot for kayaking as well as snorkeling. Morning is the best time to see dolphins.

Surfing is popular on the Big Island.

DEEP-SEA FISHING

The Kona Coast has some of the world's most exciting "blue-water" fishing. Although July, August, and September are peak months, with the best fishing and a number of tournaments, charter fishing goes on year-round. You don't have to compete to experience the thrill of landing a Pacific blue marlin or other big-game fish. Some 60 charter boats, averaging 26 to 58 feet, are available for hire, all of them out of **Honokohau Harbor**, north of Kailua-Kona.

The Kona Coast is world-famous for the presence of large marlin, particularly the Pacific blue. In fact, it's also known as "Grander Alley" for the fish caught here that weigh more than 1,000 pounds. The largest blue marlin on record was caught in 1984 and weighed 1,649 pounds. In total, more than 60 Granders have been reeled in here by top sport-fishing teams.

For an exclusive charter, prices generally range from $600 to $950 for a half-day trip (about four hours) and $800 to $1,600 for a full day at sea (about eight hours). For share charters, rates are about $100 to $140 per person for a half day and $200 for a full day. If fuel prices increase, expect charter costs to rise. Most boats are licensed to take up to six passengers, in addition to the crew. Tackle, bait, and ice are furnished, but you usually have to bring your own lunch. You won't be able to keep your catch, although if you ask, many captains will send you home with a few fillets.

Hawaiian International Billfish Tournament. Pacific blue marlin are sought after by deep-sea anglers the world over, who come to Kona's fabled waters, most notably during this five-day tournament in August. Since 1959, this granddaddy of big-game-fishing tourneys has attracted supercompetitive teams in the finest boats imaginable. The powerful animals are caught or tagged and released. Occasionally, Kona waters produce a grander—over 1,000 pounds. ☎ *808/836–1723* ⊕ *www.hibtfishing.com.*

Honokohau Harbor's Fuel Dock. Show up around 11 am and watch the weigh-in of the day's catch from the morning charters, or around 3:30 pm for the afternoon charters, especially during the summer tournament season. Weigh-ins are fun when the big ones come in, but these days, with most of the marlin being released, it's not a sure thing. ■**TIP→** On Kona's Waterfront Row, look for the "Grander's Wall" of anglers with their 1,000-pound-plus prizes. There's also a display at the Kona Inn. ✉ *Honokohau Harbor, Kealakehe Pkwy. at Hwy. 11, Kailua-Kona.*

BOATS AND CHARTERS

Before you sign up with anyone, think about the kind of trip you want. Looking for a romantic cruise? A rockin' good time with your buddies? Serious fishing in one of the "secret spots?" A family-friendly excursion? Be sure to describe your expectations so a booking agent can match you with a captain and a boat that suit your style.

FAMILY **Bite Me Sportfishing Fleet.** This multifaceted sportfishing company offers a full fleet with shared, half-day, three-quarter-day, and invitational championships; they know how, when, and where to catch fish along the Kona Coast. They specialize in a family-friendly experience and can accommodate large, private parties of six or more. Lots of charters for different excursions are also available, and they follow catch-and-release practices to help sustain local fisheries. ■**TIP→** Bonus: They let you keep your catch, and will help you clean and package it should you wish to ship it back on your flight. There's also a cool retail store where you can buy everything from logo T-shirts to hats. ✉ *Honokahau, 74-425 Kealakehe Pkwy., Suite 17, Kailua-Kona* ☎ *808/960-2464* ⊕ *www.bitemesportfishing.com* 🖃 *From $100.*

Bwana Sportfishing. Full-, half-, quarter-, three-quarter-day, and overnight charters are available on the 46-foot *Bwana*. The boat features the latest electronics, top-of-the-line equipment, and air-conditioned cabins. Captain Teddy comes from a fishing family; father Pete was a legend on Kona waters for decades. ✉ *Honokohau Harbor, Slip H-17, 74-381 Kealakehe Pkwy., just south of Kona airport, Kailua-Kona* ☎ *808/936–5168* 🖃 *From $1,250.*

The Charter Desk at Honokohau Harbor. With about 60 big-name boats on the books, this place will book just the right charter for you. Due to their location near the weigh scales, they know which boats are the most active and have the best daily catches. They will also weigh your catch, take photos, and give you souvenir tags to take home; the small shop has souvenir T-shirts. ■**TIP→** You can make arrangements through hotel activity desks, but it's better to come here and look things over for

8

yourself. ✉ *Honokohau Harbor Fuel Dock, 74-381 Kealakehe Pkwy., Kailua-Kona* ☎ *808/329–5735, 888/566–2487* ⊕ *www.charterdesk. com* 🖙 *From $499.*

Charter Locker. This experienced company offers half- and full-day charter fishing trips on 36- to 53-foot vessels. Featured boats include *Kona Blue, JR's Hooker, Strong Persuader,* and *Kila Kila.* Rates depend on the boat. ✉ *Honokohau Harbor #16, 74-381 Kealakehe Pkwy., just south of Kona airport, Kailua-Kona* ☎ *808/326–2553* ⊕ *www.charterlocker. com* 🖙 *From $395.*

Humdinger Sportfishing. This game-fisher guide has more than five decades of fishing experience in Kona waters, and the expert crew are marlin specialists. The 37-foot *Humdinger* has the latest in electronics and top-line rods and reels. Book online for discounts and specials. ✉ *Honokohau Harbor, Slip B-4, 74-381 Kealakehe Pkwy., Kailua-Kona* ☎ *808/425–9225, 800/926–2374, 808/425–9228 boat phone* ⊕ *www. humdingersportfishing.com* 🖙 *From $399.*

Jeff Rogers Charters. One of Kona's friendliest "old salts," Captain Jeff has been leading personalized big game and other fishing charters since 1982. Using a few tricks of the trade (including targeting the bottom), he's able to find the right fish in the right place, nearly without fail. You may ask him to fillet part of your catch. Holder of six world records and six state records, one of his marlins was even a grander (over 1,000 lbs.). He is also one of the few captains in Kona who will allow groups of guests to share a charter to save costs, so check online for the updated list of available shares. ☎ *808/895–1852* ⊕ *www.fishinkona. com* 🖙 *From $375.*

KAYAKING

The leeward (west coast) areas of the Big Island are protected for the most part from the northeast trade winds, making for ideal near-shore kayaking conditions. There are miles and miles of uncrowded Kona and Kohala coastline to explore, presenting close-up views of stark, raw, lava-rock shores and cliffs; lava-tube sea caves; pristine, secluded coves; and deserted beaches. There's even guided kayaking in a hand-built irrigation ditch dating from the early 1900s.

Ocean kayakers can get close to shore—where the commercial snorkel and dive cruise boats can't reach. This opens up all sorts of possibilities for adventure, such as near-shore snorkeling among the expansive coral reefs and lava rock formations that teem with colorful tropical fish and Hawaiian green sea turtles. You can pull ashore at a quiet cove for a picnic and a plunge into turquoise waters. With a good coastal map and some advice from the kayak vendor, you might paddle by ancient battlegrounds, burial sites, bathing ponds for Hawaiian royalty, or old villages.

Kayaking can be enjoyed via a guided tour or on a self-guided paddling excursion. Either way, the kayak outfitter can brief you on recommended routes, safety, and how to help preserve and protect Hawaii's ocean resources and coral reef system.

Whether you're a beginning or experienced kayaker, choose appropriate location, distance, and conditions for your excursion.

Ask the outfitter about local conditions and hazards, such as tides, currents, and advisories.

Beginners should practice getting into and out of the kayak and capsizing (called a *huli,* the Hawaiian word for "flip") in shallow water.

Before departing, secure the kayak's hatches to prevent water intake.

Use a line to attach the paddle to the kayak to avoid losing it.

Always use a life vest or jacket, and wear a rash guard and plenty of sunblock.

Carry appropriate amounts of water and food.

Don't kayak alone. Create a float plan; tell someone where you're going and when you will return.

BEST SPOTS

Hilo Bay. This is a favorite kayak spot. The best place to put in is at **Reeds Bay Beach Park.** Parking is plentiful and free at the bayfront. Most afternoons you'll share the bay with local paddling clubs. Stay inside the breakwater unless the ocean is calm (or you're feeling unusually adventurous). Conditions range from extremely calm to quite choppy. ✉ *Banyan Way and Banyan Dr., 1 mile from downtown Hilo.*

Kailua Bay and Kamakahonu Beach. The small sandy beach that fronts the Courtyard King Kamehameha's Kona Beach Hotel is a nice place to rent or launch kayaks. You can unload in the cul-de-sac and park in nearby free or paid lots. The water here is especially calm, and the surroundings are historical and scenic. ✉ *Alii Dr., next to Kailua Pier, Kailua-Kona.*

Kealakekua Bay State Historical Park. The excellent snorkeling and likelihood of seeing dolphins (morning is best) make Kealakekua Bay one of the most popular kayaking spots on the Big Island. An ocean conservation district, the bay is usually calm and tranquil. (Use caution and common sense during surf advisories.) Tall coral pinnacles and clear visibility surrounding the monument also make for stupendous snorkeling. Regulations permit only a few operators to lead kayak tours in the park. ✉ *Napoopoo Rd. and Manini Bch. Rd., Captain Cook* ⊕ *dlnr. hawaii.gov/dsp/parks/hawaii.*

Oneo Bay. Right downtown, this is usually a placid place to kayak. It's fairly easy to get to. If you can't find parking along the road, there's a free lot across the street from the library and farmers' market. ✉ *Alii Dr., Kailua-Kona.*

EQUIPMENT, LESSONS, AND TOURS

There are several rental outfitters on Highway 11 between Kainaliu and Captain Cook, but only a few are specially permitted to lead kayak trips in Kealakekua Bay.

Aloha Kayak Co. This outfitter is one of the few permitted to guide tours to the stunningly beautiful Kealakekua Bay, leaving from Napoopoo, including about 1½ hours at the Captain Cook Monument. The 3½-hour morning and afternoon tours include snacks and drinks, while the 5-hour tour includes lunch. Local guides discuss the area's cultural, historical, and natural significance. You may see dolphins, but you must observe them from a distance only, as this is a protected marine reserve. Keauhou Bay tours are also available, including a two-hour evening manta ray tour. ✉ 79-7248 *Mamalahoa Hwy., across from Teshima's Restaurant, Honalo* ☎ 808/322–2868 ⊕ *www.alohakayak. com* 🖃 *Tours from $99.*

Flumin' Kohala. The Kohala Ditch was built by hand in the early 1900s to bring water from the cloud forests of the Kohala watershed to the arid lands where sugarcane grew. Like no other in Hawaii, this kayak tour takes you through miles of these fascinating concrete tunnels and flumes in four-man kayaks. ☎ 808/933–4294 ⊕ *fluminkohala. com* 🖃 *From $135.*

Fodor's Choice ★ **Kona Boys.** On the highway above Kealakekua Bay, this full-service, environmentally conscious outfitter handles kayaks, body boards, surfboards, stand-up paddleboards, and snorkeling gear. Single-seat and double kayaks are offered. Surfing and stand-up paddleboarding lessons are available for private or group instruction. Tours such as their Morning Magic and Midday Meander include two half-day guided kayaking and snorkeling trips with gear, lunch, snacks, and beverages. Kona Boys also run a beach shack fronting the King Kamehameha's Kona Beach Hotel and are happy to give advice on the changing regulations regarding South Kona bay usage. ■TIP➔ **The Kailua-Kona location offers Hawaiian outrigger canoe rides, SUP lessons, and rentals of beach mats, chairs, and other gear.** ✉ 79-7539 *Mamalahoa Hwy., Kealakekua* ☎ 808/328–1234, 808/329–2345 ⊕ *www.konaboys.com* 🖃 *Tours from $189.*

Ocean Safari's Kayak Adventures. On the guided 3½-hour morning sea-cave tour that begins in Keauhou Bay, you can visit lava-tube sea caves along the coast, then swim ashore for a snack. The kayaks are already on the beach, so you won't have the hassle of transporting them. They also offer stand-up paddleboard lessons. ✉ *End of Kamehameha III Rd., Kailua-Kona* ✛ *Next to Sheraton Kona Resort & Spa at Keauhou Bay* ☎ 808/326–4699 ⊕ *www.oceansafariskayaks.com* 🖃 *From $79.*

SAILING

For old salts and novice sailors alike, there's nothing like a cruise on the Kona or Kohala Coast. Calm waters, serene shores, and the superb scenery of Mauna Kea, Mauna Loa, and Hualalai, the Big Island's primary volcanic peaks, make for a great sailing adventure. You can drop a line over the side and try your luck at catching dinner, or grab some snorkel gear and explore when the boat drops anchor in one of the quiet coves and bays. A cruise may well be the most relaxing and adventurous part of a Big Island visit.

Honu Sail Charters. The fully equipped 32-foot cutter-rigged sloop *Honu* (Hawaiian for sea turtle) carries six passengers on full-day, half-day, and sunset sailing excursions along the scenic Kona Coast, which include time to snorkel in clear waters over coral reefs. This friendly outfitter allows passengers to get some hands-on sailing experience or just to kick back and relax. Prices include food, snorkel equipment, towels, etc. ⊠ *Honokōhau Harbor, Kailua-Kona* ☎ *808/896–4668* ⊕ *www. sailkona.com* ⊠ *Tours from $100.*

Kohala Sail & Sea. Based at the new Kawaihae South Small Boat Harbor, this company offers morning snorkeling, day sailing, and sunset cruises, and humpback whale-watching in season. Owned and operated by Captain Steve Turner, the crew aboard the 34-foot Riva focuses on sharing the wonders of the Kawaihae area, including the impressive Puukohola Heiau National Historic Site, the Puako reef, and views of Big Island volcanoes and even Maui's Haleakala. ⊠ *Kawaihae Harbor South, Slip #8, 61-3527 Kawaihae Rd., Kawaihae* ☎ *808/895–1781* ⊕ *kohalasailandsea.com* ⊠ *From $106.*

SCUBA DIVING

The Big Island's underwater world is the setting for a dramatic diving experience. With generally warm and calm waters, vibrant coral reefs and rock formations, and plunging underwater drop-offs, the Kona and Kohala coasts offer premier scuba diving. There are also some good dive locations in East Hawaii, not far from the Hilo area. Divers find much to occupy their time, including marine reserves teeming with tropical reef fish, Hawaiian green sea turtles, an occasional and critically endangered Hawaiian monk seal, and even some playful spinner dolphins. On special night dives to see manta rays, divers descend with bright underwater lights that attract plankton, which in turn attract these otherworldly creatures. The best spots to dive are all on the west coast.

BEST SPOTS

Garden Eel Cove. Accessible only by boat, this is a great place to see manta rays somersaulting overhead as they feast on a plankton supper. It's also home to hundreds of tiny garden eels darting out from their sandy homes. There's a steep drop-off and lots of marine life. ⊠ *Rte. 19, near the Kona Airport, Kailua-Kona.*

Manta Village. Booking with a night-dive operator is required for the short boat ride to this area, one of Kona's best night-dive spots. If you're a diving or snorkeling fanatic, it's well worth it to experience manta rays drawn by the lights of the hotel. ■ TIP➔ **If night swimming isn't your cup of tea, you can catch a glimpse of the majestic creatures from the Sheraton's viewing areas.** (No water access is allowed from the hotel's property.) ⊠ *78-128 Ehukai St., off Sheraton Kona Resort & Spa at Keauhou Bay, Kailua-Kona.*

Pawai Bay Marine Perserve. Clear waters, abundant reef life, and interesting coral formations make protected Pawai Bay Marine Preserve ideal for diving. Explore sea caves, arches, and lava rock formations and dive into lava tubes. An easy, boat-only dive spot is ½ mile north of Old Airport. (No shoreline access to protected Pawai Bay is available due

HAWAII'S MANTA RAYS

Manta rays, one of Hawaii's most fascinating marine-life species, can be seen on some nighttime diving excursions along the Kona and Kohala coasts. They are generally completely harmless to divers, though of course no wild animal is totally predictable. If you don't want to get wet, head to the beach fronting the Mauna Kea Beach Hotel, on the Kohala Coast, or to the Sheraton Kona Resort & Spa at Keauhou Bay, where each evening, visitors gather by the hotel's lights to watch manta rays feed in the shallows.

■ The manta ray (*Manta birostris*), called the devil fish by some, is known as *hahalua* by Hawaiians.

■ Its winglike fins, reaching up to 20 feet wide, allow the ray to skim through the water like a bird gliding through air.

■ The manta ray uses the two large flap-like lobes extending from its eyes to funnel food to its mouth. It eats microscopic plankton, small fish, and tiny crustaceans.

■ Closely related to the shark, the manta can weigh more than 3,000 pounds.

■ Its skeleton is made of cartilage, not bone.

■ A female ray gives birth to one or two young at a time; pups can be 45 inches long and weigh 20 pounds at birth.

to its cultural and environmental significance.) ⊠ *Kuakini Hwy., north of Old Kona Airport Park, Kailua-Kona.*

Puako. Just south of Hapuna Beach State Recreation Area, beautiful Puako offers easy entry to some fine reef diving. Deep chasms, sea caves, and rock arches abound with varied marine life. ⊠ *Puako Rd., off Hwy. 19, Kailua-Kona.*

EQUIPMENT, LESSONS, AND TOURS

There are quite a few good dive shops along the Kona Coast. Most are happy to take on all customers, but a few focus on specific types of trips. Trip prices vary, depending on whether you're already certified and whether you're diving from a boat or from shore. Instruction with PADI, SDI, or TDI certification in three to five days costs $600 to $850. Most instructors rent dive equipment and snorkel gear, as well as underwater cameras. Most organize otherworldly manta ray dives at night and whale-watching cruises in season.

Big Island Divers. This company offers several levels of certification as well as numerous excursions, including night dives, two-tank charters, and in-season whale watching. ⊠ *74-5467 Kaiwi St., Kailua-Kona* ☎ *808/329–6068* ⊕ *bigislanddivers.com* ⊡ *From $135.*

Jack's Diving Locker. Good for novice and intermediate divers, Jack's has trained and certified tens of thousands of divers since 1981, with classrooms and a dive pool for instruction. Four boats that accommodate up to 18 divers and 6 snorkelers visit more than 80 established dive sites along the Kona coast, yielding sightings of turtles, manta rays,

The Kona Coast's relatively calm waters and colorful coral reefs offer excellent scuba diving.

garden eels, and schools of barracuda. They even take you lava tube diving. Snorkelers can accompany their friends on the dive boats or take guided morning trips and manta night trips, and dolphin-watch and reef snorkels. Combined sunset/night manta ray dives are offered as well. ■TIP➜ Kona's best deal for scuba newbies is Jack's two-part introductory dive from Kailua Pier. ⊠ *75-5813 Alii Dr., Kailua-Kona* ☎ *808/329–7585, 800/345–4807* ⊕ *www.jacksdivinglocker.com* ✉ *Tours from $135.*

Kohala Divers. The Kohala Coast's lava-tube caves, vibrant coral reefs, and interesting sea life make it a great diving destination. This full-service PADI dive shop has been certifying divers since 1984. A one-day intro dive course has you in the ocean the same day. A four-day, full certification course is offered, too. The company also rents equipment and takes divers to the best diving spots. ⊠ *Kawaihae Harbor Shopping Center, Hwy. 270, Kawaihae* ☎ *808/882–7774* ⊕ *www.kohaladivers. com* ✉ *One-day dive course, from $185.*

Nautilus Dive Center. Across from Hilo Bay, Nautilus Dive Center is the oldest and most experienced dive shop on the island. It offers a broad range of services for both beginners and experienced divers. Owner Bill De Rooy has been diving around the Big Island since 1982, has personally certified more than 2,000 divers, and can provide you with underwater maps and show you the best dive spots in Hilo. He also provides PADI instruction, one- and two-tank dives, and snorkeling tours. ⊠ *382 Kamehameha Ave., Hilo* ☎ *808/935–6939* ⊕ *www.nautilusdivehilo.com* ✉ *Certification from $400.*

Shan's Scuba. For a personalized scuba-certification experience, certified PADI MSDT instructor Shannon Rhodes-Velasquez offers complete certification; cost includes book, training materials, and most dive equipment. Specializing in small groups, she's particularly good with those who feel intimidated about learning to dive. If you plan ahead, you can learn online with PADI before arrival, and Shannon will certify you in the water for a discounted price. ⊠ *Captain Cook* ☎ *808/938–8119* 🗺 *From $450.*

Torpedo Tours. Owner-operators Mike and Nikki Milligan, both dive instructors, love to take divers out on their 40-foot custom dive boat, the *Na Pali Kai II.* They specialize in small groups, which means you'll get personalized attention and spend more time diving and less time waiting to dive. Morning excursions feature two-tank dives. Both snorkelers and divers can try the torpedo scooters—devices that let you cover more area with less kicking. Manta ray night diving and snorkeling at Garden Eel Cove are offered. This is the only company that fishes between dives. ⊠ *Honokohau Harbor, 74-425 Kealakehe Pkwy., Kailua-Kona* ☎ *808/938–0405* ⊕ *www.torpedotours.com* 🗺 *Dives from $129.*

SNORKELING

A favorite pastime on the Big Island, snorkeling is perhaps one of the easiest and most enjoyable water activities for visitors. By floating on the surface, peering through your mask, and breathing through your snorkel, you can see lava rock formations, sea arches, sea caves, and coral reefs teeming with colorful tropical fish. While the Kona and Kohala coasts boast more beaches, bays, and quiet coves to snorkel, the east side around Hilo and at Kapoho are also great places to get in the water.

If you don't bring your own equipment, you can easily rent all the gear needed from a beach activities vendor, who will happily provide directions to the best sites for snorkeling in the area. For access to deeper water and assistance from an experienced crew (to say nothing of typically great food and drink), you can opt for a snorkel cruise. Excursions generally range from two to five hours; be sure to ask what equipment and food is included.

BEST SPOTS

Puako Tide Pools. There's a large shelf of extensive reef and tide pools at this sleepy beach town along the Kohala Coast, where you'll find fantastic snorkeling as long as conditions are calm. ⊠ *South end of Puako Beach Rd., off Hwy. 11.*

Kahaluu Beach Park. Since ancient times, the waters around Kahaluu Beach have provided traditional throw net–fishing grounds. With super-easy access, the bay offers good swimming and outstanding snorkeling, revealing turtles, angelfish, parrotfish, needlefish, puffer fish, and many

Continued on page 206

SNORKELING IN HAWAII

Molokini Crater

The waters surrounding the Hawaiian Islands are filled with life—from giant manta rays cruising off the Big Island's Kona Coast to humpback whales giving birth in the waters around Maui. Dip your head beneath the surface to experience a spectacularly colorful world: pairs of miletseed butterflyfish dart back and forth, redlipped parrotfish snack on coral algae, and spotted eagle rays flap past like silent spaceships. Sea turtles bask at the surface while tiny wrasses give them the equivalent of a shave and a haircut. The water quality is typically outstanding; many sites afford 30-foot-plus visibility. On snorkel cruises, you can often stare from the boat rail right down to the bottom.

Certainly few destinations are as accommodating to every level of snorkeler as Hawaii. Beginners can tromp in from sandy beaches while more advanced divers descend to shipwrecks, reefs, craters, and sea arches just offshore. Because of Hawaii's extreme isolation, the island chain has fewer fish species than Fiji or the Caribbean—but many of the fish that live here exist nowhere else. The Hawaiian waters are home to the highest percentage of endemic fish in the world.

The key to enjoying the underwater world is slowing down. Look carefully. Listen. You might hear the strange crackling sound of shrimp tunneling through coral, or you may hear whales singing to one another during winter. A shy octopus may drift along the ocean's floor beneath you. If you're hooked, pick up a waterproof fishkey from Long's Drugs. You can brag later that you've looked the Hawaiian turkeyfish in the eye.

Picasso Triggerfish

Milletseed Butterflyfish*

Yellow Tang

Moorish Idol

Hawaiian Whitespotted Toby*

Saddleback Wrasse*

Redlip Parrotfish

Hawaiian Turkeyfish*

Zebra Moray Eel

Stocky Hawkfish

Green Sea Turtle (Honu)

Spotted Eagle Ray

*endemic to Hawaii

POLYNESIA'S FIRST CELESTIAL NAVIGATORS: HONU

Honu is the Hawaiian name for two native sea turtles, the hawksbill and the green sea turtle. Little is known about these dinosaur-age marine reptiles, though snorkelers regularly see them foraging for *limu* (seaweed) and the occasional jellyfish in Hawaiian waters. Most female honu nest in the uninhabited Northwestern Hawaiian Islands, but a few sociable ladies nest on Maui and Big Island beaches. Scientists suspect that they navigate the seas via magnetism—sensing the earth's poles. Amazingly, they will journey up to 800 miles to nest—it's believed that they return to their own birth sites. After about 60 days of incubation, nestlings emerge from the sand at night and find their way back to the sea by the light of the stars.

SNORKELING

Many of Hawaii's reefs are accessible from shore.

The basics: Sure, you can take a deep breath, hold your nose, squint your eyes, and stick your face in the water in an attempt to view submerged habitats . . . but why not protect your eyes, retain your ability to breathe, and keep your hands free to paddle about when exploring underwater? That's what snorkeling is all about.

Equipment needed: A mask, snorkel (the tube attached to the mask), and fins. In deeper waters (any depth over your head), life jackets are advised.

Steps to success: If you've never snorkeled before, it's natural to feel a bit awkward at first, so don't sweat it. Breathing through a mask and tube, and wearing a pair of fins take getting used to. Like any activity, you build confidence and comfort through practice.

If you're new to snorkeling, begin by submerging your face in shallow wa-ter or a swimming pool and breathing calmly through the snorkel while gazing through the mask.

Next you need to learn how to clear water out of your mask and snorkel, an essential skill since splashes can send water into tube openings and masks can leak. Some snorkels have built-in drainage valves, but if a tube clogs, you can force water up and out by exhaling through your mouth. Clearing a mask is similar: lift your head from water while pulling forward on mask to drain. Some masks have built-in purge valves, but those without can be cleared underwater by pressing the top to the forehead and blowing out your nose (charming, isn't it?), allowing air to bubble into the mask, pushing water out the bottom. If it sounds hard, it really isn't. Just try it a few times and you'll soon feel like a pro.

Now your goal is to get friendly with

fins—you want them to be snug but not too tight—and learn how to propel yourself with them. Fins won't help you float, but they will give you a leg up, so to speak, on smoothly moving through the water or treading water (even when upright) with less effort.

Flutter stroking is the most efficient underwater kick, and the farther your foot bends forward the more leg power you'll be able to transfer to the water and the farther you'll travel with each stroke. Flutter kicking movements involve alternately separating the legs and then drawing them back together. When your legs separate, the leg surface encounters drag from the water, slowing you down. When your legs are drawn back together, they produce a force pushing you forward. If your kick creates more forward force than it causes drag, you'll move ahead.

Submerge your fins to avoid fatigue rather than having them flailing above the water when you kick, and keep your arms at your side to reduce drag. You are in the water—stretched out, face down, and snorkeling happily away—but that doesn't mean you can't hold your breath and go deeper in the water for a closer look at some fish or whatever catches your attention. Just remember that when you do this, your snorkel will be submerged, too, so you won't be breathing (you'll be holding your breath). You can dive head-first, but going feet-first is easier and less scary for most folks, taking less momentum. Before full immersion, take several long, deep breaths to clear carbon dioxide from your lungs.

If your legs tire, flip onto your back and tread water with inverted fin motions while resting. If your mask fogs, wash condensation from lens and clear water from mask.

TIPS FOR SAFE SNORKELING

- Snorkel with a buddy and stay together.
- Plan your entry and exit points prior to getting in the water.
- Swim into the current on entering and then ride the current back to your exit point.
- Carry your flippers into the water and then put them on, as it's difficult to walk in them, and rocks may be slippery.
- Make sure your mask fits properly and is not too loose.
- Pop your head above the water periodically to ensure you aren't drifting too far out, or too close to rocks.
- Think of the water as someone else's home—don't take anything that doesn't belong to you, or leave any trash behind.
- Don't touch any sea creatures; they may sting.
- Wear a T-shirt over your swimsuit to help protect you from being fried by the sun.
- When in doubt, don't go without a snorkeling professional; try a guided tour.
- Don't go in if the ocean seems rough.

Green sea turtle (Honu)

8

IN FOCUS SNORKELING IN HAWAII

types of tang. ■TIP➡ Stay inside the breakwater and don't stray too far, as dangerous and unpredictable currents swirl outside the bay. ⊠ *Alii Dr., Kailua-Kona.*

Kapoho Tide Pools. Here you'll find the best snorkeling on the Hilo side. Fingers of lava from the 1960 flow that destroyed the town of Kapoho jut into the sea to form a network of tide pools. Conditions near the shore are excellent for beginners, while farther out is challenging enough for experienced snorkelers. ⊠ *End of Kapoho-Kai Rd., off Hwy. 137, Hilo.*

Kealakekua Bay State Historical Park. This protected Marine Life Conservation District is hands-down one of the best snorkeling spots on the island, thanks to clear visibility, fabulous coral reefs, and generally calm waters. Pods of dolphins can be abundant, but they're protected under federal law and may not be disturbed or approached. Access to the area is restricted, but a few companies are permitted to escort tours to the bay. ■TIP➡ Overland access is difficult, so opt for one of the guided snorkel cruises permitted to moor here. ⊠ *Napoopoo, at end of Beach Rd. and Hwy. 160, Kailua-Kona.*

Magic Sands Beach Park. Also known as White Sands or Disappearing Sands Beach Park, this is a great place for beginning and intermediate snorkelers. In winter, it's also a prime spot to watch for whales. ⊠ *Alii Dr., Kailua-Kona.*

EQUIPMENT, LESSONS, AND TOURS

FAMILY **Body Glove Cruises.** This operator is a good choice for families; kids love the waterslide and the high-dive platform. On the Snorkel & Dolphin Watch Adventure, the 65-foot catamaran sets off for uncrowded Red Hill in stunning South Kona from Kailua-Kona pier daily for a morning snorkel cruise that includes breakfast and a BBQ burger lunch, with vegetarian options. A three-hour historical dinner cruise to Kealakekua Bay is a great way to relax, watch the sunset, and learn about Kona's history. It includes a Hawaiian-style buffet, complimentary cocktail, and live music. (A lunch version is also available.) Seasonal whale-watch cruises and all dolphin snorkel cruises guarantee you will see the featured mammals or you can go again for free; the company implements a NOAA-approved Dolphin SMART policy on all of their cruises. Children under five are always free. ⊠ *75-5629 Kuakini Hwy., Kailua-Kona* ☎ *808/326–7122, 800/551–8911* ⊕ *www.bodygloveha-waii.com* ⊠ *From $132.*

FAMILY **Fair Wind Cruises.** In business since 1971, Fair Wind offers morning and
Fodor's Choice afternoon snorkel trips into breathtaking Kealakekua Bay. Great for
★ families with small kids, the custom-built, 60-foot catamaran has two 15-foot waterslides, freshwater showers, and a staircase descending directly into the water for easy access. Snorkel gear is included, along with flotation equipment and prescription masks. The 4½-hour cruise is known for its delicious meals; 3½-hour snack cruises are offered, too. For ages seven and older, the company also operates the *Hula Kai* snorkel cruise, a 55-foot luxury hydrofoil catamaran that takes guests to several remote South Kona locations. Their five-hour morning

snorkel cruise includes a gourmet breakfast buffet and barbecue lunch. ✉ *Keauhou Bay, 78-7130 Kaleiopapa St., Kailua-Kona* ☎ *808/322–2788, 800/677–9461* ⊕ *www.fair-wind.com* 🖃 *Cruises from $145.*

Sea Quest. Careful stewardship of the Kona Coast and its sea life is a major priority for this company, which provides catamaran charters and other snorkeling excursions. Trips leave from Keauhou Bay and head to Captain Cook Monument and other points south. ☎ *808/329–7238* ⊕ *www.seaquesthawaii.com* 🖃 *From $78.*

Snorkel Bob's. You're likely to see Snorkel Bob's wacky ads in your airline in-flight magazine. The company offers a wide selection of rental gear packages and options; they often run specials so be sure to ask. There are two Big Island locations, one in Kona and one at Mauna Lani. ✉ *75-5831 Kahakai St., Kailua-Kona* ☎ *808/329–0770, 800/262–7725* ⊕ *www.snorkelbob.com* 🖃 *From $38/week.*

STAND-UP PADDLEBOARDING

Stand-up paddleboarding (or SUP for short), a sport with roots in the Hawaiian Islands, has grown popular worldwide in recent years. It's available for all skill levels and ages, and even novice stand-up paddleboarders can get up, stay up, and have a great time paddling around a protected bay or exploring the gorgeous coastline. All you need to get started is a large body of calm water, a board, and a paddle. The workout tests your core strength as well as your balance and offers an unusual vantage point from which to enjoy the beauty of island and ocean.

8

BEST SPOTS

Anaehoomalu Bay Beach (A-Bay). In this well-protected bay, even when surf is rough on the rest of the island, it's usually fairly calm here, though trades pick up heartily in the afternoon. Boards are available for rent at the north end, and the safe area for stand-up paddling is marked by buoys. ✉ *Off Waikoloa Beach Dr., south of Waikoloa Beach Marriott, Kohala Coast.*

Hilo Bay. At this favorite among locals, the best place to put in is at **Reeds Bay Beach Park.** Most afternoons you'll share the bay with local paddling clubs. Stay inside the breakwater unless the ocean is calm (or you're feeling unusually adventurous). Conditions range from extremely calm to quite choppy. ✉ *Banyan Way and Banyan Dr., 1 mile from downtown Hilo.*

Kailua Bay and Kamakahonu Beach. The small sandy beach that fronts the Courtyard King Kamehameha's Kona Beach Hotel is great for kids; the water here is especially calm and gentle. If you're more daring, you can easily paddle out of the bay and along the coast for some great exploring. ✉ *Alii Dr., next to Kailua Pier, Kailua-Kona.*

Passengers aboard the *Atlantis VII* submarine can visit the aquatic world without getting wet.

EQUIPMENT AND LESSONS

Fodor's Choice ★ **Hypr Nalu Hawaii.** SUP master Ian Foo is the king of the stand-up paddle-board in downtown Kailua-Kona. At his small oceanfront shop across from the pier, he stocks paddleboards and surfboards, all beautifully custom-made. They also offer OC1 lessons, rentals, active ocean gear, and apparel. He and his family are serious and enthusiastic about ocean sports and are awesome teachers. ⊠ *75-5663A Palani Rd., Kailua-Kona* ☎ *808/960–4667* ⊕ *www.hyprnalu.com.*

Ocean Sports. This outfitter rents equipment, offers lessons, and has the perfect location for easy access to the bay. Ocean Sports also operates rental shacks at the Hilton Waikoloa Village, Whale Center Kawai-hae, Queens' MarketPlace, and at Anaehoomalu Bay. They can also set you up with cruises, dives, and charters elsewhere on the island. ⊠ *Waikoloa Beach Marriott, 69-275 Waikoloa Beach Dr., Waikoloa* ☎ *808/886–6666* ⊕ *www.hawaiioceansports.com* ☎ *SUP rental $50/hr.*

SUBMARINE TOURS

FAMILY **Atlantis Submarines.** Want to stay dry while exploring the tropical under-sea world? Climb aboard the 48-passenger *Atlantis X* submarine, anchored off Kailua Pier, across from Courtyard King Kamehameha's Kona Beach Hotel. A large glass dome in the bow and 13 viewing ports on each side allow clear views of the aquatic world more than 100 feet down. This is a great trip for kids and nonswimmers. ⊠ *75-5669 Alii Dr., Kailua-Kona* ☎ *808/326–7939, 800/381–0237* ⊕ *www.atlantisad-ventures.com* ☎ *$119.*

SURFING

The Big Island does not have the variety of great surfing spots found on Oahu or Maui, but it does have decent waves and a thriving surf culture. Local kids and avid surfers frequent a number of places up and down the Kona and Kohala coasts of West Hawaii; some have become famous surf champions. Expect high surf in winter and much calmer activity during summer. The surf scene is much more active on the Kona side.

BEST SPOTS

Honolii Cove. North of Hilo, this is the best surfing spot on the eastern side of the island. It hosts many exciting surf contests. ⊠ *Off Hwy. 19, near mile marker 4, Hilo.*

Kahaluu Beach Park. Slightly north of this beach park and just past the calm lagoon filled with snorkelers, beginning and intermediate surfers can have a go at some nice waves. *Alii Dr., Kailua-Kona.*

Kohanaiki Also known as Pine Trees, this community beach park is among the best places to catch waves. Keep in mind that it's a very popular local surf spot on an island where there aren't all that many surf spots, so be respectful. ⊠ *Off Hwy. 11, Kohanaiki entrance gate, about 2 miles south of Kona airport, Kailua-Kona.*

Old Kona Airport Park. This park is a good place for catching wave action. A couple of the island's outfitters conduct surf lessons here, as the break is far from potentially dangerous rocks and reefs. ⊠ *Kuakini Rd., Kailua-Kona.*

EQUIPMENT, LESSONS, AND TOURS

Hawaii Lifeguard Surf Instructors. This family-owned, lifeguard-certified school helps novices become wave riders at Kahaluu Beach Park and offers lessons for more experienced riders at Kona's top surf spots. A two-hour introductory lesson has one instructor per two to four students. Private instruction is available as well. If the waves are on the smaller side, they convert to stand-up paddleboard lessons for the same prices as surfing. ⊠ *75-5909 Alii Dr., Kailua-Kona* ☎ *808/324–0442, 808/936–7873* ⊕ *www.surflessonshawaii.com* ✉ *From $75.*

Fodor's Choice ★ **Ocean Eco Tours Surf School.** Family-owned and -operated, Kona's oldest surf school emphasizes the basics and specializes in beginners. It's one of a handful of operators permitted to conduct business in Kaloko-Honokohau National Historical Park, which gets waves even when other spots on the west side are flat. All lessons are taught by certified instructors, and the school guarantees that you will surf. If you're hooked, sign up for a three-day package. There's an authentic soul surfer's vibe to this operation, and they are equally diehard about teaching you about the ocean and having you standing up riding waves on your first day. Group, private, and semiprivate lessons available. ⊠ *King Kam Hotel, 75-5660 Palani Rd., Suite 304, Kailua-Kona* ☎ *808/324–7873* ⊕ *www. oceanecotours.com* ✉ *From $95.*

8

Humpback whales are visible off the coast of the Big Island between December and April.

Fodor's Choice
★

Orchidland Surfboards & Surf Shop. On Big Island radio stations, you're likely to hear the familiar voice of shop owner and local surf legend Stan Lawrence delivering the daily surf reports. Around since the 1970s, his shop, located in the heart of Hilo's historic district, is a veritable testament to Big Island surfing, with surf culture/Hawaiiana on the walls, along with vintage boards, old photos, and plenty of stories. The shop offers custom surfboards, body boards, and other gear for sale or rent along with the latest surf apparel. ✉ *262 Kamehameha Ave., Hilo* ☎ *808/935–1533* ⊕ *www.orchidlandsurf.com.*

WHALE- AND DOLPHIN-WATCHING

Each winter, some two-thirds of the North Pacific humpback whale population (about 4,000–5,000 animals) migrate over 3,500 miles from the icy Alaska waters to the warm Hawaiian ocean to mate and, the following year, give birth to and nurse their calves. Recent reports indicate that the whale population is on the upswing—a few years ago one even ventured into the mouth of Hilo Harbor, which marine biologists say is quite rare. Humpbacks are spotted here from early December through the end of April, but other species, like sperm, pilot, and beaked whales as well as spinner, spotted, and bottlenose dolphins, can be seen year-round. ■TIP→ **If you take a morning cruise, you're more likely to see dolphins.** *In addition to the outfitters listed below, see Snorkeling for more outfitters that offer whale- and dolphin-watching cruises.*

BE DOLPHIN SMART

DOLPHIN SMART

The idea of swimming with Hawaii's wild spinner dolphins may seem like an amazing experience, but in actuality it's neither ecologically conscious, nor safe for the animals. Oh, and did we mention that it's illegal to feed, chase, harass, or swim too closely to wild dolphins? Instead, visitors should follow the Dolphin SMART guidelines ⊕ *sanctuaries.noaa.gov/dolphinsmart* developed by NOAA, the Whale and Dolphin Conservation, and the Dolphin Ecology Project. These guidelines break down the cans and cannots when it comes to wildlife, and the rules are proudly followed by most tour operators and businesses; if you're looking into a company that does not follow these practices, we suggest you look elsewhere.

S is for Stay Away. People must stay at least 50 yards from dolphins at all times.

M is for Move Cautiously Away. Move away cautiously from dolphins who are showing signs of disturbance.

A is for Always Put Your Engine in Neutral. Always put your boat engine in neutral when dolphins are near. The same can be said for humans—put yourself in neutral and stop to think about the negative impact you may have by getting too close.

R is for Refrain. This means refrain from swimming with, feeding, or touching dolphins.

T is for Teach. Share your knowledge with others.

Keep these guidelines in mind for Hawaii's other protected species such as sea turtles, humpback whales (and other whales and dolphins), and Hawaiian monk seals.

TOURS

Captain Dan McSweeney's Whale Watch Learning Adventures. Captain Dan McSweeney, self-described whale researcher and conservationist, offers three-hour trips on his double-decker, 40-foot cruise boat. In addition to humpbacks (in winter), he'll try to show you dolphins and some of the six other whale species that live off the Kona Coast throughout the year. McSweeney guarantees you'll see whales or he'll take you out again for free. ⊠ *Honokōhau Harbor, 74-381 Kealakehe Pkwy., Kailua-Kona* ☎ *808/322–0028, 888/942–5376* ⊕ *www.ilovewhales.com* ⤴ *$120.*

Hawaii Nautical. The only NOAA-designated "Dolphin SMART" operator in Hawaii, this company practices strict guidelines for viewing protected marine animals, including dolphins and whales. You can be assured that you'll enjoy a wonderful ocean tour, see plenty of animals, and not be a part of harming or impacting the animal's activities or habitats. ⊠ *74-425 Kealakehe Parkway, Slip I-10, Kailua-Kona* ☎ *808/234-7245* ⊕ *www.hawaiinautical.com* ⤴ *From $79.*

Living Ocean Adventures. Captain Tom Bottrell, a U.S. Merchant Marine officer who also holds a bachelor's degree in meteorology and oceanography, and a master's in ecology from the University of Michigan, is ideally qualified to lead whale-watching tours in Kona waters. Excursions on board the six-person *Spinner* last about four hours and can be booked as private or shared charters; each tour focuses on the biology, ecology, and conservation of these magnificent creatures. The company practices responsible marine mammal viewing in line with NOAA's Dolphin SMART guidelines. ✉ *Kailua-Kona* ☎ *808/325–5556* ⊕ *www. livingoceanadventures.com* 💲 *From $110.*

GOLF, HIKING, AND OUTDOOR ACTIVITIES

Visit Fodors.com for advice, updates, and bookings

Updated
by Kristina
Anderson

With the Big Island's predictably mild year-round climate, it's no wonder you'll find an emphasis on outdoor activities. After all, this is the home of the annual Ironman World Championship triathlon. Whether you're an avid hiker or a beginning bicyclist, a casual golfer or a tennis buff, you'll find plenty of land-based activities to lure you away from the sand and surf.

You can explore by bike, helicopter, ATV, zip line, or horse, or you can put on your hiking boots and use your own horsepower. No matter how you get around, you'll be treated to breathtaking backdrops along the Big Island's 266-mile coastline and within its 4,028 square miles (and still growing!). Aerial tours take in the latest eruption activity and lava flows, as well as the island's gorgeous tropical valleys, gulches, and coastal plains. Trips into the backcountry wilderness explore the rain forest, private ranch lands, and coffee farms, while sleepy sugar-plantation villages offer a glimpse of Hawaii's bygone days.

Golfers will find acclaimed championship golf courses at the Kohala coast resorts—Mauna Kea Beach Hotel, Hapuna Beach Prince Hotel, Mauna Lani Bay Hotel & Bungalows, and Waikoloa Beach Resort, among others. And during the winter, if snow conditions allow, you can even go skiing on top of Maunakea (elevation: 13,796 feet). It's a skiing experience unlike any other.

AERIAL TOURS

There's nothing quite like the aerial view of a waterfall crashing down a couple of thousand feet into cascading pools, or watching lava flow to the ocean as exploding clouds of steam billow into the air. You can get this bird's-eye view from a helicopter or a fixed-wing small plane. All operators pay strict attention to safety. So how to get the best experience for your money? ■ TIP→ Before you choose a company, be a savvy

DID YOU KNOW?

A helicopter tour is one of the best ways to see the Big Island's most inaccessible areas. It's hard to beat an aerial view of a 2,600-foot waterfall plunging down a sheer cliff face into the valley below.

traveler and ask the right questions. What kind of aircraft do they fly? What is their safety record?

Big Island Air Tours. This small company, in business since the 1980s, offers fixed-wing tours of the island, including a circle island, Kilauea sunset tour, or Maui-Big Island tour. They also feature charter or cargo service between all the major islands except Kauai. This is a good alternative to the pricier helicopter tours. ☎ 808/329–4868 ⊕ *www.bigislandair.com* ✉ *From $345.*

Blue Hawaiian Helicopters. Hawaii Island's premier flight is on the roomy, $3-million Eco-Star helicopter—so smooth and quiet you hardly realize you're taking off. No worries about what seat you get because there are great views from each. Pilots are also state of Hawaii–certified tour guides, so they are very knowledgeable and experienced but not overly chatty. In the breathtaking Waimanu Valley, the helicopter hovers amazingly close to 2,600-foot cliffs and cascading waterfalls. The two-hour Big Island Spectacular also takes in Kilauea Volcano lava flows as well as the valleys; you can even choose an optional waterfall landing as part of it. Most tours leave from Blue Hawaiian's Waikoloa heliport, but the 50-minute Circle of Fire tour departs from Hilo for the volcano's wonders. Tours on the company's A-Star helicopters are less expensive. ⊠ *Waikoloa Heliport, Hwy. 19, Waikoloa* ☎ *808/961–5600* ⊕ *www.bluehawaiian.com* ✉ *From $259.*

Fodor'sChoice
★

Paradise Helicopters. This locally owned adventure tour company offers numerous helicopter tour options, many of which are completely unique. The "Doors-off Lava & Rainforests Adventure" shows guests Hilo's rain forests and Waianuenue (Rainbow Falls) before getting you so close to the lava flows that you can feel the heat, while the Sunset Experience allows you to experience glowing lava plus a Kona sunset over Puuhonua o Honaunau. Pilots, many of whom have military backgrounds, are fun and knowledgeable. ■ TIP➔ The only helicopter company in Hawaii certified by the Hawaii Ecotour Association, Paradise offers you the option to offset your tour's carbon footprint by having a tree planted in Hawaii for each ride you take. ☎ 808/969–7392, 866/876–7422 ⊕ *www.paradisecopters.com* ✉ *From $274.*

Safari Helicopters. Based at the Hilo airport, Safari offers a 45-minute tour of the volcanic activity, craters, and lava tree forest or a 60-minute tour that visits these attractions plus the waterfalls. ■ TIP➔ Book online for substantial discounts. ⊠ *Hilo International Airport, 2350 Kekuanaoa St., Hilo* ☎ *808/969–1259* ⊕ *www.safarihelicopters.com* ✉ *From $189.*

ATV TOURS

A fun way to experience the Big Island's rugged coastline and wild ranch lands is through an off-road adventure—a real backcountry experience. At higher elevations, the weather gets nippy and rainy, but views can be awesome. Protective gear is provided, and everyone gets a mini driving lesson. Generally, you must be 16 or older to ride your own ATV; some outfitters allow children seven and older as passengers.

ATV Outfitters Hawaii. These trips take in the scenic beauty of the rugged North Kohala Coast, traveling along coastal cliffs and the Kohala Ditch Trail into the forest in search of waterfalls, along 22 miles of trails. ATV Outfitters also offers double-seater ATVs for parents traveling with children or adults who don't feel comfortable operating their own vehicle. Knowledgeable guides stop at various points of interest and share the fascinating history of the region. The company also offers a Waterfall and Rainforest tour and a Deluxe Ocean and Waterfall adventure. ✉ *51-324 Lighthouse Rd., Kapaau* ☎ *808/889–6000, 888/288–7288* ⊕ *www. atvoutfittershawaii.com* 💲 *From $179.*

Fodor'sChoice
★ **Waipio Ride the Rim.** A fabulous way to experience the extraordinary beauty atop lush Waipio Valley, the tour is led by fun and knowledgeable guides along private trails to the headwaters of the twin Hiilawe Falls, Hawaii's highest single-fall waterfall. You'll stop for a snack and swim in a ginger-laden grotto with a refreshing waterfall (disclaimer: it's freezing cold!) and travel to a series of lookouts; bring a bathing suit and be prepared to get wet and muddy. Beginners are welcome, but to drive your own ATV, you must be 16 or over. Adults who don't wish to drive may book the buggy. ✉ *Waipio Valley Artworks Bldg., 48-5416 Kukuihaele Rd., Kukuihaele* ☎ *808/775–1450, 877/775–1450* ⊕ *www. ridetherim.com* 💲 *From $199.*

BIKING

The Big Island's biking trails and road routes range from easy to moderate coastal rides to rugged backcountry wilderness treks that challenge the most serious cyclists. You can soak up the island's storied scenic vistas and varied geography—from tropical rain forest to rolling ranch country, from high-country mountain meadows to dry lava deserts. It's dry, windy, and hot on Kona's and Kohala's coastal trails, mountainous through South Kona, and cool, wet, and muddy in the upcountry Waimea and Volcano areas, as well as in lower Puna. There are long distances between towns, few bike lanes, narrow single-lane highways, and scanty services in the Kau, Puna, South Kona, and Kohala Coast areas, so plan accordingly for your weather, water, food, and lodging needs before setting out. ■ TIP➔ **Your best bet is to book with an outfitter who has all the details covered.**

Hawaii Cycling Club. This nonprofit club has tons of information on biking the Big Island, along with scheduled rides and events such as picnics. ⊕ *www.hawaiicyclingclub.com.*

BEST SPOTS

Fodor'sChoice
★ **Kulani Trails.** This has been called the best ride in the state—if you really want to get gnarly. The technically demanding ride, which passes majestic eucalyptus trees, is for advanced cyclists; muddy conditions prevail. To reach the trailhead from the intersection of Highway 11 and Highway 19, take Highway 19 south about 4 miles, turn right on Stainback Highway, continue 2½ miles, turn right at the Waiakea Arboretum, and park near the gate. A permit is required, available from the Department

of Land and Natural Resources at Kawili Street and Kilauea Avenue in Hilo. ⊠ *Stainback Hwy., Hilo.*

Old Puna Trail. A 10½-mile ride through the subtropical jungle in Puna, this trail leads into one of the island's most isolated areas. It starts on a cinder road, which becomes a four-wheel-drive trail. If it's rained recently, you'll have to deal with puddles—the first few of which you'll gingerly avoid until you give in and go barreling through the rest for the sheer fun of it. This is a great ride for all abilities and takes about 90 minutes. To get to the trailhead from Highway 130, take Kaloli Road to Beach Road. ⚠ **Ride at your own risk; this is not a maintained trail.** ⊠ *Kaloli Rd. at Hwy. 130, Pahoa.*

EQUIPMENT AND TOURS

There are rental shops in Kailua-Kona and a couple in Waimea and Hilo. Many resorts rent bicycles that can be used around the properties. Most outfitters can provide a bicycle rack for your car, and all offer reduced rates for rentals longer than one day. All retailers offer excellent advice about where to go; they know the areas well.

BikeVolcano.com. This outfitter leads three- or five-hour bike rides through Hawaii Volcanoes National Park, mostly downhill, that take in fantastic sights, from rain forests to craters. Equipment, support van, and food are included; pickup locations in Hilo and Volcano (and Kona by request). The company also coordinates and leads rides to the active lava flows. ⊠ *Hilo* 🕾 *808/934–9199, 888/934–9199* ⊕ *www. bikevolcano.com* 🖃 *From $115.*

Bike Works. This company caters to cyclists of all skill levels with race services, suggested rides for moderate to advanced riders, and rentals of deluxe road bikes, full-suspension mountain bikes, and high-end triathlon bikes. Their retail space, located in Kona's "Old" Industrial Area, is huge and impressive. ⊠ *Hale Hana Center, 74-5583 Luhia St., Kailua-Kona* 🕾 *808/326–2453* ⊕ *www.bikeworkskona. com* 🖃 *From $55.*

Hilo Bike Hub. An enthusiast shop specializing in servicing bikes to fit the ruggedness of Hawaii's East side terrain, they are a good resource for those wishing to mountain bike in these off-the-beaten-path areas. Sponsors of rides and local events, they were instrumental in helping to establish Kulani Trails, part of the Waiakea Forest reserve, as an official mountain biking area. They also carry gear and accessories. ⊠ *318 East Kawili St., Hilo* 🕾 *808/961–4452* ⊕ *www.hilobikehub.com.*

Kona Beach & Sports. For those who prefer comfort over speed, Kona Beach & Sports rents seven-speed city cruisers and "Specialized" brand 24-speed hybrids perfect for cruising the waterfront. ⊠ *Kona Inn Shopping Village, 75-5744 Alii Dr., Kailua-Kona* 🕾 *808/329–2294* ⊕ *www. konabeachandsports.com.*

Mid Pacific Wheels. The oldest bike shop on the Big Island, this community-oriented shop near the university carries a full line of bikes and accessories and rents mountain bikes for exploring the Hilo area. The friendly staff provides expert advice on where to go and what to see and do on a self-guided tour. They also carry a large selection of cycling accesssories, bikes, and repair parts. ✉ *1133C Manono St., Hilo* ☎ *808/935–6211* ⊕ *www.midpacificwheelsllc.com* 🖻 *From $35.*

CAVING

The Kanohina Lava Tube system is about 1,000 years old and was used by the ancient Hawaiians for water collection and for shelter. More than 40 miles of these braided lava tubes have been mapped so far in the Kau District of the Big Island, near South Point. About 45 miles south of Kailua-Kona, these lava tubes are a great experience for cavers of all age levels and abilities.

Fodor's Choice **Kula Kai Caverns.** Expert cave guides lead groups into the fantastic under-
★ world of these caverns near South Point. The braided lava-tube system attracts scientists from around the world, who come to study and map them (more than 40 miles so far). Tours range from the "Lighted Trail" (in the lighted show cave, which is easy walking), to the "Two Hour," a deep-down-under spelunking adventure that often takes closer to three hours and allows you to see archaeological evidence of the ancient Hawaiians. Longer, customized tours are also available and programs are tailored to each group's interest and abilities; all gear is provided. Tours start at an Indiana Jones–style expedition tent, complete with a topographic map and divulge fascinating details about the caves' geologic and cultural history. Reservations are required. ✉ *Kula Kai Estates, Lauhala Dr. at Kona Kai Blvd.* ☎ *808/929–9725* ⊕ *www.kulakaicaverns.com* 🖻 *From $20.*

GOLF

For golfers, the Big Island is a big deal—starting with the Mauna Kea Golf Course, which opened in 1964 and remains one of the state's top courses. Black lava and deep blue sea are the predominant themes on the island. In the roughly 40 miles from the Kona Country Club to the Mauna Kea resort, nine courses are carved into sunny seaside lava plains, with four more in the hills above. Indeed, most of the Big Island's best courses are concentrated along the Kohala Coast, statistically the sunniest spot in Hawaii. Vertically speaking, although the majority of courses are seaside or at least near sea level, three are located above 2,000 feet, another one at 4,200 feet. This is significant because in Hawaii temperatures drop 3°F for every 1,000 feet of elevation gained.

Green Fee: Green fees listed here are the highest course rates per round on weekdays for U.S. residents. Courses with varying weekend rates are noted in the individual listings. (Some courses charge non–U.S. residents higher prices.) ■ TIP→ **Discounts are often available for resort guests and for those who book tee times online, as well as for those willing to play in the afternoon. Twilight rates are also usually offered.**

Big Island Country Club. Set 2,000 feet above sea level on the slopes of Hualalai, this course is out of the way but well worth the drive. In 1997, Pete and Perry Dye created a gem that plays through upland

TIPS FOR THE GREEN

Golf is golf, and Hawaii is part of the United States, but island golf nevertheless has its own quirks. Here are a few tips to make your golf experience in the Islands more pleasant.

■ Wear sunscreen, even in December. We recommend zinc-based, with a minimum SPF of 30, and that you reapply on the 10th tee.

■ Stay hydrated. Spending four-plus hours in the sun and heat means you'll perspire away considerable fluids and energy.

■ Private courses may allow you to play at their discretion.

■ All resort courses and many daily-fee courses provide rental clubs. In many cases, they're the latest lines from Titleist, Ping, Callaway, and the like. This is true for both men and women, as well as left-handers, which means you don't have to schlep clubs across the Pacific.

■ Pro shops at most courses are stocked with balls, tees, and other

accoutrements, so even if you bring a bag, it needn't weigh a ton.

■ Come spikeless—very few Hawaii courses permit metal spikes.

■ Resort courses, in particular, offer more than the usual three sets of tees, sometimes four or five. So bite off as much or little challenge as you like. Tee it up from the tips and you'll end up playing a few 600-yard par-5s and see a few 250-yard forced carries.

■ In theory, you can play golf in Hawaii 365 days a year. But there's a reason the Hawaiian Islands are so green. Better to bring an umbrella and light jacket and not use them than to not bring them and get soaked.

■ Unless you play a muni or certain daily-fee courses, plan on taking a cart. Carts are mandatory at most courses and are included in the green fee.

woodlands—more than 2,500 trees line the fairways. On the par-5 16th, a giant tree in the middle of the fairway must be avoided with the second shot. Five lakes and a meandering natural mountain stream bring water into play on nine holes. The most dramatic is the par-3 17th, where Dye created a knockoff of his infamous 17th at the TPC at Sawgrass. ⊠ 71-1420 Hawaii Belt Rd., Kailua-Kona ☎ 808/325–5044 ⊕ www. bigislandcountryclub.com ⚑ $135 with cart, bottled water, range balls ⚐ 18 holes, 7075 yards, par 72.

FAMILY **Hamakua Country Club.** While the typical, modern 18-hole golf course requires at least 250 acres, this public course fits into just 19. Compact is the word, and with several holes crisscrossing, this place may require you to BYO hard hat. Holes run up and down a fairly steep slope overlooking the ocean—the views are spectacular. Cheerfully billed as an Old World golf experience, the course works on the honor system ("if no one is there, put your money in the slot") and the 9th green is square, but for 20 bucks (under 17 plays free), whaddaya expect? Most golfers prefer to walk, but there are carts available. ⊠ Hwy. 19, at mile marker 41, Honokaa ✛ 43 miles north of Hilo ☎ 808/775–7244 ⊕ hamakuagolf.com ⚑ $20 ⚐ Two sets of 9 holes, 4800 yards, par 66 (men), 74 (women).

Most of the Big Island's top golf courses are located on the sunny Kohala Coast.

Hapuna Golf Course. Hapuna's challenging play and environmental sensitivity make it one of the island's most unusual courses. Designed by Arnold Palmer and Ed Seay, it is nestled into the natural contours of the land from the shoreline to about 700 feet above sea level. There are spectacular views of mountains and sea (Maui is often visible in the distance). Holes wind through kiawe scrub, beds of jagged lava, and tall fountain grasses. Hole 12 is favored for its beautiful views and challenging play. ⊠ *62-100 Kanunaoa Dr., Waimea (Hawaii County)* ☎ *808/880–3000* ⊕ *www.hapunabeachresort.com/golf* ⊇ *$160, $100 after 1 pm* ⚑ *18 holes, 6875 yards, par 72.*

Hilo Municipal Golf Course. Hilo Muni is proof that you don't need sand bunkers to create a challenging course. Trees and several meandering creeks are the danger here. The course, which offers views of Hilo Bay from most holes, has produced many of the island's top players over the years. Taking a divot reminds you that you're playing on a volcano—the soil is dark black crushed lava. ⊠ *340 Haihai St., Hilo* ☎ *808/959–7711* ⊕ *www.hawaiicounty.gov/pr-golf* ⊇ *$35 weekdays, $40 weekends* ⚑ *18 holes, 6325 yards, par 71.*

Kona Country Club. This recently renovated William F. Bell–designed golf course is perched high above historic Keauhou Bay with spectacular views of the sea from almost every hole. Stands of mature coco trees, several remarkable lava features, wide fairways, and challenging Bermuda greens make this course a classic Hawaii golf experience that's open to the public. The most prominent feature is the "blowhole" (*puka* in Hawaiian), fronting the par-4 13th tee, where seawater propelled through a lava tube formation erupts forcefully like a geyser—try timing your drive to penetrate the shooting water! In the winter months, golfers may also be treated to the sights of migrating humpback whales splashing and breaching within a tee shot of the shoreline. Amici's, the onsite restaurant, and the Vista Bar—both favorites of locals, whether they golf or not—have some of the best sunset views on the Kona Coast. ⊠ *78-7000 Alii Dr., Kailua-Kona* ☎ *808/322–2595* ⊕ *www.konacountryclub.com* ⊠ *$180* ♟ *18 holes, 6613 yds, Par 72.*

Makalei Golf Club. Set on the slopes of Hualalai, at an elevation of 2,900 feet, Makalei is one of the rare Hawaii courses with bent-grass putting greens, which means they're quick and without the grain associated with Bermuda greens. Former PGA Tour official Dick Nugent (1992) designed holes that play through thick forest and open to wide ocean views. Elevation change is a factor on many holes, especially the par-3 8th, whose tee is 80 feet above the green. In addition to fixed natural obstacles, wild peacocks and turkeys can make for an entertaining game. ▮TIP➔ **Ask about summer rates.** ⊠ *72-3890 Hawaii Belt Rd., Kailua-Kona* ☎ *808/325–6625* ⊕ *www.makalei.com* ⊠ *$109, $89 after 12, $69 after 2* ♟ *18 holes, 7091 yards, par 72.*

Fodor'sChoice
★
Mauna Kea Golf Course. Originally opened in 1964, this golf course is one of the most revered in the state. It underwent a tee-to-green renovation by Rees Jones, son of the original architect, Robert Trent Jones Sr. Hybrid grasses were planted, the number of bunkers increased, and the overall yardage was expanded. The par-3 3rd is one of the world's most famous holes—and one of the most photographed. You play from a cliffside tee across a bay to a cliffside green. Getting across the ocean is just half the battle because the green is surrounded by seven bunkers, each one large and undulated. The course is a shot-maker's paradise and follows Jones's "easy bogey, tough par" philosophy. ▮TIP➔ **Since you're in Hawaii, try the new Golfboard, a surf-inspired alternative to a golf cart.** ⊠ *62-100 Kaunaoe Dr., Waimea (Hawaii County)* ☎ *808/882–5400* ⊕ *www.maunakeagolf.com* ⊠ *$285, $195 after 1:30 pm, add Golfboard for $35* ♟ *18 holes, 7250 yards, par 72.*

Fodor'sChoice
★
Mauna Lani Resort. Black lava flows, lush green turf, white sand, and the Pacific's multihues of blue define the 36 holes at Mauna Lani. The South Course includes the par-3 15th across a turquoise bay, one of the most photographed holes in Hawaii. But it shares "signature hole" honors with the 7th, a long par 3, which plays downhill over convoluted patches of black lava, with the Pacific immediately to the left and a dune to the right. The North Course plays a couple of shots tougher. Its most distinctive hole is the 17th, a par 3 with the green set in a lava pit 50 feet deep. The shot from an elevated tee must carry a pillar of lava that rises from the pit and partially blocks a view of the green. ⊠ *68-1310 Mauna Lani Dr., Waimea (Hawaii County)* ☎ *808/885–6655* ⊕ *www.maunalani.com* ⊠ *$235 before 1, $155 after 1* ♟ *North Course: 18 holes, 6057 yards, par 72. South Course: 18 holes, 6025 yards, par 72.*

Volcano Golf & Country Club. Just outside Hawaii Volcanoes National Park—and barely a stone's throw from Halemaumau Crater—this is by far Hawaii's highest course. At 4,200-feet elevation, shots tend to fly a bit farther than at sea level, even in the often cool, misty air. Because of the elevation and climate, this Hawaii course features Bermuda and seashore Paspalum grass putting greens. The course is mostly flat, and holes play through stands of *ohia lehua* (flowering evergreen trees), and multitrunk hau trees. The uphill par-4 15th doglegs through a tangle of hau. ⊠ *Pii Mauna Dr., off Hwy. 11, Hawaii Volcanoes National Park* ☎ *808/967–7331* ⊕ *www.volcanogolfshop.com* ✉ *$61, including cart* ⚐ *18 holes, 6106 yards, par 72.*

Fodor'sChoice **Waikoloa Beach Resort.** Robert Trent Jones Jr. built the Beach Course
★ at Waikoloa (1981) on an old flow of crinkly *aa* lava, which he used to create holes that are as artful as they are challenging. The par-5 12th hole is one of Hawaii's most picturesque and plays through a chute of black lava to a seaside green. At the Kings' Course (1990), Tom Weiskopf and Jay Morrish built a links-esque track. It turns out lava's natural humps and declivities replicate the contours of seaside Scotland. But there are a few island twists—such as seven lakes. This is "option golf," as Weiskopf and Morrish provide different risk-reward tactics on each hole. ■TIP➜ Fees vary depending on the time of day, the cheapest being a midday tee-time. ⊠ *600 Waikoloa Beach Dr., Waikoloa* ☎ *808/886–7888* ⊕ *www.waikoloabeachgolf.com* ✉ *From $125, including cart* ⚐ *Beach Course: 18 holes, 6566 yards, par 70; Kings' Course: 18 holes, 7074 yards, par 72.*

Waikoloa Village Golf Course. Robert Trent Jones Jr., who created some of the most expensive courses on the Kohala Coast, also designed this little gem 20 minutes from the coast. At a 450-foot elevation, it offers ideal playing conditions year-round; ask about summer rates. Holes run across rolling hills with sweeping mountain and ocean views. ⊠ *68-1792 Melia St., Waikoloa* ☎ *808/883–9621* ⊕ *www.waikoloavillagegolf.com* ✉ *$100, $66 twilight* ⚐ *18 holes, 6230 yards, par 72.*

HIKING

Ecologically diverse, Hawaii Island has four of the five major climate zones and 8 of 13 sub-climate zones—a lot of variation for one island—and you can experience them all on foot. The ancient Hawaiians cut trails across the lava plains, through the rain forests, and up along the mountain heights. Many of these paths are still in use today. Part of the King's Trail at Anaehoomalu winds through a field of lava rocks covered with ancient petroglyphs. Many other trails, historic and modern, crisscross the huge Hawaii Volcanoes National Park and other parts of the island. Plus, the serenity of remote beaches, such as Papakolea Beach (Green Sands Beach), is accessible only to hikers. Check the statewide trail system website at ⊕ *hawaiitrails.ehawaii.gov* for up-to-date information for hiking trails.

Department of Land and Natural Resources, State Parks Division. The division provides information on all the Big Island's state parks and jurisdictions. Check online for the latest information and advisories. ⊠ *75 Aupuni St., Hilo* ☎ *808/961–9544* ⊕ *www.dlnr.hawaii.gov/dsp/parks/hawaii.*

BEST SPOTS

Hawaii Volcanoes National Park. Perhaps the Big Island's premier area for hikers, the park has more than 155 miles of trails providing close-up views of fern and rain forest environments, cinder cones, craters, steam vents, lava fields, rugged coastline, and current eruption activity. Day hikes range from easy to moderately difficult, and from one or two hours to a full day. For a bigger challenge, consider an overnight or multiday backcountry hike with a stay in a park cabin (available en route to the remote coast, in a lush forest, or atop frigid Mauna Loa). To do so, you must first obtain a permit at the backcountry office in the Visitor Emergency Operations Center. ■TIP➔ Daily guided hikes are led by knowledgeable, friendly park rangers. The bulletin boards outside Kilauea Visitor Center and inside Jaggar Museum have

HIKING BIG ISLAND TRAILS

■ Trails on the eastern, or windward, side of the island are often wet and muddy, making them slippery and unstable, so wear good hiking shoes or boots.

■ Bring plenty of water, rain protection, a hat, sunblock, and a cellphone (but be aware that service can be spotty).

■ Don't eat any unknown fruits or plants, or drink unfiltered water from streams.

■ Darkness comes suddenly here, so carry a flashlight if you'll be out after sunset.

■ Always obey posted warning signs.

the day's schedule. Perhaps the Big Island's premier area for hikers, the park has 150 miles of trails providing close-up views. ✉ *Hwy. 11, 30 miles south of Hilo, Hawaii Volcanoes National Park* ☎ *808985–6000* ⊕ *www.nps.gov/havo/index.htm.*

Kekaha Kai State Park. A 1.8-mile unimproved road leads to Mahaiula Bay, a gorgeous little piece of paradise, while on the opposite end of the park is lovely Kua Bay. Connecting the two is the 4½-mile Ala Kahakai historic coastal trail. Midway between the two white-sand beaches, you can hike to the summit of Puu Kuili, a 342-foot-high cinder cone with an excellent view of the coastline. Mahaiula has picnic tables and vault toilets. It's dry and hot with no drinking water, so pack sunblock, hats, and extra water. Gates close at 7 pm sharp. ✉ *Trailhead on Hwy. 19, About 2 miles north of Kona airport, Kailua-Kona* ⊕ *dlnr.hawaii.gov/dsp/parks/hawaii.*

Muliwai Trail. On the western side of mystical Waipio Valley, this trail leads to the back of the valley, then switchbacks up through a series of gulches, and finally emerges at Waimanu Valley. Only very experienced hikers should attempt the very remote entire 18-mile trail, the hike of a lifetime. It can take two to three days of backpacking and camping, which requires camping permits from the Division of Forestry and Wildlife in Hilo. ✉ *Trailhead at end of Hwy. 240, Honokaa* ☎ *808/974–4221* ⊕ *hawaiitrails.ehawaii.gov.*

Hawaii Volcanoes National Park's 150 miles of trails offer easy to moderately difficult hikes.

Onomea Bay Trail. This short but beautiful trail is packed with stunning views of the cliffs, bays, and gulches of the Hamakua Coast, on the east side of the island. The trail is just under a mile and fairly easy, with access down to the shore if you want to dip your feet in, although we don't recommend swimming in the rough waters. Unless you pay the $15 entry fee to the nearby botanical garden, entering its gates (even by accident) will send one of the guards running after you to nicely but firmly point you back to the trail. ⊠ *Trailhead on Old Hawaiian Belt Rd., just before botanical garden.* ⊕ *hawaiitrails.ehawaii.gov.*

GOING WITH A GUIDE

To get to some of the best trails and hiking spots (some of which are on private property), it's worth going with a skilled guide. Costs range from $95 to $179, and some hikes include picnic meals or refreshments, and gear, such as binoculars, ponchos, and walking sticks. The outfitters mentioned here also offer customized adventure tours.

Fodor's Choice ★ **Hawaii Forest & Trail.** Since 1993, this locally owned and operated outfit has built a reputation for outstanding nature tours and eco-adventures. Sustainability, cultural sensitivity, and forging island connections are company missions. They have access to thousands of acres of restricted or private lands and employ expert, certified guides who are entertaining and informative. Choose an Endangered Native Habitats bird-watching tour, or journey deep into the Hakalau Forest National Wildlife Refuge. Other tours include a Twilight Volcano Adventure excursion, Kohala waterfall trip, or the Kohala Canopy adventure. If you want to see it all in one day, you can't beat the circle-island Epic Island Volcano Journey, which visits spots off the beaten path—three national parks/historic sites combined with caving in a lava tube. Breakfast, lunch, and a farm-to-fork dinner prepared by a renowned chef are included. ✉ *73-5593 A Olowalau St., Kailua-Kona* ☎ *808/331–8505, 800/464–1993* ⊕ *www.hawaii-forest.com* 💲 *From $69.*

KapohoKine Adventures. This friendly outfitter offers several hiking adventures in Hawaii Volcanoes National Park and surrounding areas, including a 12-hour tour that explores the region by day and sees the lava at night. The Kilauea Hike & Glow tour leads guests to an enormous, still-steaming crater and into areas of the park not normally visited by tour groups. The Evening Volcano Explorer takes you to what remains of the lava-inundated town of Kalapana, explores the park, and ends with dinner at the historic Volcano Winery. The Lava Expedition tour traverses the flow fields looking for lava breakouts while the Secrets of Puna takes you along the rugged coast where you experience a region that's been besieged by lava flows over the years. Tours depart from both Hilo and Kona. ✉ *Grand Naniloa Hotel, 93 Banyan Dr., Hilo* ☎ *808/964–1000* ⊕ *www.kapohokine.com* 💲 *From $149.*

HORSEBACK RIDING

With its *paniolo* (cowboy) heritage and the ranches it spawned, the Big Island is a great place for equestrians. Riders can gallop through green pastures or saunter through Waipio Valley for a taste of old Hawaii.

TOURS

Paniolo Adventures. Paniolo Adventures offers riders of all levels an open-range horseback ride on a working Kohala Mountain cattle ranch, spectacular views of three volcanoes and the coastline, and an authentic paniolo experience from 3,000 feet up. You don't ride nose-to-tail and can spread out and trot or canter if you wish. ✉ *Kohala Mountain Road (Hwy. 250), at mile marker 13.2, Waimea (Hawaii County)* ☎ *808/889–5354* ⊕ *www.panioloadventures.com* 💲 *From $69.*

RUNNING

Ironman 70.3 Hawaii. The only Hawaii qualifier for the World Championship, the spring Ironman 70.3 Hawaii triathlon begins with a swim at Hapuna Beach, then moves to biking for 56 miles on Queen Ka'ahumanu Highway with turnaround in Hawi, and finishes with a 13-mile run through the Fairmont Orchid resort grounds. ☎ ⊕ *www.ironman703hawaii.com.*

Ironman World Championship. Staged annually since 1978, the Ironman World Championship is the granddaddy of all triathlons. For about two weeks in early October, Kailua-Kona takes on the vibe of an Olympic Village as 2,000 top athletes from across the globe and their supporters roam the town, carb-loading, training, and prepping in advance of the world's premier swim-bike-run endurance event. The competition starts at Kailua Pier with a 2.4-mile open-water swim, followed by a 112-mile

Continued on page 230

HAWAII'S PLANTS 101

Tropical Hibiscus

IN FOCUS HAWAII'S PLANTS 101

9

Hawaii is a bounty of rainbow-colored flowers and plants. The evening air is scented with their fragrance. Just look at the front yard of almost any home, travel any road, or visit any local park and you'll see a spectacular array of colored blossoms and leaves. What most visitors don't know is that many of the plants they are seeing are not native to Hawaii; rather, they were introduced during the last two centuries as ornamental plants, or for timber, shade, or fruit.

Hawaii boasts nearly every climate on the planet, excluding the two most extreme: arctic tundra and arid desert. The Islands have wine-growing regions, cactus-speckled ranchlands, icy mountaintops, and the rainiest forests on earth.

Plants introduced from around the world thrive here. The lush lowland valleys along the windward coasts are predominantly populated by non-native trees including yellow- and red-fruited **guava**, silvery-leafed **kukui**, and orange-flowered **tulip trees**.

The colorful **plumeria flower**, very fragrant and commonly used in lei making, and the giant multicolored **hibiscus flower** are both used by many women as hair adornments, and are two of the most common plants found around homes and hotels. The umbrella-like **monkeypod tree** from Central America provides shade in many of Hawaii's parks including Kapiolani Park in Honolulu. Hawaii's largest tree, found in Lahaina, Maui, is a giant **banyan tree.** Its canopy and massive support roots cover about two-thirds of an acre. The native **ohia tree**, with its brilliant red brush-like flowers, and the **hapuu**, a giant tree fern, are common in Hawaii's forests and are also used ornamentally in gardens.

Naupaka, Limahuli Garden

Bougainvillea

Guava

Monkeypod

Banyan

Ohia Lehua*

Tulip Tree

Plumeria

Pandanus

Hibiscus

Anthurium

Kukui

Hapuu

*endemic to Hawaii

DID YOU KNOW?

More than 2,200 plant species are found in the Hawaiian Islands, but only about 1,000 are native. Of these, 320 are so rare, they are endangered. Hawaii's endemic plants evolved from ancestral seeds arriving in the Islands over thousands of years as baggage with birds, floating on ocean currents, or drifting on winds from continents thousands of miles away. Once here, these plants evolved in isolation, creating many new species known nowhere else in the world.

bicycle ride and a 26.2-mile marathon. The week prior is filled with fun community events such as the Underpants Run, in which locals and visitors—as well as well-known celebrities—run through town in only their knickers. ■ TIP→ Only qualified athletes may participate, but if you are visiting during Ironman and want to volunteer, contact kona@ironmanvolunteers.com. 🎫 ⊕ *www.ironmanworldchampionship.com.*

Peaman Running Events. Beloved by the Kona community, Sean "Peaman" Pagett has been a Kona icon for decades, putting on no-cost running and biathlon events, suitable for the whole family. All events are free and have no entry forms. ☎ *808/938–2296* ⊕ *www.kona5k.com.*

SKIING

Where else but Hawaii can you surf, snorkel, and snow ski on the same day? In winter, the 13,796-foot Maunakea (Hawaiian for "white mountain") usually has snow at higher elevations—and along with that, skiing. No lifts, no manicured slopes, no faux-alpine lodges, no après-ski nightlife, but the chance to ski some of the most remote (and let's face it, unlikely) runs on the planet.

Ski Guides Hawaii. With the motto, "Pray for pineapple powder," Christopher Langan of Mauna Kea Ski Corporation is the only licensed outfitter providing transportation, guide services, and ski equipment on Mauna Kea. Snow can fall from Thanksgiving to June, but the most likely months are February and March. With "springlike" conditions, some runs can be 2 miles long and offer 2,500–4,500 feet of "vertical." You may be able to see Haleakala, Kilauea Crater, and Mauna Loa from this surreal place. Langan charges $450 per person for a daylong experience that includes lunch, equipment, guide service, transportation from Waimea, and a four-wheel-drive shuttle back up the mountain after each ski run. Ski or snowboard rentals are $50 per day. ☎ *808/885–4188* ⊕ *www.skihawaii.com* 🎫 *$450.*

ZIP LINE TOURS

Kohala Zipline. This tour features nine zips and five suspension bridges for a thrilling, within-the-canopy adventure in the forest. You'll bounce up to the site in a six-wheel-drive, military-style vehicle. Two certified guides accompany each small group. Designed for all ability levels, the Kohala Zipline focuses on fun and safety, offering a dual line for efficient confident braking. You'll soar more than 100 feet above the ground and feel like a pro by the last platform. A quickie lesson in rappelling is included. Zip and Dip tours (combining zip line, nature walk, lunch, snacks, and waterfall swim) are available. ✉ *54-3676 Akoni Pule Hwy., Kapaau* ☎ *808/331–3620, 800/464–1993* ⊕ *www.kohalazipline.com* 🎫 *From $185.*

Zipline Through Paradise. In addition to offering volcano hikes, waterfall swims, and helicopter tours, this company does zipping exceptionally well, in combinations or via à la carte adventures. It has one of the longest zip lines on the island, at 2,400 feet, as well as the only

DID YOU KNOW?

Waipio Valley is a popular place to go horseback riding. Waipio means "curved water"; the valley is named for the Waipio River, which flows through it.

all-dual-track zip, which means you'll be able to traverse the eight stations more quickly and have a friend at your side the whole way. You'll soar over the lush rain forests of Hilo's Honolii River gorge, complete with thundering waterfalls, and get views of the smoking vent at Kilauea Volcano. This is the one big-name celebrities have been known to book, so you might share the platform with someone famous. Tours depart from both Hilo and Kona. ⊠ *224 Kamehameha Ave., Hilo* ☎ *808/964–1000* ⊕ *www.ziplinehi.com* 🖃 *From $179.*

UNDERSTANDING
THE BIG ISLAND

HAWAIIAN VOCABULARY

HAWAIIAN VOCABULARY

Although an understanding of Hawaiian is by no means required on a trip to the Aloha State, a *malihini*, or newcomer, will find plenty of opportunities to pick up a few of the local words and phrases. Traditional names and expressions are widely used in the Islands. You're likely to read or hear at least a few words each day of your stay.

With a basic understanding and some uninhibited practice, anyone can have enough command of the local tongue to ask for directions and to order from a restaurant menu. One visitor announced she would not leave until she could pronounce the name of the state fish, the *humuhumunukunukuāpua'a*.

Simplifying the learning process is the fact that the Hawaiian language contains only seven consonants—H, K, L, M, N, P, W, and the silent *'okina*, or glottal stop, written '—plus one or more of the five vowels. All syllables, and therefore all words, end in a vowel. Each vowel, with the exception of a few diphthongized double vowels such as *au* (pronounced "ow") or *ai* (pronounced "eye"), is pronounced separately. Thus *'Iolani* is four syllables (ee-oh-la-nee), not three (yo-la-nee). Although some Hawaiian words have only vowels, most also contain some consonants, but consonants are never doubled.

Pronunciation is simple. Pronounce A "ah" as in *father*; E "ay" as in *weigh*; I "ee" as in *marine*; O "oh" as in *no*; U "oo" as in *true*.

Consonants mirror their English equivalents, with the exception of W. When the letter begins any syllable other than the first one in a word, it is usually pronounced as a V. *'Awa*, the Polynesian drink, is pronounced "ava," *'ewa* is pronounced "eva."

Almost all long Hawaiian words are combinations of shorter words; they are not difficult to pronounce if you segment them. *Kalaniana'ole*, the highway running east from Honolulu, is easily understood as *Kalani ana 'ole*. Apply the standard pronunciation rules—the stress falls on the next-to-last syllable of most two- or three-syllable Hawaiian words—and Kalaniana'ole Highway is as easy to say as Main Street.

Now about that fish. Try *humu-humu nuku-nuku āpu a'a*.

The other unusual element in Hawaiian language is the *kahakō*, or macron, written as a short line (ˉ) placed over a vowel. Like the accent (´) in Spanish, the kahakō puts emphasis on a syllable that would normally not be stressed. The most familiar example is probably *Waikīkī*. With no macrons, the stress would fall on the middle syllable; with only one macron, on the last syllable, the stress would fall on the first and last syllables. Some words become plural with the addition of a macron, often on a syllable that would have been stressed anyway. No Hawaiian word becomes plural with the addition of an S, since that letter does not exist in the language.

The Hawaiian diacritical marks are not printed in this guide.

Pidgin

You may hear pidgin, the unofficial language of Hawai'i. It is a Creole language, with its own grammar, evolved from the mixture of English, Hawaiian, Japanese, Portuguese, and other languages spoken in 19th-century Hawai'i, and it is heard everywhere.

Glossary

What follows is a glossary of some of the most commonly used Hawaiian words. Hawaiian residents appreciate visitors who at least try to pick up the local language.

'a'ā: rough, crumbling lava, contrasting with *pāhoehoe,* which is smooth.

'ae: yes.

aikane: friend.

āina: land.

akamai: smart, clever, possessing savoir faire.

akua: god.

ala: a road, path, or trail.

ali'i: a Hawaiian chief, a member of the chiefly class.

aloha: love, affection, kindness; also a salutation meaning both greetings and farewell.

'ānuenue: rainbow.

'a'ole: no.

'apōpō: tomorrow.

'auwai: a ditch.

auwē: alas, woe is me!

'ehu: a red-haired Hawaiian.

'ewa: in the direction of 'Ewa plantation, west of Honolulu.

hala: the pandanus tree, whose leaves (*lau hala*) are used to make baskets and plaited mats.

hālau: school.

hale: a house.

hale pule: church, house of worship.

hana: to work.

haole: foreigner. Since the first foreigners were Caucasian, *haole* now means a Caucasian person.

hapa: a part, sometimes a half; often used as a short form of *hapa haole*, to mean a person who is part-Caucasian.

hau'oli: to rejoice. *Hau'oli Makahiki Hou* means Happy New Year. *Hau'oli lā hānau* means Happy Birthday.

heiau: an outdoor stone platform; an ancient Hawaiian place of worship.

he mea iki or he mea 'ole: you're welcome.

holo: to run.

holoholo: to go for a walk, ride, or sail.

holokū: a long Hawaiian dress, somewhat fitted, with a yoke and a train. Influenced by European fashion, it was worn at court, and at least one local translates the word as "expensive mu'umu'u."

holomū: a post–World War II cross between a *holokū* and a mu'umu'u, less fitted than the former but less voluminous than the latter, and having no train.

honi: to kiss; a kiss. A phrase that some tourists may find useful, quoted from a popular hula, is *Honi Ka'ua Wikiwiki:* Kiss me quick!

honu: turtle.

ho'omalimali: flattery, a deceptive "line," bunk, baloney, hooey.

huhū: angry.

hui: a group, club, or assembly. A church may refer to its congregation as a *hui* and a social club may be called a *hui*.

hukilau: a seine; a communal fishing party in which everyone helps to drive the fish into a huge net, pull it in, and divide the catch.

hula: the dance of Hawai'i.

iki: little.

ipo: sweetheart. Commonly seen as "ku'uipo," or "my sweetheart."

ka: the. This is the definite article for most singular words; for plural nouns, the definite article is usually *nā*. Since there is no S in Hawaiian, the article may be your only clue that a noun is plural.

kahuna: a priest, doctor, or other trained person of old Hawai'i, endowed with special professional skills that often included prophecy or other supernatural powers; the plural form is kāhuna.

kai: the sea, saltwater.

kalo: the taro plant from whose root *poi* (paste) is made.

kamā'aina: literally, a child of the soil; it refers to people who were born in the Islands or have lived there for a long time.

kanaka: originally a man or humanity, it is now used to denote a male Hawaiian or part-Hawaiian, but is occasionally taken as a slur when used by non-Hawaiians. *Kanaka maoli,* originally a full-blooded Hawaiian person, is used by some Native Hawaiian rights activists to embrace part-Hawaiians as well.

kāne: a man, a husband. If you see this word on a door (or kane), it's the men's room.

kapa: also called by its Tahitian name, *tapa,* a cloth made of beaten bark and usually dyed and stamped with a repeat design.

kapakahi: crooked, cockeyed, uneven. You've got your hat on *kapakahi*.

kapu: keep out, prohibited. This is the Hawaiian version of the more widely known Tongan word *tabu* (taboo).

kēia lā: today.

keiki: a child; *keikikāne* is a boy, *keiki-wahine* a girl.

kōkua: to help, assist. Often seen in signs like "Please *kōkua* and throw away your trash."

kolohe: mischievous, naughty.

kona: the leeward side of the Islands, the direction (south) from which the *kona* wind and *kona* rain come.

kula: upland.

kuleana: a homestead or small plot of ground on which a family has been installed for some generations without necessarily owning it.

kupuna: grandparent; elder.

lā: sun.

lamalama: to fish with a torch.

lānai: a porch, a balcony, an outdoor living room.

lani: heaven, the sky.

lau hala: the leaf of the *hala*, or pandanus tree, widely used in handicrafts.

lei: a garland of flowers.

limu: seaweed.

lōlō: feeble-minded, crazy.

luna: a plantation overseer or foreman.

mahalo: thank you.

mahina: moon.

makai: toward the ocean.

mālama: to take care of, preserve, protect

malihini: a newcomer to the Islands.

mana: the spiritual power that the Hawaiians believe inhabits all things and creatures.

manō: shark.

manuahi: free, gratis.

mauka: toward the mountains.

mauna: mountain.

mele: a Hawaiian song or chant, often of epic proportions.

Mele Kalikimaka: Merry Christmas.

Menehune: a Hawaiian pixie. The *Menehune* were a legendary race of little people who accomplished prodigious work, such as building fishponds and temples in the course of a single night.

moana: the ocean.

mu'umu'u: the voluminous dress in which the missionaries enveloped Hawaiian women. Now made in bright printed cottons and silks, it is an indispensable garment.

nani: beautiful.

nui: big.

'ohana: family.

'ono: delicious.

pāhoehoe: smooth, unbroken, satiny lava.

palapala: document, printed matter.

pali: a cliff, precipice.

pānini: prickly pear cactus.

paniolo: a Hawaiian cowboy, a rough transliteration of *español*, the language of the Islands' earliest cowboys.

pau: finished, done.

pilikia: trouble. The Hawaiian word is much more widely used here than its English equivalent.

pū: large conch shell used as trumpet before start of luau and other special events.

puka: a hole.

pule: prayer, blessing. Often performed before a meal or event.

pupule: crazy, like the celebrated Princess Pupule. This word has replaced its English equivalent in local usage.

pu'u: volcanic cinder cone.

tūtū: grandmother.

waha: mouth.

wahine: a female, a woman, a wife, and a sign on the ladies' room door; the plural form is *wāhine*.

wai: freshwater, as opposed to saltwater, which is *kai*.

wailele: waterfall.

wikiwiki: to hurry, hurry up (since this is a reduplication of *wiki*, quick, neither W is pronounced as a V).

TRAVEL SMART
BIG ISLAND

GETTING HERE AND AROUND

Unless you have a travel agent in the family, you're probably among millions who book arrangements online. But it pays to know the options, especially for complicated destinations like Hawaii. Online Travel Agencies (OTAs) and discounters (like Priceline, Expedia, and Pleasant Holidays) have websites for booking airline, hotel, and car reservations without directly contacting the company itself. Aggregators (like Kayak and Hipmunk) compare travel offerings so you don't have to. These businesses offer good prices from their relationships with wholesalers, who make cheap, bulk reservations for resale. Yet another option is to consult a Hawaii-based inbound travel company. Because the travel industry has changed so much over the years, these companies can give you the best of both worlds—the personal service of an old-fashioned travel agent and connections to wholesalers as well as to the local travel industry. Often, they offer deals that beat what you can find yourself.

Hawaii Aloha Travel. ✉ *6800 Kalanianaole Hwy., Honolulu* ☎ *800/843–8771* ⊕ *www.hawaii-aloha.com.*

▌ AIR TRAVEL

Flying time to the Big Island is about 10 hours from New York, 8 hours from Chicago, 5 hours from Los Angeles, and 15 hours from London, not including layovers. Some of the major airline carriers serving Hawaii fly direct to the Big Island, allowing you to bypass connecting flights out of Honolulu and Maui. If you're a more spontaneous traveler, island-hopping flights depart daily every 20 to 30 minutes or so.

Although the Big Island's airports are smaller and more casual than Honolulu International, during peak times they can also get quite busy. Allow extra travel time getting to all airports during morning and afternoon rush-hour traffic periods. Due to increased security measures and inadequate

staff, TSA screening can often become backed up significantly. Plan to arrive at the airport 90 minutes before departure for interisland or domestic flights. If your interisland flight is part of an international itinerary, then you must check in to your interisland flight at least two hours prior.

Plants and plant products are highly restricted by the U.S. Department of Agriculture, both upon entering and leaving Hawaii. When you leave the Islands, both checked and carry-on bags will be screened and tagged at the airport's agricultural inspection stations. Pineapples and coconuts with the packer's agricultural inspection stamp pass freely; papayas must be treated, inspected, and stamped. All other fruits are banned for export to the U.S. mainland. Flowers pass except for gardenia, rose leaves, jade vine, and mauna loa. Also banned are insects, snails, soil, cotton, cacti, sugarcane, and all berry plants.

You'll have to leave dogs and other pets at home. A 120-day quarantine is imposed to prevent the introduction of rabies, which is nonexistent in Hawaii. If specific pre- and post-arrival requirements are met, animals may qualify for a 30-day or 5-day-or-less quarantine; this includes service animals.

Airline Security Issues Transportation Security Administration (TSA). ☎ *866/289–9673* ⊕ *www.tsa.gov.* **U.S. Department of Agriculture.** ☎ *808/326–1252* ⊕ *www.aphis. usda.gov.*

AIRPORTS

Daniel K. Inouye International Airport (HNL) is the main gateway for most domestic and international flights into Hawaii. From Honolulu, interisland flights to the Big Island depart regularly from early morning through mid-evening. From Honolulu, the travel time is about 35 minutes. From Maui, it's about 20 minutes. Many carriers now offer nonstop service directly from the mainland to the Ellison Onizuka Kona International Airport at Keahole (KOA) and Hilo International Airport (ITO). The two Big Island airports are currently "jetway free," meaning you can enjoy those balmy trade winds the moment you step off the plane, a welcome and rather quaint way to arrive in the Islands.

DANIEL K. INOUYE INTERNATIONAL AIRPORT

Hawaii's major airport is Daniel K. Inouye International Airport, on Oahu, 20 minutes (9 miles) west of Waikiki. To travel to the Big Island from Honolulu, you will depart from either the interisland terminal or the commuter-airline terminal (also called the "old interisland terminal" by locals), located in two separate structures adjacent to the main overseas terminal building. A free shuttle bus, the Wiki Wiki Shuttle, operates between terminals, or stretch your legs with a short walk.

Information Daniel K. Inouye International Airport (HNL). ✉ *300 Rodgers Blvd., Honolulu* ☎ *808/836-6413* ⊕ *hawaii.gov/hnl.*

BIG ISLAND AIRPORTS

Those flying to the Big Island regularly land at one of two fields. Ellison Onizuka Kona International Airport at Keahole, on the west side, serves Kailua-Kona, Keauhou, the Kohala Coast, North Kohala, Waimea, and points south. There are Visitor Information Program (VIP) booths located by all baggage-claim areas to assist travelers. Additionally, the airport offers news and lei stands, Laniakea By Centerplate, and a small gift and sundries shop. A modernization project launched in 2017 aims to join the two terminals (now separate) so that baggage and passenger screening can be streamlined and retail options enhanced.

Hilo International Airport is more appropriate for those planning visits based on the east side of the island. Here, you'll find VIP booths across from the Centerplate Coffee Shop near the departure lobby and in the arrival areas at each end of the terminal. In addition to the coffee shop,

services include a Bank of Hawaii ATM, a gift shop, newsstands, and lei stands.

Waimea-Kohala Airport, called Kamuela Airport by residents, is used primarily for private flights between islands, but has recently welcomed one commercial carrier with a single route.

Contacts Hilo International Airport (ITO). ☎ *808/961-9300* ⊕ *hawaii.gov/ito.* **Ellison Onizuka Kona International Airport at Keahole (KOA).** ☎ *808/327-9520* ⊕ *hawaii.gov/koa.* **Waimea-Kohala Airport (MUE).** ☎ *808/887-8126* ⊕ *hawaii.gov/mue.*

GROUND TRANSPORTATION

Check with your hotel to see if it runs an airport shuttle. If you're not renting a car, you can choose from multiple taxi companies serving the Hilo Airport. The approximate taxi rate is $3 for the initial 1/8th mile, plus $3 for each additional mile, with surcharges for waiting time (40¢ per minute) and baggage ($1 per bag) for up to six people. Call or calculate online for fares to popular destinations. The local Hele-On county bus also services the Hilo airport. Uber and Lyft serve Hilo, but they are not allowed to operate at the airport. You may have to walk some distance to catch one.

At the Kona airport, taxis are available. SpeediShuttle also offers transportation between the airport and hotels, resorts, and condominium complexes from Waimea to Keauhou. Uber or Lyft are not available on the west side of the island yet.

Contacts SpeediShuttle. ☎ *877/242-5777, 808/329-5433* ⊕ *www.speedishuttle.com.*

FLIGHTS

Serving Kona are Air Canada, Alaska Airlines, American Airlines, Delta Airlines, Hawaiian Airlines, Japan Airlines, Mokulele, United Airlines, Virgin Atlantic, and Westjet. Hawaiian, Mokulele, and United fly into Hilo. Airlines schedule flights seasonally, meaning the number of daily flights—and sometimes the carriers themselves—vary according to demand.

Airline Contacts Air Canada. ☎ 888/247–2262 ⊕ www.aircanada.com. **Alaska Airlines.** ☎ 800/252–7522 ⊕ www.alaskaair.com. **American Airlines.** ☎ 800/433–7300 ⊕ www.aa.com. **Delta Airlines.** ☎ 800/221–1212 for U.S. reservations ⊕ www.delta.com. **United Airlines.** ☎ 800/864–8331 for U.S. reservations, 800/241–6522 arrival and departure information ⊕ www.united.com. **Westjet.** ☎ 888/937–8538 ⊕ www.westjet.com.

INTERISLAND FLIGHTS

Should you wish to visit neighboring islands, Hawaiian Airlines and Mokulele offer regular service. Prices for interisland flights have increased quite a bit in recent years, while flight schedule availability has been reduced. Mokulele now serves Waimea. Planning ahead is your best bet.

Interisland Carriers Mokulele Airlines. ☎ 888/435–9462 ⊕ www.mokuleleairlines.com. **Hawaiian Airlines.** ☎ 800/367–5320 ⊕ www.hawaiianair.com.

CHARTER FLIGHTS

Big Island Air, in addition to offering air tours of the Big Island, offers on-demand service between all the islands via a Cessna Caravan. Nine passengers can ride comfortably, and the charter has plenty of room for luggage.

Charter Companies Big Island Air. ☎ 808/329–4868 ⊕ www.bigislandair.com.

▌ BUS TRAVEL

Depending on where you're staying, you can take advantage of the affordable Hawaii County Mass Transit Agency's Hele-On Bus, which travels several routes throughout the island. Mostly serving local commuters, the Hele-On Bus costs $2 per person (students and senior citizens pay $1). Just wait at a scheduled stop and flag down the bus. A one-way journey between Hilo and Kona takes about four hours. There's regular service in and around downtown Hilo, Kailua-Kona, Waimea, North and South Kohala, Honokaa, and Pahoa. However, some routes are served only once a day so if

you are planning on using the bus, be sure to study up carefully before assuming the bus serves your area.

Visitors staying in Hilo can take advantage of the Transit Agency's Shared Ride Taxi program, which provides door-to-door transportation in the area. A one-way fare is $2, and a book of 15 coupons can be purchased for $30. Visitors to Kona can also take advantage of free trolleys operated by local shopping centers.

Contacts Hele-On Bus. ☎ 808/961–8744 ⊕ www.heleonbus.org.

▌ CAR TRAVEL

It's essential to rent a car when visiting the Big Island. As the name suggests, it's a very big island, and it takes a while to get from point A to point B.

Fortunately, when you circle the island by car, you are treated to miles and miles of wondrous vistas of every possible description. In addition to using standard compass directions such as north and south, Hawaii residents often refer to places as being either *mauka* (toward the mountains) or *makai* (toward the ocean).

It's difficult to get lost along the main roads of the Big Island. Although their names may challenge the visitor's tongue, most roads are well marked; in rural areas look for mile marker numbers. Free publications containing basic road maps are given out at car rental agencies, but if you are doing a lot of driving, invest about $4 in the standard Big Island map available at local retailers. GPS is often unreliable.

For those who want to travel from the west side to the east side, or vice versa, the newly rerouted and repaved Saddle Road, now known as the Daniel K. Inouye Highway, is a nice shortcut across the middle of the island. This is especially convenient if you are staying on the Kohala side of the island and wish to visit the east side. Hazardous conditions such as fog are common.

Turning right on a red light is legal, except where noted. Hawaii has a strict seat-belt law that applies to both drivers and passengers. The fine for not wearing a seat belt is $102. Mobile phone use is strictly limited to talking on a hands-free mobile device, and only for those over 18. Many police officers drive their own cars while on duty, strapping the warning lights to the roof. Because of the color, locals call them "blue lights."

GASOLINE

You can count on having to pay more at the pump for gasoline on the Big Island than almost anywhere on the U.S. mainland except for California. Prices tend to be higher in Kailua-Kona and cheaper in Hilo. Gas stations in rural areas can be few and far between, and it's not unusual for them to close early. If you notice that your tank is getting low, don't take any chances: Keep your tank filled.

PARKING

Parking can be limited in historic Kailua Village. A few municipal lots near Alii Drive offer convenient parking on an honor system. (You'll be ticketed if you don't pay.) There is one free county lot downtown. In Hilo, you'll find plenty of free parking along the scenic bayfront.

ROAD CONDITIONS

Roads on the Big Island are generally well maintained and can be easily negotiated. Most of the roads are two-lane highways with limited shoulders—and yes, even in paradise, there is traffic, especially during the morning and afternoon rush hours and before and after school. Major roadworks have been ongoing in the five-mile stretch between the Kona airport and town, so give yourself extra time if you need to catch a flight. Jaywalking and hitchhiking are very common, so pay careful attention to the roads, especially while driving in rural areas. Also use caution during heavy downpours, especially if you see signs warning of flash floods and falling rocks. These can also occur suddenly, even if it's not raining, and take you by surprise. Stay clear of ponding or rising water on roadways and heed emergency weather advisories not to cross flooded roads.

RENTALS

Should you plan to sightsee around the Big Island, it is best to rent a car. With more than 260 miles of coastline—and attractions as varied as Hawaii Volcanoes National Park, Akaka Falls State Park, Puuhonua o Honaunau National Historic Park, and Puukohola Heiau National Historic Site—ideally you should split up your stay between the east and west coasts of the island. Even if all you want to do is relax at your resort, you may want to hop in the car to check out one of the island's popular restaurants.

While on the Big Island, you can rent anything from an econobox to a sports car to a motorcycle. Rates are usually better if you reserve though a rental agency's website, and most sites allow you to reserve for free. It's wise to make reservations in advance and make sure that a confirmed reservation guarantees you a car, especially if visiting during peak seasons or for major conventions or sporting events. It's not uncommon to find several car categories sold out during major events on the island, such as the Merrie Monarch Festival in Hilo in April or the Ironman World Championship triathlon in Kailua-Kona in October. ∎TIP➡ If you're planning on driving to the 13,796-foot summit of Mauna Kea for stargazing, you'll need a four-wheel-drive vehicle. Harper Car and Truck Rental, with offices in Hilo and Kona, is the *only* company that allows its vehicles to be driven to the summit.

If exploring the island on two wheels is more your speed, Big Island Motorcycle Company rents motorcycles and mopeds.

Rates begin at about $30 to $35 a day for an economy car with air-conditioning, automatic transmission, and unlimited mileage. This does not include the airport concession fee, general excise tax, rental vehicle surcharge, or vehicle license fee.

CAR RENTAL RESOURCES

Automobile Associations

American Automobile Association	☏ 315/797–5000	⊕ www.aaa.com

Local Agencies

AA Aloha Cars-R-Us	☏ 800/655–7989	⊕ www.hawaiicarrental.com
Big Island Motorcycle Co.	☏ 866/886–2011	⊕ www.thrillseekershawaii.com
Harper Car and Truck Rental (Big Island)	☏ 800/852–9993	⊕ www.harpershawaii.com
Hawaiian Discount Car Rentals	☏ 800/955–3142	⊕ www.hawaiidrive-o.com

Major Agencies

Alamo	☏ 888/233–8749	⊕ www.alamo.com
Avis	☏ 808/327–3000	⊕ www.avis.com
Budget	☏ 800/214–6094	⊕ www.budget.com
Dollar	☏ 800/800–5252	⊕ www.dollar.com
Enterprise	☏ 808/331–2509	⊕ www.enterprise.com
Hertz	☏ 808/329–2042	⊕ www.hertz.com
National Car Rental	☏ 888/826–6890	⊕ www.nationalcar.com
Thrifty	☏ 808/331–0531	⊕ www.thrifty.com

When you reserve a car, ask about cancellation penalties and drop-off charges should you plan to pick up the car in one location and return it to another. Many rental companies in Hawaii offer coupons for discounts at various attractions.

In Hawaii, you must be 21 years of age to rent a car, and you must have a valid driver's license and a major credit card. Those under 25 pay a daily surcharge of $27 to $30. Request car seats and extras such as GPS when you book. Hawaii's Child Restraint Law requires that all children three years and younger be in an approved child safety seat in the backseat of a vehicle. Children ages four to seven must be seated in a rear booster seat or child restraint such as a lap and shoulder belt. Car seats and booster rentals range from $8 to $10 per day.

In Hawaii, a mainland driver's license is valid for a rental for up to 90 days.

Because the road circling the Big Island can be two-lane, narrow, and windy in places, allow plenty of time to return your vehicle so that you can make your flight. Traffic can be heavy during morning and afternoon rush hours, especially in the Kona area. Roadwork is ongoing and often unscheduled. ■TIP➔ **Give yourself about 3½ hours before departure time to return your vehicle.**

CAR RENTAL INSURANCE

Everyone who rents a car wonders whether the insurance that the rental companies offer is worth the expense. No one—including us—has a simple answer. It all depends on how much regular insurance you have, how comfortable you are with risk, and whether or not money is an issue.

If you own a car and carry comprehensive car insurance for both collision and liability, your personal auto insurance probably covers a rental, but call your auto insurance company to confirm. If you don't have auto insurance, then you will need to buy the collision- or loss-damage waiver (CDW or LDW) from the rental company. The CDW allows you to walk away from most incidents, so it might be worth the peace of mind. Some credit cards offer CDW coverage, but it's usually supplemental to your own insurance and rarely covers SUVs, minivans, and luxury models. If your coverage is secondary, you may still be liable for loss-of-use costs from the car-rental company (again, read the fine print). But no credit-card insurance is valid unless you use that card for *all* transactions, from reserving to paying the final bill.

■TIP→ Diners Club offers primary CDW coverage on all rentals reserved and paid for with the card. This means that Diners Club's company—not your own car insurance—pays in case of an accident. It doesn't mean that your car insurance company won't raise your rates once it discovers you had an accident.

You may also be offered supplemental liability coverage; the car-rental company is required to carry a minimal level of liability coverage insuring all renters, but it's rarely enough to cover claims in a really serious accident if you're at fault. Your own auto-insurance policy will protect you if you own a car; if you don't, you have to decide whether or not you are willing to take the risk.

U.S. rental companies sell CDWs and LDWs for about $15 to $25 a day; supplemental liability is usually more than $10 a day. The car-rental company may offer you all sorts of other policies, but they're rarely worth the cost. Personal accident insurance, which is basic hospitalization coverage, is an especially egregious rip-off if you already have health insurance.

RIDESHARES

Both Uber and Lyft introduced service on the Big Island in 2017 but are not permitted to pick up at the airport. There is more service in Hilo and limited service in Kona, but those who plan on traveling long distances may find that regular taxis are a bit cheaper.

ESSENTIALS

■ COMMUNICATIONS

INTERNET

If you've brought your laptop or tablet with you to the Big Island, you should have no problem checking email or connecting to the Internet. Most of the major hotels and resorts offer high-speed access in rooms or lobbies. You should check with your hotel in advance to confirm that access is wireless; if not, ask whether in-room cables are provided. It's a good idea to bring your own ethernet cable. In some cases, there will be an hourly or daily charge posted to your room. The latest unhappy trend is for the major hotels to charge a resort fee, a mandatory daily fee that is supposed to cover Wi-Fi and parking and may range from $25 to $40. If you're staying at a small inn or bed-and-breakfast without Internet access, ask the proprietor for the nearest café or shopping center with wireless access.

■ HEALTH

Hawaii is known as the Health State. The life expectancy here is 79 years, the longest in the nation. Balmy weather makes it easy to remain active year-round, and the low-stress aloha attitude certainly contributes to general well-being. When visiting the Islands, however, there are a few health issues to keep in mind.

The Hawaii State Department of Health recommends that you drink 16 ounces of water per hour to avoid dehydration when hiking or spending time in the sun. Use zinc-based sunblock, wear UV-reflective sunglasses, and protect your head with a visor or hat for shade. If you're not acclimated to warm humid weather you should allow plenty of time for rest stops and refreshments. When visiting freshwater streams, be aware of the tropical disease leptospirosis, which is spread by animal urine and carried into streams and mud. Symptoms include fever, headache,

> **BOX TITLE**
>
> Did the resort look as good in real life as it did in the photos? Did you sleep like a baby, or were the walls paper-thin? Did you get your money's worth? Rate hotels and write your own reviews in Travel Ratings or start a discussion about your favorite places in the Forums on ⊕ *www. fodors.com.* Your comments might even appear in our books. Yes, you, too, can be a correspondent!

nausea, and red eyes. If left untreated, it can cause liver and kidney failure, respiratory failure, internal bleeding, and even death. To avoid this, don't swim or wade in freshwater streams or ponds if you have open sores and don't drink from any freshwater streams or ponds. Wash all locally grown leafy vegetables thoroughly to protect yourself against rat-lungworm disease.

On the Big Island, you may experience the effects of "vog," an airborne stew of gases released from volcanic vents at Kilauea. Depending on your location and the level of volcanic activity, you may notice a sulfur smell and hazy horizons. These gases can exacerbate respiratory and other health conditions, especially allergies, asthma or emphysema. Pregnant women are sometimes advised to avoid visiting the volcano, but ask your doctor to be certain. If susceptible, skip the volcano, stay indoors, and get emergency assistance if needed.

The Islands have their share of bugs and insects that enjoy the tropical climate as much as visitors do. Most are harmless but annoying. When planning to spend time outdoors in hiking areas, wear long-sleeve shirts and pants and use mosquito repellent. In very damp or rocky places, you may encounter the dreaded local centipede. Blue or brown in color, the centipedes can grow as long as eight inches but are not overly aggressive. If surprised, they might sting, which might feel like a bee or wasp sting. When camping, shake out your sleeping bag before climbing in, and check your shoes in the morning, as centipedes like warm, moist places. If planning on hiking or traveling in remote areas, always carry a first-aid kit and appropriate medications for sting reactions.

▌ HOURS OF OPERATION

Even people in paradise have to work. Generally local business hours are weekdays 8–5. Banks are usually open Monday through Thursday 8:30–4 and until 6 on Friday. Some banks offer Saturday morning hours.

Only a handful of service stations are open around the clock. Many operate from around 7 am until 10 pm. U.S. post offices are open weekdays 8:30 am–4:30 pm and Saturday 8:30–noon.

Most museums generally open their doors between 9 am and 10 am and stay open until 5 pm Tuesday through Saturday. Many museums operate with afternoon hours only on Sunday and close on Monday. Visitor-attraction hours vary throughout the state, but most sights are open daily with the exception of major holidays such as Christmas and New Year's Day.

Stores in resort areas sometimes open as early as 8 am, with shopping-center opening hours varying from 9:30 to 10 am on weekdays and Saturday, a bit later on Sunday. Bigger malls stay open until 9 pm Monday through Saturday and close at 5 pm on Sunday. Boutiques in resort areas may stay open as late as 11 pm.

▌ MONEY

Automatic teller machines for easy access to cash are everywhere in the Islands. ATMs can be found in shopping centers, small convenience and grocery stores, and hotels and resorts as well as outside most bank branches. Also, you can get cash back at point of purchase in larger stores. For a directory of locations, call ☎ 800/424–7787 for the MasterCard/Cirrus/Maestro network or ☎ 800/843–7587 for the Visa/Plus network.

CREDIT CARDS

It's a good idea to notify your credit-card and debit-card companies before you travel. Otherwise, they might put a hold on your card owing to unusual activity—not a good thing halfway through your trip. Record all your credit-card numbers—as well as the phone numbers to call if your cards are lost or stolen—in a safe place, so you're prepared should something go wrong. Both MasterCard and Visa have general numbers you can call if your card is lost, but you're better off calling the number of your issuing bank, since MasterCard and Visa usually just transfer you to your bank. Your bank's number is usually printed on your card.

Reporting Lost Cards American Express. ☎ 800/528–4800 in the U.S., 336/393–1111 collect from abroad ⊕ www.americanexpress. com. **Diners Club International.** ☎ 800/234–6377 in the U.S., 303/799–1504 collect from abroad ⊕ www.dinersclub.com. **Discover.** ☎ 800/347–2683 in the U.S., 801/902–3100 collect from abroad ⊕ www.discover.com. **MasterCard.** ☎ 800/622–7747 in the U.S., 636/722–7111 collect from abroad ⊕ www. mastercard.com. **Visa.** ☎ 800/847–2911 in the U.S., 303/967–1096 collect from abroad ⊕ www.visa.com.

▌ PACKING

Hawaii is casual: sandals, bathing suits, and comfortable informal clothing are the norm. Year-round, clothing of cotton or rayon proves very comfortable. Local women love to wear the *pareau*, or sarong. For men, you'll look right at home in T-shirts and board shorts.

One of the most important things to tuck in your suitcase is sunscreen. Recent research has indicated that some traditional sunscreens are harming coral reefs; indeed there's legislation currently being

LOCAL DO'S AND TABOOS

GREETINGS

Hawaii is a very friendly place and this is reflected in the day-to-day encounters between friends, family, and even business associates. Women will often hug and kiss one another on the cheek and men will shake hands and sometimes combine that with a friendly hug. Children may refer to elders as "aunty" or "uncle," even if they aren't related, which reflects an ingrained sense of respect for family.

When you disembark from a long flight, perhaps a bit groggy and stiff, nothing quite compares with a fragrant Hawaiian-lei greeting. This charming custom ranks as one of the fastest ways to make the transition from the worries of home to the joys of being on a tropical holiday.

If you've booked a vacation with a wholesaler or tour company, a lei greeting might be included in your package, so check before you leave. If not, it's easy to arrange a lei greeting for yourself or for your companions before you arrive. Contact Hawaiian Lei Greetings if you're arriving at Kona International Airport. A plumeria or dendrobium orchid lei is considered standard and starts at about $19 per person. Hilo International Airport does not allow companies to provide lei greeting services, but there are lei vendors at the airport should you wish to purchase one upon arrival.

INFORMATION

Hawaiian Lei Greetings. ☎ 865/665–7959 ⊕ www.leigreeting.com.

LANGUAGE

Hawaii was admitted to the Union in 1959, so residents can be sensitive when visitors offer that their own hometowns are "back in the States." When in Hawaii, refer to the contiguous 48 states as "the mainland" and not as the United States. When you do, you won't appear to be such a *malahini* (newcomer).

English is the primary language on the Islands. Making the effort to learn some Hawaiian words can be rewarding, however. Despite the length of many Hawaiian words, the Hawaiian alphabet is actually one of the world's shortest, with only 12 letters: the five vowels, *a, e, i, o, u,* and seven consonants, *h, k, l, m, n, p, w.* Hawaiian words you're most likely to encounter during your visit to the Islands are *aloha, mahalo* (hello, thank you), *keiki* (child), *haole* (Caucasian or foreigner), *mauka* (toward the mountains), *makai* (toward the ocean), and *pau* (finished, all done).

Hawaii's history includes waves of immigrants, each bringing their own languages. To communicate with each other, they developed a sort of slang known as "pidgin." If you listen closely, you'll know what is being said by the inflections and by the extensive use of body language. For example, when you know what you want to say but don't know how to say it, just say "you know, da kine." For an informative and sometimes hilarious view of things Hawaiian, check out Jerry Hopkins's series of books titled *Pidgin to the Max* and *Fax to the Max,* available on most local bookshelves in the Hawaiiana sections.

introduced to ban the sale of these products in the Islands. So if you do want to use sunscreen, buy products that are zinc-based or reef approved. Even better? Buy a long-sleeved rash guard, available at all major retailers. No gunky lotions or harmful chemicals to deal with while out enjoying the reefs. Hats and sunglasses offer important sun protection, too. Both are easy to find in island shops, but if you already have a favorite packable hat or sun visor, bring it with you. All major hotels in Hawaii (and most small ones) provide beach towels.

As for clothing in the Hawaiian Islands, there's a saying that when a man wears a suit during the day, he's either going for a loan or he's a lawyer trying a case. Only a few upscale restaurants require a jacket for dinner. The *aloha* shirt is accepted dress in Hawaii for business and most social occasions. Shorts are acceptable daytime attire, along with a T-shirt or polo shirt. There's no need to buy expensive sandals on the mainland—here you can get flip-flops (called "slippers" by locals) for under $5. Golfers should remember that many courses have dress codes requiring a collared shirt; call courses you're interested in for details. If you're not prepared, you can pick up appropriate clothing at resort pro shops. If you're visiting in winter, bring a sweater or light- to medium-weight jacket. A polar fleece pullover is ideal, and makes a great impromptu pillow.

If your vacation plans include Hilo, you'll want to pack a compact umbrella and a light poncho. And if you'll be exploring Hawaii Volcanoes National Park, make sure you pack appropriately as weather ranges from hot and dry along the shore to chilly, foggy, and rainy at the 4,000-foot summit. Sturdy boots are recommended if you'll be hiking or camping in the park.

▌ SAFETY

Hawaii is generally a safe tourist destination, but it's still wise to stick to the same commonsense safety precautions you would normally follow in your own hometown. Hotel and visitor-center staff can provide information should you decide to head out on your own to more remote areas. Because their models and colors are obvious, rental cars are magnets for break-ins, so don't leave any valuables in them, not even in a locked trunk. Thieves watch these areas and can pop your hood and be gone in 60 seconds. Avoid poorly lighted areas, beach parks, and isolated areas after dark as a precaution. When hiking, stay on marked trails, no matter how alluring the temptation might be to stray; changing weather conditions can cause landscapes to become muddy, slippery, and tenuous, so staying on marked trails lessens the possibility of a fall or getting lost. This is especially true on the wetter, windward side. Heed warnings about dangerous currents in rivers and swimming holes.

Ocean safety is of the utmost importance when visiting any island destination. Visitors often get into trouble because the beach looks benign and they can't wait to get in the water so they throw caution to the wind and jump in. We urge you to avoid swimming if the conditions seem rough or dangerous. Most beaches on the Big Island do not have lifeguards. Unfortunately, most of the drowning deaths that occur in Hawaii are visitors—and this is not by chance. Winter brings higher, more dangerous surf, so please exercise caution. Don't swim alone, and follow the international signage posted at beaches, which alerts swimmers to strong currents, man-of-war or box jellyfish, sharp coral, high surf, sharks, and dangerous shore breaks. At coastal lookouts along cliff tops, heed the signs indicating that waves can climb over the ledges. Check with lifeguards at each beach for current conditions, and if the red flags are up, or if a high surf advisory has been issued by civil defense agencies indicating swimming and surfing are not allowed, don't go in. Waters that look calm on the surface can harbor strong currents and undertows, and not a few people who were "just wading" have been dragged out to sea and never seen again. When in doubt, don't go out!

Women traveling alone are generally safe in Hawaii, but always follow the same safety precautions you would use in any major destination. When booking hotels, request rooms closest to the elevator, and always keep your hotel-room door and balcony doors locked. Stay away from isolated areas after dark. If you stay out late at a nightclub or bar, use caution when exiting and returning to your car or lodging; most establishments will be glad to give you an escort to your car.

▌TAXES

Businesses on Hawaii Island collect a 4.167% general excise tax on all purchases, including food and services. A hotel transient accommodations tax of 10.25%, combined with the excise tax, totals a 14.42% rate added to your room bill. Even vacation rentals and B&Bs are required to collect this tax. A $3-per-day road tax is also assessed on each rental vehicle, in addition to an airport concession recovery tax, and other fees that are not technically taxes but are tacked on to the base rate.

▌TIME

Hawaii is on Hawaii Standard Time, 5 hours behind New York, 2 hours behind Los Angeles, and 10 hours behind London.

When the U.S. mainland switches to daylight saving time, Hawaii does not, so add an extra hour of time difference between the Islands and U.S. mainland destinations.

▌TIPPING

Tipping is not only common but expected: Hawaii is a major vacation destination and many of the people who work at the hotels and resorts rely on tips to supplement their wages. Give $1 to bartenders, bellhops, and maids (more in an expensive luxury resort). Tip 15%–20% in restaurants and in taxis.

▌TOURS

GENERAL-INTEREST TOURS

A guided tour can be a hassle-free way to see lots of attractions on all the islands without having to worry about the details yourself. Plus it's a great way of making new friends. Globus visits the main Hawaiian Islands, including the Big Island, on their Grand Hawaii Vacation. Aloha Hawaiian Vacations offers an all-inclusive, seven-day adventure to the Big Island. Trafalgar also offers several Hawaii itineraries that include two to three nights on the Big Island, depending on the tour. Usually, visits to Hawaii Volcanoes National Park are included.

Recommended Companies Globus.
☎ 866/755–8581 ⊕ www.globusjourneys.com. **Aloha Hawaiian Vacations.** ☎ 800/256–4211 ⊕ www.aloha-hawaiian.com. **Trafalgar.** ☎ 866/809–8426 ⊕ www.trafalgar.com. **YMT Vacations.** ☎ 877/322–6185 ⊕ www.ymtvacations.com.

SPECIAL-INTEREST TOURS
ADVENTURE STUDY

A tour of Kilauea Volcano—the most active volcano on earth—is even better when led by an actual geologist, volcanologist, retired ranger, or even botanist. Mother Nature does not offer a money-back guarantee, so keep in mind that seeing active lava cannot be promised.

Contacts Friends of Hawaii Volcanoes National Park. ☎ 808/985–7373 ⊕ fhvnp. org. **Kapoho Kine Adventures.** ✉ 224 Kamehameha Ave., Hilo ☎ 808/964–1000 ⊕ www.kapohokine.com.

ART

Artists and free spirits have made Hawaii Island a known and respected haven for the arts, including printmaking, jewelry making, oil painting, sculpture, pottery, photography, and glassworks. The tiny hamlet of Volcano, across from the national park, draws the fantastically talented, many of whom live in the village and sell their works at the Volcano Art Center gallery or at their own small shops.

Contact Volcano Art Center. ☎ 866/967–8222 Administration, 808/967–7565 Gallery ⊕ www.volcanoartcenter.org.

BIKING

If you're a bicycling enthusiast, you've got exciting options on the Big Island. ■TIP➔ Most airlines accommodate bikes as luggage, provided they're dismantled and boxed.

Contacts Bicycle Adventures. ☎ 800/443–6060 ⊕ www.bicycleadventures.com. **Woman-Tours.** ☎ 800/247–1444 ⊕ www.womantours.com.

BIRD-WATCHING

Because of its isolated location, nearly 2,500 miles from any major landmass, Hawaii's unique habitats have encouraged many unusual species of birds to evolve. Although many bird species have been lost due to hunting, introduced predators, or loss of habitat, some highly endangered birds still thrive, mostly in the Hakalau National Wildlife Refuge on the slopes of Mauna Kea, where their natural forest habitats have been replanted and protected. Birders from around the world come here and to other parts of the island to spot these amazing creatures—and you can, too, with the help of expert guides.

Contacts Hawaii Forest & Trail. ✉ 73-5598 Olowalu St., Kailua-Kona ☎ 800/464–1993 ⊕ www.hawaii-forest.com. **Victor Emanuel Nature Tours.** ☎ 800/328–8368 ⊕ www.ventbird.com.

CULTURE

Some tour companies cater to culturally inclined visitors interested in discovering the island beyond the usual tourist track.

Contacts Road Scholar. ☎ 800/454–5766 ⊕ www.roadscholar.org.

ECO TOURS

Contacts Sierra Club Outings. ☎ 415/977–5522 ⊕ www.sierraclub.org/outings.

HIKING

If you love to hike and want to experience the wonders of walking on the major Hawaiian Islands without the hassles of finding flights and hotels yourself, consider booking with a tour company that specializes in hiking. They can get better rates on hotels, interisland flights, and ground transportation than you can by booking it all separately on your own.

■ VISITOR INFORMATION

Before you go, contact the Island of Hawaii Visitors Bureau to request a free official vacation planner with information on accommodations, transportation, sports and activities, dining, arts and entertainment, and culture. A virtual visit on the bureau website can be helpful, and it includes a calendar section that shows which local events will coincide with your visit. ■TIP➔ To experience the aloha spirit firsthand, connect the old-fashioned way—by phone.

The Hawaii Island Chamber of Commerce has links to dozens of museums, attractions, bed-and-breakfasts, and parks on its website. The Kona-Kohala Chamber of Commerce lists local activities. The Volcano Art Center offers a host of activities within the park, including classes and workshops; music, dance, and theater performances; art shows; and volcano runs.

Contacts Island of Hawaii Visitors Bureau. ☎ 800/648–2441 ⊕ www.gohawaii.com. **Hawaii Island Chamber of Commerce.** ☎ 808/935–7178 ⊕ www.hicc.biz. **Kona-Kohala Chamber of Commerce.** ☎ 808/329–1758 ⊕ www.kona-kohala.com.

INDEX

PHOTO CREDITS

Front cover: Russ Bishop/agefotostock [Description: Pacific, Kailua, Kona, Hawaii]. **Back cover, from left to right:** Shutterstock / lauraslens; John Almarez/Four Seasons Hotels & Resorts; Castle Resorts & Hotels. **Spine:** Shutterstock / aquatic creature. 1, Blakerandall81 I Dreamstime.com. 2, Fremme/Shutterstock. 4, Chadc I Dreamstime.com. 5 (top), Swaengpic I Dreamstime.com. 5 (bottom), Michael DeFreitas North America / Alamy Stock Photo. 6 (top left), Barsik I Dreamstime.com. 6 (top right), Kailua village business improvement District. 6 (bottom left), Melissa Burovac. 6 (bottom right), Kilauea Military Camp. 7, Gardendreamer I Dreamstime.com. 8 (top left), Big Island Gravity. 8 (top right), Anita Gould/Flickr, [CC BY-NC 2.0]. 8 (bottom), Michael Hanano / Shutterstock. 9 (top), Samantoniophotography I Dreamstime.com. 9 (bottom), Picturist21 I Dreamstime.com. 10 (top left), Vacclav I Dreamstime.com. 10 (top right), Icemanj I Dreamstime.com. 10 (bottom), Kate Russell. 11, John Elk III / Alamy Stock Photo. 13, John Elk III / Alamy Stock Photo. **Chapter1: Experience Big Island:**16-17, Ademyan I Dreamstime.com. 33 and 34, Hawaii Visitors & Convention Bureau. 35, Thinkstock LLC. 37 (top), Linda Ching/HVCB. 37 (bottom), Sri Maiava. 38 (1), Leis Of Hawaii. 38 (2), Kelly alexander photography. 38 (3-6), Leis Of Hawaii. 39, Polynesian Cultural Center. 40 (1-5), Dana Edmunds/Polynesian Cultural Center's/Alii Luau. 41 (1-3), HTJ. 41 (4), Oahu Visitors Bureau. **Chapter 2: Exploring the Big Island:** 43, Unclejay I Dreamstime.com. 44, George Burba/Shutterstock. 47and 55, Big Island Visitors Bureau. 57, Hawaii Tourism Authority (HTA) / Tor Johnson. 58, Island of Hawaii Visitors Bureau (IHVB) / Tyler Schmitt. 61, Alexander Demyanenko/Shutterstock. 62, Maria Luisa Lopez Estivill I Dreamstime.com. 67, Island of Hawaii Visitors Bureau (IHVB) / Tyler Schmitt. 68, Photo Resource Hawaii/Alamy. 75, Russ Bishop/Alamy. 76, Cornforth Images/Alamy. 84, SuperStock/age fotostock. 91, Interfoto Pressebildagentur/Alamy. 92, Big Island Visitors Bureau. 93, Russ Bishop/age fotostock. 95, Photo Resource Hawaii/Alamy. 96, Cornforth Images/Alamy. 97 (top), Pacific Stock/SuperStock. New photo no attribution. 97 (bottom), Linda Robshaw/Alamy. **Chapter 3: Beaches:** 103, Preferred Hotels & Resorts Worldwide. 104, Kushch Dmitry/Shutterstock. 107, Luis Castanedox/agefotostock. 111, Cornforth Images/Alamy. 114, MNStudio I Dreamstime.com. **Chapter 4: Where to Eat:** 117, Four Seasons Hualalalai. 118, Don Riddle Images/Four Seasons Hotels & Resorts. **Chapter 5: Where to Stay:** 141, Four Seasons Hualalalai. 142, Blake Marvin. **Chapter 6: Entertainment& Nightlife:** 163, Hilton Hawaii. 164, Hawaii Tourism Authority (HTA)/ Tor Johnson. **Chapter 7: Shops & Spas:** 171, Hilton Hawaii. 172, Fairmont Hotel & Resorts. **Chapter 8: Water Sports & Tours:** 187, WaterFrame/Alamy. 188, Hawaii Tourism Authority (HTA) / Tor Johnson. 191, Russ Bishop/Alamy. 192, Blaine Harrington III/Alamy. **199,** Andre Seale/Alamy. **201,** Ron Dahlquist/ HVCB. 202, Shane Myers Photography/Shutterstock. 204 (top), SPrada/iStockphoto. 204 (bottom), Gert Vrey/iStockphoto. 205, sweetlifephotos/iStockphoto. 209, David Fleetham/Alamy. 210, Stephen Frink Collection/Alamy. **Chapter 9: Golf, Hiking & Outdoor Activities:** 213, Hawaii Tourism Authority (HTA) / Tor Johnson. 214, Kushch Dmitry/Shutterstock. 215, Cameron Nelson. 221, Russ Bishop / Alamy Stock Photo. 226 and 227, MNStudio I Dreamstime.com. 228, Kaua'i Visitors Bureau. 229, Jack Jeffrey. 231, McPHOTO. **About Our Writers:** All photos are courtesy of the writers.

ABOUT OUR WRITERS

Karen Anderson is a Kona resident who enjoys horseback riding in the hills of the Big Island. She is the managing editor of *At Home, Living with Style in West Hawaii* and has written for a variety of publications including *West Hawaii Today, Big Island Weekly, Hawaii* magazine and the Kona-Kohala Chamber of Commerce. She's also the best-selling author of *The Hawaii Home Book, Practical Tips for Tropical Living*, which received an award for excellence from the Hawaii Book Publishers Association. Her monthly editor's column and chef/restaurant profiles are known throughout West Hawaii. For this edition, Karen updated the Shops and Spas, Entertainment and Nightlife, Where to Eat, and Where to Stay chapters.

Kristina Anderson has been writing professionally for more than 25 years. After working as an advertising copywriter and creative director in Southern California for more than a decade, she moved to Hawaii in 1992, freelancing copy and broadcast for Hawaii agencies. Since 2006, she's written for national and regional publications, most notably for *At Home in West Hawaii* magazine, which profiles a variety of homes—from coffee shacks to resort mansions—and for USAToday.com Travel Tips. She also fills in here and there as a substitute teacher, which keeps her busy, as does being a single mom to two teenage boys. When there's time, she paddles outrigger canoes competitively and plays tennis very noncompetitively. For this book, Kristina updated the Experience; Golf, Hiking, and Outdoor Activities; and Travel Smart chapters.